THE PSYCHOLOGY OF ADAPTATION TO ABSURDITY

Tactics of Make-Believe

THE PSYCHOLOGY OF ADAPTATION TO ABSURDITY

Tactics of Make-Believe

Seymour Fisher
State University of New York
Health Science Center at Syracuse

Rhoda L. Fisher
Private practice, Syracuse, New York

LEA LAWRENCE ERLBAUM ASSOCIATES, PUBLISHERS
1993   Hillsdale, New Jersey   Hove and London

Lawrence Erlbaum Associates, Inc., Publishers
365 Broadway
Hillsdale, New Jersey 07642

Library of Congress Cataloging-in-Publication Data

Fisher, Seymour.
    The psychology of adaptation to absurdity : tactics of make-
believe / Seymour Fisher, Rhoda L. Fisher.
        p.   cm.
    Includes bibliographical references and index.
    ISBN 0-8058-1205-9
    1. Fantasy. 2. Adjustment (Psychology). I. Fisher, Rhoda L.
(Rhoda Lee), 1924–   . II. Title.
    [DNLM: 1. Adaptation, Psychological. 2. Fantasy. WM 193.5.S8
    F536p]
    BF175.5.F36F57   1993
    155.2'4–dc20
    DNLM/DLC
    for Library of Congress   92-30295
                                                                   CIP

Books published by Lawrence Erlbaum Associates are printed on acid-free
paper, and their bindings are chosen for strength and durability.

Printed in the United States of America
10 9 8 7 6 5 4 3 2 1

To our family—Drs. Jerid Fisher, Eve Fisher-Whitmore, and Mark Whitmore. Also special regards to all the court jesters and other expert practitioners of absurdity out there.

CONTENTS

PREFACE

All cultures are infused with make-believe and magic. Even infants learn quickly that they must learn how to pretend; and they shortly become experts in fantasy construction. Daily life is filled with the fictions of novels, television, theater, and religious myths. We all learn to dissimulate, put on facades and masks, and daydream. People are forever toying with the potential unreality and, not infrequently, the absurdity of what they are experiencing. The comedians and dramatists of the world are fond of reminding us that all is not what it appears to be.

What is the significance of our preoccupation with make-believe? Why do we flirt so often with images depicting radical new versions of the world? Why are we so fascinated with fiction and pretense?

The major goal of this book is to explore and integrate all that is scientifically known about the utility of magical plans and strategies for coping with life's inevitable absurdities. Obviously, make-believe has great adaptive value. We wish to probe in detail how it helps the average individual to function better in a world saturated with contradiction and paradox. We trace the origins of pretending (illusion construction) and the developmental phases of this skill. We analyze how parents depend on pretending to secure conformity and self-control from their children. We unravel the ways in which make-believe is utilized to defend against death anxiety and feelings of fragility and insignificance. We examine the relationship between pretending and classical defense mechanisms. We test the protective powers of illusory constructs by investigating how well they have functioned in the context of religious myths. We also define the diverse contributions of make-believe to the construction of the self-concept, the defensive maneuvers of the psychologically distressed, and the maintenance of somatic health.

In short, this book pulls together all of the available scientific information and data concerning the defensive value of illusory make-believe in coping with those aspects of life that are experienced as unreasonable and beyond understanding.

An undertaking of this sort calls for the integration of a striking spectrum of research. We have drawn on literatures from such diverse sources as social, clinical, developmental, and cognitive psychology, psychiatry, anthropology, religion, psychosomatics, and the history of magic. This means that we often have had to bridge between concepts that are ordinarily not considered to be contiguous. The very diversity of the materials examined represented an obstacle to putting all of the pieces neatly together.

ACKNOWLEDGMENTS

We are appreciative of the support for our work that was provided by the Department of Psychiatry and Behavioral Sciences of the State University of New York Health Science Center (Syracuse). We had the benefit of a comfortable scholarly setting in which there was the right mix of those elements that facilitate the cycle of producing a book. Special thanks to the Health Science Center's library that patiently delivered superb service. Further, we would like to acknowledge Dr. Roger Greenberg's helpful observations concerning the relationship between absurdity and psychopathology.

Seymour Fisher
Rhoda L. Fisher

1

WHAT TO DO ABOUT ABSURDITY?

The comedians of the world have known from the beginning that the conditions of human existence, if viewed directly and rationally, appear somewhat absurd. In an earlier book (Fisher & Fisher, 1981), we studied a variety of comedians and clowns by means of interviews and formal psychological tests and learned a good deal about their personal conflicts and comedic strategies. One of the points that particularly impressed us about these people, who are so dedicated to being funny, is that they forever feel called upon to shield people from the threats and forebodings typifying modal life on this planet. As the result of early transactions with their parents they feel obligated to soothe others and to interpose themselves against the bad things "out there." They are weighted down by a poignant sense of duty to help those who come asking for the antidote provided by humor against human misfortune.

It is apropos in this respect that the early court jesters were assigned the role of protecting the king against the chaotic and uncontrolled forces in the universe. The jesters were considered to be qualified for such a role because their foolish strangeness and deviance intimated they were in contact with, and could potentially influence, analogous outlandish phenomena. Paradoxically, even as the funny ones soothe and protect, they also provoke. They go out of their way to conjure up images of threatening, forbidden stuff (variously relating to sex, death, anality, and hypocrisy). But each provocation is bathed in humor and the reassurance that there is nothing to fear from the threatening theme because it is, after all, only one more example of something ridiculous and absurd. The provocation functions in a fashion analogous to an injection of an attenuated virus intended to initiate the body's manufacture of a proper antibody. Much of the power of comedians resides in the fact that they can infuse images of the world with the flavor of unreal absurdity. We (Fisher & Fisher, 1981) originally depicted comedians as "Einsteins of the moral world" who do not respect one set of rules or moral principles more than any other. They communicate to their audiences that nothing is sacred. They scorn convention. They repeatedly shift their perspectives on events. With one joke they belittle the radical and in the next they make fun of the conservative. They are loyal only to the novel and the paradoxical.

Comedians revel in their play with potentially universal nonsense. They dramatize this apparent nonsense and simultaneously tell us it is nothing to worry about. We have suggested further (Fisher & Fisher, 1981) that comics love to intimate that anything is possible. They dramatize the unpredictable nature of things. They tell people that they are involved with forces that inevitably will go off into unexpected trajectories. They conjure up images of a Dali-like landscape pervaded by the surrealistic. They know that stark surprise faces all of us. Their comedy leads one to expect novel intrusion by highlighting that customary and apparently dependable rules are illusory. Because they ridicule the very nature of logic, how is it possible to reason or control? Basically, comedians prepare their audiences for chaos and perhaps even persuade them that chaos can be fun.

It is an interesting paradox that although comics are sensitizing the audience to the unexpected they imply that they have control over it. Court jesters and similar funny fools had a special, although strange status, because it was widely believed that they were capable of defending against chaos. Modern comics, in their play with funny images and nonsensical unpredictability, also convey a sense of ease with the chaotic stuff. They are apparently relaxed and happy in the midst of this stuff. They imply that they can influence what will happen and that there is probably nothing to fear. They arouse anxiety about concealed dangers, but at the same time provide soothing reassurance.

In other words, comics stand before us as outstanding practitioners of absurd images. They tease us with the idea that life is silly and ridiculous. They mock us with the possibility that there is only absurdity. But more fundamentally, they seduce us with the illusory protective promises of humor. They even suggest that absurdity is preferable to worse things that exist.

We know (Fisher & Fisher, 1981) that just about all cultures have reserved a valued niche for clowns and other kinds of clever "fools" in one guise or another. The near universality of the comic role is intriguing. It is as if there is a need in most cultures to have people around who are experts at playing with the idea of absurdity: to propose it, retract it, and experiment with it in all sorts of creative ways. Relatedly, it is obvious that there is a widespread fascination in everyday life with nonsense and potential absurdity. As people interact, much "kidding" and joking prevail in which it is implied that what appears to be serious and important has little or no significance. Such kidding often iconoclastically implies too that certain basic value systems and beliefs are just plain silly. It is not unusual in the course of a joking exchange to challenge persons' long-held beliefs about self and also about the solidity and meaningfulness of honored customs and institutions. People are forever titillating each other with the possibility that things are not what they appear to be, that there is the potential for reality to be turned upside down. In short, people keep alerting each other to consider that accepted world structures and values may be illusory. Solid meanings are humorously, cyclically, and repeatedly dissolved for a millisecond and then restored. Images highlighting the possibility that life is jumbled nonsense are featured in dreams, in The Theater of the Absurd (Esslin, 1961), in modern paintings, in schizophrenic imaginings, in the special context of children's television cartoons, and so forth. Of course, an opposite trend is even more strongly present. Tremendous quantities of societal energy go into affirming that basic values, ideas, and institutions are sensibly sound. We see this in many aspects of the community's educational apparatus, in the divinely reinforced pronouncements of the established religions, and in the confident urgings of parents.

Why are people so preoccupied with absurdity? Is it because they entertain secret doubts about whether their values, their beliefs, and even their very existence are meaningful? Does flirting with absurdity mirror persistent suspicions? Do we toy with absurdity as a way of preparing ourselves? That is, do we practice touching and tasting it with the hope that we can develop some expertise in coping with it as a chronically imminent event? As is well known, numerous observers (e.g., Frankl, 1955) have commented on what a struggle it is to make consistent sense of the whole process of living. Indeed, they have further suggested that unless individuals infiltrate their life perceptions with good solid self-protective illusions they become overwhelmed by the absurdity of it all. They argue that one can survive psychologically only by elaborate self-deceptions designed to put an acceptable face on what living is all about. Literary figures have been in the forefront of those urging the need for such illusory self-deception (e.g., Eugene O'Neill in The Iceman Cometh; Henrik Ibsen in The Wild Duck; Pirandello in Henry IV). Using a more empirical framework, Lazarus (1983) and others (e.g., Becker, 1973; Tiger, 1979) similarly hypothesized the need for defensive illusions to buffer life's sheer toughness.

They picture humans as having to face up to the gnawing implications of being biologically anchored creatures inhabiting an astral speck and inevitably subject not only to illness but also death. No one has more vividly pictured the dilemma posed by existential threats than has Becker (1973):

> Man is reluctant to move out into the overwhelmingness of his world, the real dangers of it; he shrinks back from losing himself in the all-consuming appetites of others, from spinning out of control in the clutchings and clawings of

men, beasts, and machines. As an animal organism man senses the kind of planet
he has been put on, the nightmarish, demonic frenzy of individual organismic
appetites of all kinds—not to mention earthquakes, meteors, and hurricanes—
Above all there is the danger of a slip-up, an accident, a chance disease, and
of course death, the final sucking up, the total submergence and negation.
(pp. 53–54)

Becker referred, in addition, to the illusory strategies people have to adopt
in order to shut out the threat of the world:

Everything that man does in his symbolic world is an attempt to deny and overcome his grotesque fate. He literally drives himself into a blind obliviousness
with social games, psychological tricks, personal preoccupations so far removed
from the reality of his situation that there are forms of madness—agreed madness, shared madness, disguised and signified madness, but madness all the same.
(p. 27)

Becker's statement is theatrical in its intensity and well beyond the tone of
scientific discourse. However, this intensity may have a useful function in
alerting the theoreticians and practitioners of the social sciences that they
have been grossly blind to the role of existential anxiety in human behavior.
Scientific journals are crammed full of studies concerned with the mediating
effects upon behavior of variables like family structure, socioeconomic status, ethnic background, intelligence, personality, and so forth. However, one
rarely finds studies concerned with the impact on behavior of the fact that
humans live on a tiny planet moving in an untracked endlessness. The sheer
fragility of the human condition is largely dismissed, as if it were a mere background factor. There seems to have been reluctance to get seriously involved
with such a potentially overwhelming theme. From a common sense perspective, it is hard to believe that persons are not shadowed by their cognitive maps of where they stand in the universe and how far along they are
on the mortal line into the future. A detailed analysis of the empirical data
bearing on these matters is presented later.

THE DISCOMFORT OF REALISM

Is there any scientific evidence that human psychological survival requires
the creation of self-reassuring myths? Does a sense of safety or happiness
require a lot of pretending and the Pollyannish shutting out of life's negativi-
ties? Let us, by way of introduction to this matter, look at several sectors
of relevant research.

One area that has been thoroughly reviewed by Watson and Clark (1984)
relates to negative affectivity, which is a disposition to experience aversive
emotional states. Multiple studies have shown that a whole variety of meas-

ures pertaining to psychological discomfort (e.g., trait anxiety, neuroticism, maladjustment) are highly intercorrelated and really refer to the same basic tendency to feel distress and discomfort over time, regardless of the situation and even when specific identifiable stress is absent. Some individuals go around feeling persistently distressed and others do not. Investigators have tried to identify basic factors that would distinguish such persons high and low in negative affectivity. Watson and Clark, after reviewing this research, concluded that those low in negative affectivity

> are most content and satisfied with life and eschew the ruthless honesty of high-Negative Affectivity individuals, both with regard to self and others, in favor of smoothing over life's rocky road. They focus on themselves less and, when they do, are more pleased with what they find, enabling them to maintain a better mood, a more favorable self-view, perhaps to the point of glossing over (repressing?) some harsh truths. (1984, p. 484)

There is actually evidence that persons high in negative affectivity are more accurate in some of their social perceptions than are persons low in this respect. For example, Kaplan (1968) reported that individuals high in negative affectivity are significantly more accurate in ratings of peers than are those in the low to middle negative affectivity category. The low negative affectivity group is depicted by Watson and Clark as more "defensive," but "better adjusted." Block (1965) concluded from a longitudinal study that persons low in negative affectivity handle "anxiety and conflicts by, in effect, refusing to recognize their presence" (pp. 100–101). The more defensive, denying style of individuals low in negative affectivity stands out, although it is difficult to boldly generalize that these individuals are, in most respects, lower in their level of realism. Overall, it is fair to say that they evidence a lower degree of psychological disturbance and a greater degree of "glossing over" and denial in some of life's "harsh truths." Watson and Clark (1984) analogously concluded that, "Insofar as high Negative Affectivity subjects are more focused on themselves and their feelings, they are more emotionally self-aware and honest with themselves. At the same time, however, they are highly distressed and poorly adjusted" (p. 481). What emerges is the simple tendency for an inverse relationship to exist between how happy and satisfied one feels and how open and nondefensive one is in witnessing life's difficulties. Those persons who are distressed seem not to be sufficiently selective (excluding) in what they allow themselves to witness and make part of their awareness.

Relatedly, there is an even more extensive and somewhat startling body of research tying depression to enhanced realism. Incidentally, one finds an ever-increasing amount of preoccupation in the psychiatric and psychological literature with the phenomena of depression. Investigators seem to be uneasily impressed that so many people experience the blues; and they assiduously spin out explanations as to likely causes. Many of the prominent theorists (e.g., Beck, 1976; Seligman, 1975) portrayed depression as arising from distorted interpretations concerning the nature of the world. It has been proposed that depressed persons are caught up in basic disheartening biases, such as grossly underestimating their own ability to influence outcomes or unrealistically exaggerating the probability of unpleasant negative events. From this perspective, people are depressed because they have constructed a view of life that mistakenly exaggerates its down side. Indeed, there are numerous studies in the literature that, as one might expect, do demonstrate that depressed persons' cognitions are more sad and unhappy than are those of nondepressives. Such observations and others of a related character suggest that depression derives from habitually and unrealistically expecting things to be more negative than they truly are. But note that some evidence has accumulated that depressed persons have actually had more unhappy childhoods and adult lives than nondepressives (e.g., Ilfeld, 1977; Lloyd, 1980). Thus, the pessimism of depressives could be regarded as just as realistic as the relative optimism of nondepressives who have had less discouraging experiences.

A variety of studies of depressive phenomena have accumulated that point to even more surprising contradictions concerning the presumed distorted perspective of the depressed individual. Researchers have come upon the fact that depressives are *more realistic* than nondepressives in a number of judgmental areas. A particularly novel illustration of this point involves the phenomenon of "illusion of control" described by Langer (1975). She observed that when persons are asked to perform tasks with only a chance probability of success, they succumb fairly easily to the illusion that they can exert personal powers that will produce better than chance results. For example, if they are asked to pull cards from a deck in an attempt to obtain higher cards than those of a competitor, most can, after relatively simple experimental manipulations, be persuaded that there is an element of personal influence governing the cards drawn. This illusion of control is, of course, widely evident in gambling behavior.

Alloy and Abramson (1979, 1982) demonstrated in clever experiments that depressed persons are less susceptible than nondepressed to such an illusion. In one instance (1979), subjects were given the impression that they could control whether a light would go on or off by either pressing or not pressing a button. A series of trials was run and the button-pressing process was manipulated so that only chance success was achieved. Subjects rated how much control they thought their button pressing gave them over the light. A variety of special conditions (e.g., degree of effective contingency) were introduced into the several experiments. The results indicated that "Depressed students' judgments of contingency were surprisingly accurate. . . . Nondepressed students, on the other hand, overestimated the degree of contingency between their responses and outcomes when noncontingent outcomes were frequent and/or desired and underestimated the degree of contingency when contingent outcomes were undesired" (p. 441).

In another instance, Alloy and Abramson (1982) exposed depressed and nondepressed college students to either controllable noise (90 db tone), uncontrollable noise, or no noise. The students were then asked to perform a task equivalent to that just described involving the pressing of a button to turn a light on or off; and they were to judge how much control they actually exerted over the light. During certain trials it was arranged that some subjects would, despite the noncontingency, experience apparent success and other subjects would experience apparent failure. The depressed subjects showed high accuracy in their judgments of control no matter what the condition to which they were exposed. But the nondepressed "previously exposed to uncontrollable noises showed a robust illusion of control in the conditions in which events were noncontingent but associated with success" (p. 1114).[1] Analogous findings have been reported by Golin, Terrell, and Johnson (1977) and Golin, Terrell, Weitz, and Drost (1979) not only in mildly depressed individuals but also in depressed and nondepressed psychiatric patients.

Alloy, Abramson, and Viscusi (1981) showed, too, that if depressed and nondepressed persons are manipulated so that their mood states are transiently reversed, susceptibility to the illusion of control changes accordingly. Depressed subjects were exposed to statements that made them feel more elated and nondepressed subjects were exposed to statements that made them feel more depressed. While under the influence of such mood states, the subjects participated in the "press button—light on or off" procedure and judged how much control they felt they had exerted on the on–off behavior of the light. The data indicated that "naturally nondepressed women made temporarily depressed gave accurate judgments of control while naturally depressed women made temporarily elated showed an illusion of control and overestimated their impact on an objectively uncontrollable outcome" (p. 1129).

Lewinsohn, Chaplin, and Barton (1980) arranged for depressed and nondepressed patients and also normals to engage in a series of group interactions. The patients' behaviors in these group situations were rated by observers for such variables as friendliness, warmth, humor, and social skillfulness. The patients also rated themselves for the same variables. Analyses were then undertaken to ascertain how much agreement there was between observer and self-evaluations. The greater the agreement between the sets of ratings, the greater the realism implied on the part of individuals in their

---

[1]Ford and Neale (1985) reported that simply exposing normal persons to a mild failure experience (that would presumably have some depressive impact) is sufficient to render them more realistic in their judgments of how much control they have over the Langer (1975) "press button—light on or off" task designed to measure illusion of control.

appraisals of their own social behavior. Both the normals and the non-depressed psychiatric patients were found to be significantly less realistic than the depressed psychiatric patients. Lewinsohn et al. noted, "Nondepressed people may thus be characterized with a halo or glow that involves an illusory self-enhancement in which one sees oneself more positively than others see one" (p. 210).[2]

Quite a number of other studies have reinforced the image of the nondepressed surrounding themselves with an illusory glow. E. R. Nelson and Craighead (1977) discovered that a depressed group accurately recalls the frequency of negative feedback it receives in a laboratory situation, whereas a nondepressed sample underestimates the frequency of negative feedback. Rozensky, Rehm, Pry, and Roth (1977) found that nondepressed subjects in a laboratory context overreward themselves for their performance to a significantly greater degree than the depressed. Further, Rizley (1978) and Kuiper (1978) observed that although depressives regard themselves as equally responsible for their previous successes and failures on a task, nondepressives assign high responsibility to themselves for success, but low responsibility to themselves for failure. The nondepressives were clearly less objective and evenhanded in evaluating their own performance patterns. The relatively greater evenhandedness of depressives in such self-judgments is reported, too, by Tennen and Herzberger (1987) and Crocker, Alloy, and Kayne (1988). Several studies (Roth & Ingram, 1985; Sackeim, 1983; Sackeim & Gur, 1979) have even reported significant trends for degree of depression to be negatively correlated with a measure of one's general inclination to be self-deceptive.

Layne (1983), after scanning the overall pertinent literature in this area concerned with depression, remarked that, "The major implication of the empirical literature is that depressives' thoughts are painfully truthful, whereas nondepressives' thoughts are unrealistically positive" (pp. 851–852).[3] However, it should be noted that studies have appeared that raise questions about the generality of depressive realism. Campbell and Fehr (1990) failed to find that degree of depression is correlated with accuracy in individuals' judgments of how others view them. Dunning and Story (1991) did not find in a real-life, nonlaboratory context that mildly depressed college students are more accurate than the nondepressed in predicting their future actions and outcomes. Note in addition, that Alloy and Abramson (1988), after analyzing an exhaustive array of pertinent publications, suggested that the matter of depressives being more realistic than nondepressives may not be as sim-

---

[2]Interestingly, there was a trend for the depressed patients to become less realistic in their judgments as they began to improve during the course of treatment!

[3]Layne (1983) suggested, on the basis of Rorschach data compiled by Holt (1968) and Allison, Blatt, and Zimet (1968), that depressives are "highly accurate and matter-of-fact in their perceptions" (p. 850).

plistically true as it appears to be. They pointed out that several studies have found that the greater accuracy of the depressive may apply particularly when judgments about self are involved but not when judgments about others are called for. There may also be equivocal trends for the relative accuracy of depressives and nondepressives to vary as a function of whether assessments occur in private versus public settings and also whether the information supplied for the judgments is ambiguous. At the same time, Ackerman and DeRubeis (1991) concluded on the basis of their review of the pertinent literature that, "Whereas results from contingency judgment and self-other studies suggest that depressed and dysphoria individuals are more accurate than nondepressed individuals, studies examining subjects' recall of self-evaluative information indicate that the nondepressed subjects are more accurate" (p. 565). Obviously, we are confronted by divergent interpretations of the existing literature. However, despite the ambiguities, the actual data in hand do indicate that nondepressives are probably less accurate and realistic than depressives in a number of contexts.

Still another sector of research that is pertinent to the adaptive use of illusion concerns the strategies persons press into service when they encounter catastrophic threats. The value of illusion has emerged particularly well in studies of individuals with major body disturbances. R. G. Frank et al. (1987) examined the coping strategies of those who had suffered serious spinal cord injuries and ascertained how these strategies mediate degree of psychological distress experienced. Frank et al. were surprised to learn that the most adequate copers (as defined by lower levels of distress) entertain the most unrealistic ideas about how much control they have over the course of their disability. Such individuals unrealistically ascribe exaggerated powers to themselves with respect to their ability to influence their illness. Frank et al. contrasted their findings with earlier assumptions (e.g., Nemiah, 1957; Siller, 1969) that adaptation to severe injury goes best when injured persons are confronted with the stark reality of their dilemma and discouraged from the use of cushioning illusion. Note that Silver and Wortman (1980) previously obtained data also pointing up the benefits patients with spinal cord injuries derive from self-deceptive optimisms.

Taylor (1983) offered an insightful and well-documented analysis of the adaptive modes employed by persons confronted with such shocking threats as cancer or rape. The range and flexibility of these modes are underscored. But most of all, Taylor said that "successful adjustment depends, in a large part, on the ability to sustain and modify illusions that buffer not only against present threats but also against possible future setbacks" (p. 1161). There are many examples of how patients with cancer often unrealistically construct comforting images with respect to making themselves safe and invulnerable. Taylor came to the conclusion that illusion is an important positive force in the face of traumatic threat. The following quote speaks for itself:

I maintain that illusions can have a dynamic force. They can simultaneously protect and prompt constructive thought and action. As the literature on depression and the self make clear, normal cognitive processing and behavior may depend on a substantial degree of illusion, whereas the ability to see things clearly can be associated with depression and inactivity. Thus, far from impeding adjustment, illusion may be essential for adequate coping. (p. 1171)

As noted earlier, the material presented here with respect to the protective functions of illusion is by way of introduction. A more detailed analysis of such self-deceptive phenomena is spelled out later. However, the introductory illustrations provide at least initial affirmation that there are good scientific reasons for exploring the self-protective value of illusion.

In the following chapters, we document the various kinds of life absurdities that confront the average individual and what strategies are available for buffering them. We examine the absurd alternatives often associated with the threat of death, loss of physical powers, and the vicissitudes of maintaining a meaningful vision of existence. To be human means unending negotiation with comiclike surprises and paradoxes.

2

HOW DIFFICULT IS IT TO BE HUMAN?

The idea that people need to encapsulate themselves in illusory bubbles to cope with being on this planet obviously assumes that they encounter a good deal of menacing unpleasantness. If there is widespread resort to illusion, one would assume that people are, in considerable numbers, finding life to be disconcerting and even overwhelming. To what degree is this true? Do we have any dependable information as to how psychologically dangerous people experience their residence here? More to the point, what kinds of data would provide such dependable information? There are many published surveys in which people have been asked how pleasant or unpleasant their lives are; and, from time to time, interesting observations have been garnered. However, if one assumes that people are employing illusion on a widespread basis to fool themselves into believing life is not overwhelming or absurd, then simply asking them how bad things are might only sample their efforts to hide from the unpleasantness. The profusion of literature dealing with the matter of how threatening people find life to be bears witness to the complexity of the issues involved. We think it is worthwhile to explore this complexity. In this chapter we look at multiple levels of how life "feels." We probe the literature dealing not only with how people say they feel about their lives, but also dealing with the relevant images and fantasies they entertain more privately, as expressed, for example, in projective responses and dreams.

PUBLIC DECLARATIONS OF HOW ONE FEELS

Considerable information has accumulated concerning what people say when they are asked directly to estimate how happy or unhappy (satisfied–dissatisfied) they are with their existences. Multiple papers have examined the average levels of expressed happiness–unhappiness in diverse cultures, socioeconomic levels, ethnic groups, age divisions, and gender categories. There is also endless methodological scrutiny of such matters as the effects of the specific phrasings of questions upon happiness reports obtained; seasonal variations in stated happiness; stability over time of happiness judgments; and so forth (e.g., Andrews, 1986; Andrews & Withey, 1976; Bradburn, 1969; Bryant & Veroff, 1982; Campbell, Converse, & Rodgers, 1976; Cantril, 1965; Watts & Free, 1973). In general, when persons respond to questions[1] about how happy they are, the majority say they feel pretty good.[2] Inglehart and Rabier (1986) analyzed responses from thousands of individuals in Western Europe and reported that 21% judged themselves to be "very satisfied" with their lives as a whole, 57% were "fairly satisfied," 16% were "not very satisfied," and 5% were "not at all satisfied." With respect to degree of happiness, 20% said they were "very happy," 58% "fairly happy," and 20% "not too happy."

Large-scale studies carried out in the United States present a similar picture. Campbell et al. (1976) noted that in one national survey in 1972, 22% said they were "very happy," 68% "pretty happy," and 10% "not too happy." Later U.S. surveys (T. W. Smith, 1979) tend to find a greater percentage (28%–36%) in the "very happy," a smaller percentage (51%–60%) in the "pretty happy," and a slightly larger percentage (11%–18%) in the "not too happy" categories. Andrews and Withey (1976) observed, in a large U.S. sample collected in 1972, that in response to the question "How do you feel about: life in the United States today?", 7% said they were "delighted," 22% "pleased," 39% "mostly satisfied," 23% "mixed," 5% "mostly dissatisfied," 3% "unhappy," and 1% "terrible." Generally, although individuals declare they are happy and satisfied, it is noteworthy that somewhere between 10% to 20% do depict themselves as quite dissatisfied or unhappy.[3]

No one really knows what variables mediate average persons' judgments of their level of happiness when they are called on to make public statements in this regard. Hard-working researchers (Andrews & Withey, 1976; Costa & McCrae, 1980; Diener, 1984) who have looked at a broad spectrum of possible mediating variables (e.g., age, education, race, gender, socioeconomic level) have been able to account, at the most, for only about 17% of the variance of the self-happiness ratings.

---

[1]For example: "Taking all things together, how would you say things are these days—would you say you're very happy, fairly happy or not too happy these days?" (Inglehart & Rabier, 1986, p. 8).

[2]Rosenberg (1965) and other investigators observed that the majority of persons who are asked to describe how they feel about themselves respond in a clearly favorable direction.

[3]Veroff, Douvan, and Kulka (1981) stated, on the basis of a nationwide sample of opinions: "While most of us respond to life as offering zestful opportunities, a substantial group of people (19%) select responses indicating considerable depression about their existence" (p. 545).

As might be expected, there are suggestions that the very process of evaluating oneself publicly plays a role in the character of one's happiness judgments. For example, differential attitudes toward such public disclosure have apparently contributed to observed national differences in happiness judgments. Inglehart and Rabier (1986) concluded, after an analysis of relatively substantial national differences in self-rated happiness, that the differences might reflect "different cultural baselines concerning what is the normal response to questions concerning one's subjective well-being" (p. 43). That is, it is less acceptable in some cultures, than in others to testify that one is not highly satisfied with life. Actually, it has been shown (e.g., T. W. Smith, 1979) that social desirability significantly influences people to give "I feel very happy" answers when they are queried publicly about their private feelings in this area. Therefore, it is striking that, even in the face of this defensive caution, a sizable chunk of people (15%–20%) are willing to declare they are experiencing considerable discomfort with life.[4]

A number of factor analyses have been undertaken to determine the structure of self-ratings of satisfaction and happiness.[5] Such self-ratings have not proved to be unidimensional. They typically can be analyzed into a series of factors (e.g., lack of self-confidence, lack of gratification). One factor, which often emerges in various guises, involves feelings of vulnerability. Apparently, a basic constituent of feeling unhappy is a sense of "being overwhelmed" and the "perception that bad things frequently occur" (Bryant & Veroff, 1986). This sense of vulnerability could conceivably bear some relationship to the earlier discussed "modal anxiety" that seems to prevail in relation to conditions of existence on our planet.

We call attention to a special finding that emerged from a study by Campbell et al. (1976). It was observed, in a national sample of persons living in the United States, that those who had a broader "awareness of alternatives" tended to describe themselves as relatively less "satisfied" with life. Two examples of this phenomenon may be cited. In one instance, it was found that those who had at any time lived in a place where life differed from that of their current community were less likely to be satisfied with their current locale. In another instance, it was noted that there was a trend for "reported satisfaction to decline with advancing education" (p. 143). Campbell et al.

---

[4]The complexity of interpreting the meaning of public declarations concerning one's degree of happiness is pointed up by the finding (Inglehart & Rabier, 1986) that the average expressed levels of happiness of various European countries are significantly *negatively* correlated with their suicide rates.

[5]Incidentally, it has emerged that feelings of well-being are related to both the presence of positive experiences and the relative absence of negative ones, but the correlation between self-rated positive and negative elements is minimal. The positive and the negative represent separate factors. There is no simple inverse relationship between the numbers of positive and negative feelings an individual experiences during a period of time.

(1976) hypothesized that with increasing education there is heightened awareness of life alternatives, and this awareness prevents "blind and unquestion-
ing satisfaction with the status quo" (pp. 145–146). More broadly, it may be
that the opening of oneself to awareness of the full range of environmental
possibilities has some kind of a dampening effect on how positively the world
is experienced. At one level, it could be interpreted that knowing a wider
range of possibilities simply makes one more conscious of what one does not
have, and therefore less satisfied. Campbell et al. (1976) suggested such a
possibility when they related their findings to the fact that dissatisfaction in
small, remote countries has often grown sharply as the inhabitants have been
made more aware (via electronic media) of the greater range of activities
and resources available "out there." This interpretation may be valid.
However, it is also conceivable that a part of the increased dissatisfaction
of those who become "aware of alternatives" is that their increased breadth
of awareness diminishes their ability to insulate (hide) themselves from the
multiple, potentially menacing aspects of the world. We introduce this possibility for consideration and discuss it again in other contexts.

DEMORALIZATION AND SYMPTOMS

The question of how positively or negatively persons experience their lives
has been approached, too, in terms of the prevalence of "symptoms" and
various forms of discomfort. Many of the studies in this area have focused
on what Link and Dohrenwend (1980) referred to as "demoralization." Typically, subjects are asked (usually by an interviewer) to respond to a series
of questions about a variety of physical and psychological symptoms regarded as related to psychiatric disorders. For example, the individual might be
asked to respond true or false to a statement like, "You feel anxiety about
something or someone almost all the time"; or indicate "often," "sometimes,"
or "never" to the inquiry, "Have you ever been bothered by 'cold sweats'?"
Many such "screening scales" have been constructed (e.g., Dupuy, 1974; Gurin,
Veroff, & Feld, 1960; Langner, 1962). As already mentioned, Link and Dohrenwend (1980) discovered that the scores from such scales are correlated strongly with a cluster of variables (e.g., low self-esteem, sadness, anxiety) that define
how demoralized one feels about one's life. In reviewing the findings concerning the application of demoralization scales to multiple individual com-
munities and nationwide samples, Link and Dohrenwend (1980) concluded
"the rate of demoralization in the United States approaches one-quarter of
the population" (p. 126). Further analysis of the data suggested that somewhere between 16% and 20% of the population are "clinically impaired."

There is an increasingly more reliable and sophisticated literature directed at objectively ascertaining the total prevalence of formal "psychiatric

disturbance" (i.e., as defined by psychiatric criteria, like DSM-III) in representative samples (e.g., Leighton, Harding, Macklin, Macmillan, & Leighton, 1963;
Srole et al., 1975, 1977). In 1974, Dohrenwend and Dohrenwend published
an analysis of this literature and concluded that the average urban prevalence rate of formal psychiatric disturbance in North America is 21%, about
18% in South America, 15.5% in Europe, and 25.9% in Australia. They noted that the greater the direct contact with the subject by the evaluators, the
greater the amount of psychopathology uncovered.

More recently, Robins et al. (1984) found the lifetime prevalence of DSM-
III disturbance in a large sample involving three U.S. cities to be in the
29%–38% range.[6] Schwab and Schwab (1978) analyzed all of the available
cross-cultural data pertinent to the prevalence of significant emotional disturbance and judged the level to be in the 15%–20% range.[7]

Other observations document further the fairly high prevalence of diverse
forms of "symptomatology" and difficulties in functioning. Consider the following. Bixler, Kales, Soldatos, Kales, and Healey (1979) determined, on the
basis of a survey of more than 1,000 households in Los Angeles, that there was
an overall prevalence of current or previous "sleep disorders" of 52.1%. Note
that the prevalence for insomnia was 42.5% and for nightmares was 11.2%.

Costello (1982) found that fears and phobias were extremely common in
a large-scale community study of women in Canada. Thus, 675 per 1,000 of
the population had mild phobic fears; 240 per 1,000 had intense fears; and
194 per 1,000 had phobic fears so intense that they actually avoided certain
objects or situations. Animal fears were most frequent, followed by the
categories "nature," "social," "mutilation," and "separation," in decreasing
order. Telch, Lucas, and Nelson (1989) discovered that 12% of a large non-
clinical sample of college students had, at some previous time, experienced
an "unexpected panic attack." They cited studies involving other populations
that have shown similar trends for the prevalence of panic attacks.

West, Kellner, and Moore-West (1986) discovered, in a survey of 9,000
adolescents in 10 U.S. cities, that 10%–15% were "seriously lonely," 45% were
"less seriously lonely," and 54% were "often lonely." Similarly, Norman and
Harris (1981) observed, in a large sample of 160,000 adolescents, that although
68% said they liked themselves, 14% said they wished they were "someone
else," and 8% said they "sometimes" think of suicide.[8] Wells, Klerman, and

---

[6]Robins et al. (1984) also found prevalence rates for serious alcohol abuse/dependence to
be in the 11%–16% range.

[7]Campbell, Converse, and Rodgers (1976) indicated that, in nationwide samples, 12%–19%
of those interviewed report that they have, at some time, felt they were going to have a "nervous breakdown."

[8]Mishara, Baker, and Mishara (1976) observed, in a sample of 293 college students, a lifetime suicide attempt prevalence rate of 15%. In addition, about 65% of the students said they
had, at one time or another, thought of suicide.

Deykin (1987) stated that, of a sample of adolescents, 33% described themselves as significantly depressed. Weissman and Myers (1978) detected, in
an investigation of over 1,000 households in New Haven, Connecticut, a 20%
lifetime prevalence of "major depression."

Pandina, White, and Yorke (1981) appraised 1,970 students in Grades 9–12
in New Jersey and reported that 41% used alcohol, 17% used both alcohol
and marijuana, and 11% used alcohol, marijuana, and at least two other drugs.
Relatedly, the *Morbidity and Mortality Weekly Report* (Colliver, Doernberg,
Grant, Dufour, & Bertolucci, 1986) stated, on the basis of data secured between 1943 and 1983, that

> Approximately 10.6 million adults in the United States can be classified as alco-
> holics, and an additional 7.3 million either are alcohol abusers or have ex-
> perienced negative consequences of alcohol use such as arrest or involvement
> in an accident. Further, an estimated 4.6 million young people aged 14 to 17
> are problem drinkers. (p. 703)

Surveys of national, young-adult, U.S. samples (King, 1986) reveal that 21.4%
have "ever used" hallucinogens, 28.3% cocaine, 18% stimulants, 18.7% seda-
tives, and 15.1% tranquilizers.

These diverse findings dramatize the idea that significant segments of
the population get into serious psychological trouble at some point in their
life span.[9] It is beginning to look like roughly one fourth to one third of
the total population suffers significant functional maladjustments during
their life course. The percentages of people considered to be maladjusted
do vary, of course, in relation to the definitions and criteria employed.
However, no matter how they are defined, there is no question that much
of the population get grossly distressed and frequently seek remedies that
are self-destructive.

INTERNAL IMAGES AND FEELINGS

Up to this point, we have scanned what is known about how persons publicly describe their degrees of happiness or satisfaction with life. We also have
considered the major facts concerning the prevalence of overt "symptoms"
indicative of psychological disturbance. Let us turn now to another dimension, less public levels, and examine feelings about life that are minimally

---

[9]There are hints (e.g., Farberow, 1980) that even larger segments of the population, which
cannot formally be labeled as manifesting psychiatric disturbance, are engaged in behaviors (e.g.,
cigarette smoking, gambling, high-risk activities) so seriously self-destructive as to suggest major
underlying frustrations and unhappiness.

subject to censorship and personal concealment. It would be helpful to gain access to life attitudes that are perhaps not even available to the individual's own awareness. To secure such data, one must use projective tests or sample the imagery in private productions, such as dreams, imaginative ruminations, and free associations. We have attempted to survey scattered caches of data of this sort.

Dreams

Diverse interpretations have been offered concerning the nature and significance of dreams (Fisher & Greenberg, 1985; Foulkes, 1982; Hall, 1966; Winget & Kramer, 1979). Dreams have been viewed as representing the whole gamut—from wish fulfillments to pure noise. Most researchers are inclined to interpret dreams as representing an individual's thoughts, preoccupations, and images depicted in a relatively fragmented and loosely organized fashion. There is clear evidence that feelings and moods do register in dream content. Therefore it is of interest to look at some of the modal themes that have been detected in large-scale studies of dreams. Thousands of dreams of essentially normal persons have been analyzed (e.g., Hall, 1951; Hall & Van de Castle, 1966), and their contents have been subjected to myriad quantifying procedures. The findings indicate that the dreams of average adults are negatively and unpleasantly toned.[10] Fear, tension, and anger are often prominent. Hall (1951) classified the emotions that appeared in a sample of 10,000 dreams into the following categories: (a) apprehension (fear), (b) anger, (c) sadness, (d) happiness, and (e) excitement. He noted: "Apprehension predominated, accounting for 40% of all dream emotions; anger, happiness and excitement were tied with 18% each, and sadness was the least frequent, 6%. Thus, 64% of all dream emotions were negative or unpleasant (apprehension, anger, sadness), and only 18% (happiness) were positively pleasant" (p. 62).

Robbins and Kilbride (1971) concluded, after analyzing a sample of dreams of persons living in Uganda (Africa), that "conflict and anxiety" were prominent themes. Griffith, Miyagi, and Tago (1958) described the "typical dreams" of Japanese college students living in Tokyo as often involving such themes as "being attacked or pursued," "falling," and "being frozen with fright." There were also positive themes (e.g., eating delicious food, sexual experiences), but they were in the minority. Kramer (1970) concluded, after scanning the literature concerning manifest dream content, that the typical adult dream is "more hostile than friendly, and more unpleasant than pleasant"

---

[10]However, Foulkes (1982) reported that the dreams of young children and adolescents are not dominated by unhappy affects.

(p. 151). As depicted in the realm of dreams, life is a rather difficult, unhappy matter.

Projective Tests, Imaginative Stories, Spontaneous Speech

Access to the level of private thought is provided, too, by the images persons conjure up when they respond to relatively unstructured inkblots (e.g., Rorschach Inkblot Test) or pictures (Thematic Apperception Test [TAT]). Although reliable data are scarce, such projective responses do indicate a trend for negative content to predominate over positive. For example, De-Vos (1952) applied an elaborate scheme for classifying the content of Rorschach Inkblot responses to the protocols of 60 "normal" adults and found a considerably higher rate of "unpleasant" as compared with "positive affect." Relatedly, Eron (1948) discovered, in a sample of college students, that the imaginative stories they created in response to pictures (TAT) were imbued heavily with negative themes (e.g., disequilibrium, guilt, aggression, sense of being pressured, mental disturbance).

Still another potential approach to persons' private attitudes is through their spontaneous imaginative stories. What themes and feelings appear when they compose fiction? Careful quantitative studies of the themes appearing in the stories of normal individuals are hard to find. However, when Pitcher and Prelinger (1963) obtained spontaneous stories from 70 "normal" girls and 67 "normal" boys (ages 2–5), the dominant themes focused on aggression, death, and misfortune. There were also a significant number of stories concerned with morality and nurturance. The highest number of themes fell into the category "hurt or misfortune."

At a different level, Gottschalk and Gleser (1969) devised a technique to score the amount of anxiety expressed by individuals when they were asked to talk spontaneously for 5 minutes. They took the verbatim, 5-minute tape-recorded sample of each individual and analyzed the number and intensity of anxious references to such themes as shame, guilt, death, and mutilation. They found that it was normative for anxious imagery to constitute a significant part of such verbal samples. Rychlak (1973) also described a good deal of negative toning in the free fantasies of high school students.

In the anonymous context of a telephone survey of households in the San Francisco area, Scherer and Tannenbaum (1986) asked respondents for examples of a recent situation that evoked "strong emotional feelings." The researchers discovered that "the majority of the situations reported had evoked negative emotions" (p. 295).

A variety of other studies (e.g., Brandstatter, 1983; Csikszentmihalyi & Larson, 1984; Hurlburt, 1979), which used time-sampling procedures to tap the content of thought in naturalistic settings throughout the day, have revealed that negative affects are significantly, and sometimes prominently, represented. A substantial minority of individuals report a fair weighting of negative feelings and images, although they have to do so in a somewhat public, and potentially embarrassing, context.[11]

CONCLUSION

The formal research literature documents what we all individually sense on the basis of our day-to-day personal experiences and intuitions. At any given time, a fairly sizable percentage of the population is in a state of psychological distress. Behaviors indicative of pressing discomfort seem to typify one fourth to one third of the people around us. There is reasonable evidence of widespread phobic anxiety, depression, and other related forms of demoralization. Everywhere, people are medicating themselves with alcohol and buffering unpleasantness with drugs. They also are having trouble sleeping, choosing to exit via suicide, and tuning into insistent interior streams of dark imagery and ideation. Lasch's (1984) impressionistic version of this troubled psychological state of affairs is vividly phrased: "the concern with the self, which seems so characteristic of our time, takes the form of a concern with its psychic survival. People have lost confidence in the future. . . . Ever since the Second World War, the end of the world has loomed as a hypothetical possibility"; and he suggested that we have retreated simply to a "determination to survive the general wreckage or, more modestly, to hold one's life together in the face of mounting pressures" (p. 16).

---

[11]Singer and McCraven (1961) reported that "fearful content" appears frequently in daydreams.

3

WHAT IS DEATH ANXIETY
AND HOW PERVASIVE IS IT?

Innumerable commentators have considered that the awareness of death's inevitability is the central threat to experiencing a meaningful life. They portray the ability to anticipate one's death as the curse of being human and an inescapable marker of existential absurdity. Some, like Becker (1973) or Zilboorg (1943), saw every person as preoccupied with death anxiety and persistently defending against it with such strategies as simple denial, religious faith in immortality, exaggerated expectations of medical "cure," and the acting out of heroic "Nothing can terminate me" fantasies. Levinson, Darrow, Klein, Levinson, and McKee (1978) provided data indicating that by mid-life it is normative for men to be confronted with making sense of their death, which looms up ahead. He stated:

> At mid-life, the growing recognition of mortality collides with the powerful wish for immortality and the many illusions that help to maintain it. A man's fear that he is not immortal is expressed in his preoccupation with bodily decline and his fantasies of imminent death. At the most elemental level, he feels that he is fighting for survival. He is terrified at the thought of being dead, of no longer existing as this particular person. (p. 215)

The speculative literature is saturated with theories about the nature of death anxiety and how it influences people. We assign considerable priority to checking these theories, and to finding out what role the fear of death plays in human conduct and imagination. Let us be clear as to what we want to learn. Essentially, how great, on the average, is the impact of death anxiety? Is death anxiety pervasive? Is it truly a major source of tension for most individuals? Is it a substantial contributor to psychological disturbance in

Western culture? Does awareness of one's mortality become the rent through which intimations of world absurdity seep in? These are not easy questions and, some cannot be answered with genuine authority at the present time.

The appraisal of what we know about death anxiety is the first phase of an agenda intended to explore what appear to be the most basic problems linked with being a human residing in the unpredictable ambiance of a tiny planet. Obviously, our humanoid somatic fragility, with its associated mortality, stands out with particular prominence. However, we propose two other major problems. One of these derives from the fundamental unpredictability of life on our planet. We refer to this as the problem of uncertainty. The other touches on our dramatic smallness in the total scheme of the universe. We label this the problem of centrality. These issues are explored in depth in later chapters.

BODY AWARENESS

Becker (1973) told us that death anxiety is inherent in the awareness that we possess a body. He felt that consciousness of one's body as a somatic entity automatically means knowing that a biological clock is ticking. Indeed, he proposed that much of the disgust with the body, which is seen in so many cultures, is a reflection of the equation of body with potential death. He conceptualized the almost universal negative attitude toward feces and other aspects of anal functioning as a special case of this equation. Presumably, substances that come out of "my body" indicate only too vividly that I am a time-limited animal. Becker (1973) also implicated sexuality in this paradigm. He suggested that sexuality is not only a thing of the body, but also the signifier of reproduction. Therefore, birth, by its designation of the beginning of life, implicitly signals an end.

What do we actually know about body attitudes that would throw light on such speculations? If one scans the pertinent scientific literature, it becomes evident that little has been ascertained about the relationship of body attitudes to death anxiety. We do not know whether increasing persons' body awareness intensifies their concerns about death. There are a few scattered studies that tangentially suggest that certain aspects of body experience are linked with death anxiety. For example, Sarnoff and Corwin (1959) reported that increasing "castration anxiety" in men (by exposure to nude pictures of women that would presumably stir up Oedipal anxieties) significantly increased their concern about death as measured by responses to a questionnaire. The few other such studies in the literature (e.g., Harwicke, 1980) are analogously vague.

Negative hyperawareness of one's body is a well-documented phenomenon. It is referred to diversely in the literature with such terms as "hypochondriasis" and "functional somatic concern." There seem to be relatively large numbers of people who are oversensitized to the potential pathological implications of various kinds of body sensations. Anywhere from 30% to 50% of various populations that have been surveyed show unrealistic "I may be sick" interpretations of body events. These concerns may be brief and fleeting, or quite long-lasting. There is some evidence (Kellner, 1986) that those with a strong hypochondriachal orientation are also unusually concerned about death. Indeed, one would generally assume that an unrealistically elevated preoccupation with the fragility or vulnerability of one's body signals, at least indirectly, a concern about death-related themes. If so, one could interpret the wide prevalence of hypochondriacal-like anxieties as a manifestation of much corresponding death concern.[1]

Considerable research has accumulated indicating, as was predicted from Becker's (1973) speculation, that persons are inclined to react to their own bodies in a somewhat avoidant, denying fashion. This has been documented in detail elsewhere (Fisher, 1986). Studies have shown that the avoidance of one's own body may often amount to a form of cognitive stupidity. For example, one study (Lefcourt, Hogg, & Sordoni, 1975) found that as much as 10% of a sample could not, in some contexts, accurately identify a front-view photograph of their own face. Schneiderman (1956) discovered that when persons are exposed to a distorted mirror image of themselves, they have difficulty adjusting the image to its true proportions. Other studies have variously shown that persons are surprisingly inaccurate in estimating their own body size, relatively unaware of the activation levels of their interior body organs (e.g., heart), and easily duped into believing they are having body experiences that are actually illusory (Fisher, 1986). Such data indicate that persons shy away from looking at their own bodies with the same clarity or accuracy typifying their perceptions of nonself objects. Obtuseness about one's body could possibly reflect a defensive strategy to ward off connotations of death associated with matters of the body. We simply do not know at this point.[2]

HOW TO EVALUATE DEATH ANXIETY

Although theorists speak glibly of "death anxiety," it has turned out to be rather complicated to measure its presence or absence. There is a whole line

[1]There is some evidence that persons with hypochondriacal tendencies may have experienced an unusual number of deaths among their own family members (Fisher, 1986).

[2]It is pertinent to mention that males seem to be made more anxious and uncomfortable than females by increasing their body awareness (Fisher, 1986). Whether this in some way mirrors sex differences in death anxiety is not apparent. However, as is seen, there is some evidence that the two sexes may be affected differently by death stimuli.

of research (e.g., Boyar, 1964; Dickstein, 1972; Lester, 1967; Lonetto & Templer, 1986) that has equated death anxiety with the degree to which persons say, when responding to a questionnaire, that they feel anxious about death. Typically, the measurement process is based on the individual's response to such statements as the following:

I am really scared of having a heart attack.

I often think about how short life really is.

It does not make me nervous when people talk about death.

The sight of a dead body is horrifying to me.

I am often distressed by the way time flies so very rapidly.

This approach assumes, of course, that persons know, with some accuracy, how much death-related anxiety they are experiencing and are willing to reveal it to a stranger who comes bearing questionnaires.

In a variety of research reports involving one of the most widely used "death questionnaires" (Death Anxiety Scale; Lonetto & Templer, 1986), the average judgment indicated that most people are not experiencing a great deal of anxiety about death-related issues. Surprisingly, persons' death scores were not consistently correlated with measures of motivation to make a good impression (social desirability) (Lonetto & Templer, 1986). Even when it is observed that those intent on making a good impression express significantly less death anxiety, the degree of correlation was modally quite low.

Death anxiety questionnaires have been administered to a broad range of populations. The derived death scores have been correlated with a scattered hodgepodge of variables (e.g., intelligence, age, ethnic background, occupation, sex, religiosity, personality, psychopathology). Scanning the array of published correlations, there are a number that incite skepticism about the validity of asking people to report their own level of apprehension about death. They seem counter to commonsense. Consider the following: Terminally ill cancer patients are reported to have *less* death anxiety than persons in the general population (Gibbs & Achterberg-Lawlis, 1978). Patients who have lost all kidney function and require kidney dialysis are depicted as having no more death anxiety than the average person (Blakely, 1975; Lucas, 1974). No correlation is said to exist between the health status of persons and their self-reported amount of death anxiety (Neustadt, 1982; Templer, 1971). Indeed, elderly persons are described as having no greater death anxiety than younger persons (Lonetto & Templer, 1986). One study (Brown, 1977) found that prison inmates on death row described themselves as experiencing no more death anxiety than the average person. Slezak (1980) detected no relationship between persons' apparent levels of death anxiety and whether they had had a "near-death" experience themselves. It is true that the literature is also replete with a string of significant and perhaps meaningful correlations between questionnaire-defined death anxiety and such variables as religiosity, "sense of well-being," willingness to help the elderly, and general anxiety (Lonetto & Templer, 1986). However, the previously cited examples of prisoners on death row or patients with fatal illnesses who seem to be no more concerned about death than the average individual can only mean that the questionnaire mode of measuring death anxiety has serious limitations.

Many other investigators have raised similar doubts; they proposed that we find methods for measuring death anxiety that tap into a more unconscious level and are not dependent on persons' ability to sense accurately their own level of death anxiety. Congruently, an increasing number of studies have appeared in which death anxiety is measured indirectly, at what are considered to be unconscious levels. The measurement strategies variously involve the frequencies of death imagery in projective response (e.g., to inkblot or picture or incomplete sentence stimuli); speed of reaction to death versus nondeath words in word association or tachistoscopic perception tasks; and references to death themes in dreams, stories, and spontaneous verbalizations (Kastenbaum & Costa, 1977).

Let us examine the highlights of what has emerged from this approach. First of all, it has been demonstrated that words or other stimuli with death meanings evoke stronger responses than do neutral stimuli at what are considered to be unconscious levels. In one study, they also evoked stronger responses than sexual words (Feldman, 1978). Persons take longer to give associations to death than nondeath words, and they also evidence larger GSR reactions to the former than the latter (e.g., Alexander, Colley, & Alderstein, 1957; Meissner, 1958). Further, individuals react in more selective ways to death than nondeath words presented tachistoscopically (Golding, Atwood, & Goodman, 1966; Lester & Lester, 1970). Second, it has become clear that persons who consciously deny any death anxiety do reveal such anxiety in terms of responses at less conscious levels. Feifel and Branscomb (1973) reported that persons who denied any death anxiety upon direct questioning did clearly manifest elevated death concern on measures (e.g., word association) designed to sample unconscious feelings. Lowry (1965) described considerably more signs of death anxiety registering in projective stories than surface in persons' answers to direct questions about their death attitudes. It is also pertinent that exposure to stimuli that contain death themes that one might expect to increase death anxiety may register at an unconscious level but not a conscious one. Moriarity (1974) had subjects view a film full of threatening mutilation material and discovered that, while their death scores on a direct questionnaire were not affected by the film, their concern about death

intensified, as measured by number of references to death themes in spontaneous samples of their speech.[3]

Another interesting contrast between conscious and unconscious death
anxiety measures relates to changes with age. One might guess, on a purely
commonsense basis, that as people enter old age and are closer to the end
of life, their concern about death would mount. However, questionnaire
studies of death anxiety have failed to show a link between death anxiety
and age (Lonetto & Templer, 1986). Indeed, a few studies have even suggested a decrease in death anxiety in the elderly (e.g., Lonetto & Templer, 1986).
But a different picture presents itself when one measures death anxiety with
projective (more unconscious) techniques.[4] In a majority of the studies employing such techniques, the elderly seem to be more upset about death than
are younger persons (e.g., Corey, 1961; Gottschalk, 1979; Gottschalk & Gleser,
1969; Pinder & Hayslip, 1981). This trend seems closer to reality than the
data based on questionnaire responses. It may be that the elderly learn to
conceal from themselves their concern about the "end," but it is doubtful
that they can escape inner turbulence about their dilemma.

Note that although "conscious" and "unconscious" measures of death anxiety usually give different patterns of results, there are instances in which they
have correlated significantly either in a negative (e.g., Alexander & Alderstein, 1960), positive (e.g., Handal, Peal, Napoli, & Austrin, 1984–1985), or
curvilinear (Handal & Rychlak, 1971) fashion. This indicates that there may
be complex patterns of communication between conscious and unconscious
death anxiety systems. As suggested by others (e.g., Alexander & Costanzo,
1979; Hayslip & Stewart-Bussey, 1986–1987), tension in the unconscious system can perhaps "overflow" into the conscious; or the conscious can be mobilized defensively to deny concerns in the unconscious, and so forth.

A study by Mikulincer, Florian, and Tolmacz (1990) illustrated the shifting
linkages that can exist between conscious and unconscious death anxiety as
a function of mediating variables. They examined (in a sample of Israeli college students) the relationship between "attachment styles" and "fear of personal death," as measured at both a conscious (overt) level by a questionnaire
and a less conscious level by means of stories elicited with Thematic Apperception Test (TAT) pictures. The manner in which subjects presumably "attach" themselves to others (feel in close relationships) was evaluated with
self-report techniques that delineate three styles of attachment: secure, am-

---

[3]Silver and Wortman (1980) reported that a number of studies indicate that a significant
proportion of persons who are close to death show much anxiety and disturbance about what
is happening to them.

[4]They also load on different factors when factor analyses are applied to data in which both
"conscious" and "unconscious" measures have been obtained (e.g., Richardson & Sands,
1986–1987).

bivalent, and avoidant. It was found that subjects who are classified as "secure in relation to attachment" manifest relatively low death anxiety (at both conscious and less conscious levels). Those classified as "ambivalent" (i.e., reacting with both heightened attachment and anger to separation) exhibit more fear of death (at conscious and unconscious levels) than do secure subjects. However, the pattern of relationship between conscious and less conscious is different in "avoidant individuals." While they do not manifest stronger fear of death than do secure persons, they do at the level of awareness measured by the TAT. Here we see an instance in which the nature of the connection between conscious and unconscious measures of death anxiety differs as a function of style in interpersonal attachments.

Divergence in findings linked to whether one looks at conscious versus unconscious death anxiety is exemplified with respect to gender differences. A large number of studies based on questionnaire data have found that women express more death anxiety than do men (Lonetto & Templer, 1986). Incidentally, no satisfactory explanation has been given for this apparent difference, although some have speculated that it simply mirrors the greater readiness of women to publicly admit to anxiety. However, when one looks at the literature based on measures of unconscious death anxiety, the picture is mixed, and neither gender emerges as clearly more anxious than the other (e.g., Baird, 1972; Kogan & Wallach, 1961; Kreiger, Epting, & Leitner, 1974; Lowenthal, Thurnher, Chiriboga, & Associates, 1975; Selvey, 1973).

PARAMETERS OF UNCONSCIOUS DEATH ANXIETY

It is difficult, on the basis of the available research literature, to estimate the true modal prevalence and intensity of unconscious death anxiety. Most studies have dealt with small, highly selected samples (e.g., college students). Even when larger populations have been surveyed, the methods used to tap unconscious attitudes are open to criticism. Consider one of the few pertinent large-scale studies reported by Bermann and Richardson (1986–1987). In this instance, a nationally representative random sample of 1,428 Americans was examined. This was done in 1957, and again in 1976. The "salience of death" for this sample was determined by asking individuals to describe the apparent actions and feelings prevailing in a series of six pictures modeled after the TAT. None of the pictures portrayed explicit images suggestive of death; in fact, stimuli even faintly hinting of death were absent. The stories elicited by the pictures were scored for explicit references to death. In the 1976 sample, only 7.4% made even a single reference to death; in the 1957 sample, the corresponding value was lower (viz., 4.3%). Such data would seem to indicate that unconscious death anxiety ("salience of death") is a rare phenomenon. However, if one considers that the stories were obtained in a "survey" type of setting, and that the pictures themselves provided little rationale for conjuring up death themes, the significance of the findings becomes obscure. To create a story about death in the context of a picture that has no hint of death in it would require a fairly intense underlying pressure for such expression. Beyond that, the pressure would need to be great to verbalize such themes to an interviewer—a stranger outside the circle one would be inclined to confide intimate images.

Incidentally, Bermann and Richardson (1986–1987) found a statistically significant increase in "salience of death" from 1957 to 1976 (particularly among women and young adults), and attributed the shift to the increase in deaths in the 1970s due to the Vietnam War. Overall, however, they wondered if the modally low frequencies of death references indicated that images of death are either "highly suppressed" or "not so urgently experienced as to intrude into the content of—projective material" (p. 204). They added:

> Perhaps the proliferation of "death scale" research distorts one's sense of the prevalence of conscious preoccupation with death experienced by most persons. Or perhaps the projective method is not the best indicator of this variable. But it is worth considering the idea that "death anxiety" may be more the concern of psychologists than of the general population. (p. 204)

Actually, until we learn more about the conditions mediating the expression of death themes to projective stimuli, we are not in a position to offer quantitative generalizations about the modal prevalence of such themes. It is conceivable that if Bermann and Richardson (1986–1987) had arranged to introduce small cues suggestive of death into their projective pictures, there might have been a dramatic increase in the projection of death imagery.

Another possible approach to exploring the role of unconscious death anxiety in life is to look at the range of empirical correlations that has emerged between measures of such anxiety and various behavioral indices. Upon what areas of life functioning does such anxiety seem to impinge? Surveying the existing pool of published studies, in which some measure of unconscious death anxiety has been employed, one finds these measures to be significantly and positively linked with the following parameters:

Self reports of frequency of certain somatic symptoms (e.g., headaches, loss of appetite) (Rhudick & Dibner, 1961; Richardson, Bermann, & Piwowarski, 1983)[5]

---

[5]Incidentally, we have also consistently observed in three unpublished sets of data that death anxiety (as defined by responses to inkblots) is negatively correlated with frequency of self-reports of one category of "symptoms" (viz., complaints of pain or discomfort in body openings, e.g., mouth, anus, nose).

Generalized anxiety (Bermann & Richardson, 1986–1987)

MMPI indices of hypochondriasis, hysteria, dependency, and impulsivity (Rhudick & Dibner, 1961)

Separation anxiety (Mikulincer, Florian, & Tolmacz, 1990)

Belief in chance external locus of control (Hayslip & Stewart-Bussey, 1986–1987)

Low level of religiosity (Richardson, Bermann, & Piwowarski, 1983)

Schizophrenic and borderline symptomatology (Walser, 1984)

Retrospective time perspective in TAT stories (Dickstein, 1975)

References to illicit sex in TAT stories (Dickstein, 1975)

Women's degree of difficulty in attaining orgasm (Fisher, 1973)

Choice of dramatic acting as an occupation (Fisher & Fisher, 1981)

Scanning this list, one notes that unconscious death anxiety has been linked with a number of major dimensions. There seem to be ties with disturbance and maladjustment as manifested in both somatic complaints and psychological distress, religiosity, time perspective, certain attitudes toward fate, separation anxiety, passivity, occupational choice, and sexual responsiveness (in women). The relationships depicted are often such that negative consequences parallel increasing amounts of death anxiety.

Overall, what can one say about unconscious death anxiety? To begin with, there seems to be justification for concluding that concern about death can exist outside of conscious awareness. Second, one discerns that there are links between such concern and death anxiety prevailing at more conscious levels, but the nature of these links is obscure and probably of low magnitude. Third, it would appear that unconscious death anxiety may be significantly involved with a spectrum of psychological phenomena diversely including religiosity, somatic complaints, time perspective, and sexual responsiveness (in women). We do lack reasonable data as to how prevalent unconscious death anxiety is in large populations. At this stage, we can only suggest that it probably mediates a number of important areas of behavior.

ABOUT CONSCIOUS DEATH ANXIETY

Although there has been a good deal of emphasis placed on the idea that persons conceal from themselves and others how concerned they are about death, and therefore that conscious death anxiety is of interest primarily as a defensive phenomenon, we would like to examine it from a wider perspective. It would be well to begin with the earlier mentioned point that measures of conscious death anxiety, which are almost invariably based on questionnaire responses, do not consistently correlate with measures of social desirability. There are studies in which significant (but low order) relationships have been reported (e.g., Lonetto & Templer, 1986). However, the majority have not so found. This would seem to indicate that most persons, when reporting the intensity of their death concerns, are not shaping their responses to match what is "socially desirable." They are, on the average, probably responding fairly truthfully. One may presume that their responses are primarily biased because they often conceal from themselves just how much dread they experience vis-à-vis the potential of death. In any case, it might be informative to take a comparative look at those who do and do not experience elevated levels of conscious preoccupation with their mortality. Endless papers and books have been written about the correlates of self-reported individual differences in death anxiety (e.g., Feifel, 1959; Kastenbaum, 1979; Lonetto & Templer, 1986; Lowenthal et al., 1975). It should be possible to get some ideas about factors mediating variations in levels of conscious death concern and, further, the consequences of such variations.

The data in the literature quickly communicate that the greater the self-reported death anxiety, the greater the accompanying discomfort and negativity about other aspects of life. There is evidence (Lonetto & Templer, 1986) that the degree of self-reported death anxiety is positively and significantly correlated with intensified general anxiety, elevated psychological maladjustment, diminished self-esteem, limited sense of life purpose, elevated depression, heightened bodily concern, limited social adequacy, low "ego strength," and intensified use of self-defeating strategies—just to name a few of the negatives.[6] Those persons particularly aware of their death concerns have been described as "sensitizers" who are introverted and conscious of their weaknesses. Incidentally, there is evidence that conscious death anxiety is actually a multifactor entity, but for the moment it will be represented in a simplified, unitary fashion. Generally, it would appear that experiencing heightened death anxiety goes hand in hand with an unhappy view of life and of self, and perhaps a diminished ability to cope adequately.[7]

There seems to be a sensitized openness to the many negatives in life among those tuned to death images. Of course, possibly over time, such an orientation actually induces more failure and difficulty, which, in turn, rein-

---

[6]A considerable literature (e.g., Dickstein & Blatt, 1966; Hooper & Spilka, 1970; Howell, 1976; Lonetto & Templer, 1986) suggested links between conscious death anxiety and disturbed feelings about the passage of time.

[7]Lonetto and Templer (1986) offered a possible, more positive conceptualization of conscious death anxiety: "This anxiety, by its very nature, helps us to survive. It also gives us a feeling of continuity because it has always been inseparable from the human condition. This often elusive, constant, and timeless companion permits us to remain in contact with the past and present while we anticipate our future" (p. 113).

forces a negative perspective. It is striking how much conscious death anxiety seems to be tied to the individual's own adaptive style rather than to situational variables. There is little evidence that conditions that one might think would incite death concerns do so with any consistency. For example, as earlier mentioned, conscious death anxiety is not elevated in persons on death row, in those sick to the point of death, in the very elderly facing an imminent life end, or in those who have recently suffered the death of a loved one.[8] This apparent lack of impact of the situation itself suggests that individuals have effective strategies for buffering the impact. Presumably, the strategies involve well-known techniques based on denial, repression, and rationalization (illusion formation). It is also conceivable that the coping strategies involve not so much denial as acceptance and assimilation. However, we consider this less likely.

To what extent has death concern, whether conscious or unconscious, been tied to serious forms of psychological disturbance? Some clinicians (e.g., Searles, 1961) asserted that death anxiety is a core problem that plays an etiological role in schizophrenia. However, the empirical literature is a maze of contradictory findings (e.g., Feifel & Hermann, 1973; Lonetto & Templer, 1986; Pollak, 1979–1980; Schulz, 1978). One could not say with any confidence that serious forms of pathology like schizophrenia are typified by high levels of conscious death anxiety. It would be even more difficult to state that conscious death anxiety has etiological functions in this area. However, as earlier mentioned, there are clear trends for measures of conscious death anxiety to be positively correlated with indicators of psychological discomfort in normal or mildly distressed samples. As for unconscious death anxiety, the few studies (e.g., Jimakas, 1980; Lester & Schumacher, 1969; Walser, 1984) that have looked at this parameter in seriously disturbed individuals (e.g., schizophrenics) have produced conflictual findings. It would be premature to draw any conclusions from the available data. One would have to say that we still know little about whether death anxiety in any form contributes to the more extreme forms of psychopathology.

---

[8]However, one should note that the available information concerning persons with the lowest levels of conscious death anxiety indicates they are most likely to be (Lonetto & Templer, 1986):

White

Male

Well educated

From an intact family

Earning an above-average income

Of relatively high intelligence

In other words, they represent a very privileged segment of the population. As such, they were probably reared with a variety of material and psychological advantages that could conceivably have provided a good deal of basic insulation against life's threats.

DEFENSES

Perhaps the ubiquity of defense against death is better documented by historical observation than by the neat little studies we put together in our laboratories. As frequently pointed out, it has been a central preoccupation of most cultures, particularly through religious imagery, either to deny the possibility of death or to put the best possible face on it. A basic theme in Christianity is that believers can keep existing, in some form or other, forever. Relatedly, the history of the Egyptian's fascination with body preservation and their provision of lavish abodes and sustenance for the elite dead speak for themselves. There is no way to quantify the enormous energies devoted worldwide to making the fact of death less vivid and nihilistic. Everywhere one looks one sees an endless dodging and twisting to evade the image of finality.

Interestingly, some of this avoidant motivation surfaces in the literature concerned with how children come to grips with death concepts. We find that children are usually slow in arriving at a realistic notion of death. The research data suggest that, on the average, children do not fully recognize the basic concepts of death's "universality" and "immutability" until they reach the age of 7 or 8 (Lonetto, 1980; Speece & Brent, 1987). However, studies indicate that some children do, by the age of 4 or 5 or even earlier, evolve quite realistic ideas concerning the nature of death. These are children who have had unusually close contacts with the phenomenon of death, either because of the serious illness of self or others (Stambrook & Parker, 1987). Their ability to grasp the meaning of death at such an early age implies that the modal delay until age 7 or 8 may be partially the result of a defensive process—the interposing of protective shielding by parents and self.[9]

The defensive maneuvers one comes upon in the literature range widely. A majority seems to take religious or quasireligious forms. However, one novel maneuver, seen particularly among women (Greenberger, 1965), is to transform the dangerous image of death into an image of a seducer, a sexually provocative figure. Apparently, death is recast as a lover, someone who is sexually exciting and certainly more attractive than the "Grim Reaper." The presentation of death in a sexual form was first detected in the personifications of critically ill women (Greenberger, 1965), but was also subsequently identified in the fantasies of healthy females (e.g., McClelland, 1963). Somewhat analogously, there are reports that death is variously personified by others in positive terms like "gentle comforter," "attractive dancer," "formless warmth," and "good looking gay deceiver" (Lonetto & Templer, 1986). Such images are obviously equivalent to those prevalent in certain religious

---

[9]Orbach and Glaubman (1979) concluded, on the basis of their studies, that distortions in children's death concepts are due more to a "defensive process" than to deficits in ability to think abstractly.

mythologies that portray death as an attractive choice. The idea of dying obviously does have an attractive quality to some persons and may partially explain certain forms of risk taking and suicide.

Although the evidence is not unanimous, it would appear that those who are religiously oriented have less conscious death anxiety[10] than do those who are nonreligious (Lonetto & Templer, 1986).[11] This correlation seems to be strongest when religiosity is defined in terms of having faith—having a strong attachment to a religious belief system.[12] We would like to cite one study of special interest because it illustrates how religiosity can serve as an indirect mediating role in the factors moderating conscious death anxiety. Schulz (1978) tested a hypothesis that the motive to achieve helps shield Americans from conscious death anxiety. He suggested that achievement might enable one to become "productively immortal," and thereby shut out threatening images of death. Both males and females were included in the study. These subjects were classified as "religious," "nonreligious," or "not sure." When correlations were determined within each of these categories (and separately by gender) between a measure of conscious death anxiety and "achievement motivation," some surprising correlations emerged. It was discovered that in neither the male nor female "religious" category were death anxiety and achievement motivation correlated. However, for the males they were significantly negatively correlated in both the "nonreligious" and "not sure" categories. For the females, they were significantly positively correlated in the "nonreligious" category.

Schulz (1978) interpreted the data to mean that males who lack religious belief also lack a defensive "world view" to cushion the threat of death, and therefore they have a greater need to use achievement as a defensive "cognitive mediator." The greater the investment of those men without religious belief in achievement goals, the less they felt threatened by death. A similar pattern characterized the women who were in the "not sure" group. But within the group explicitly "nonreligious," there was a reversal, such that death anxiety and achievement motivation were significantly positively correlated. Schulz (1978) explained this reversal as due to the lesser social acceptability

---

[10]The relationship of religiosity to unconscious death anxiety has been barely considered. Only one pertinent study was found. Richardson et al. (1983) reported a significant negative correlation between religious attachment and unconscious death anxiety, but only within one age category (21–34 years) of the wider range they explored.

[11]However, an interesting lead has been provided by McMordie (1981), who found that conscious death anxiety was lowest in those who are either very high or very low in self-perceived religiosity. He stated: "These findings suggest a curvilinear relationship between death anxiety and religion and support the contention that the strength of conviction is an important determinant in fear of death—a strong belief system fosters perceptions of increased control and predictability which lessens the fear of death" (p. 922).

[12]It should be added that, when questioned, some individuals (although a small minority) feel their religious experiences have increased their fear of death (Wulff, 1991).

of achievement as a way of being "productively immortal" for women; and, indeed, if adopted as a major adjustment strategy (in the 1970s when the study was done), so likely to get women into frustrating dilemmas that death anxiety is increased rather than decreased. We cite this study to document an example of the potentially complex manner in which religiosity can enter into the defenses utilized against conscious death anxiety. In any case, we would reiterate that there is a basic, general trend for conscious death anxiety to be inverse to degree of religious faith.[13]

The defensive value of belief systems rooted in religion for countering concerns about death has been demonstrated with particular precision by Osarchuk and Tatz (1973). They showed, with a clarity that is unusual in this area of research, that an upsurge of death anxiety can trigger a compensatory increase in a religious type of faith. They studied college students whose degree of belief in "afterlife" had been measured by means of a standardized questionnaire. Students were asked to indicate their agreement or disagreement with a series of statements, such as the following:

Earthly existence is the only existence we have.

There must be an afterlife of some sort.

The life we now lead is but a pebble cast upon the sands of our future lives.

Subjects scoring high or low on this "afterlife" measure were assigned to one of the following three experimental conditions:

1. Exposure to a "death threat" that consisted of a taped communication about the high probabilities of meeting an early death, with an accompanying series of slides depicting auto wrecks, corpses, and murder victims.
2. Participation in a pseudo-experiment in which it was explicitly indicated that electric shocks were to be administered.
3. Neutral control activity that simply called for practicing with a child's toy that involved flipping a ball into a cup.

Following any given condition, the subject completed an alternate form of the "afterlife" questionnaire; another form had been administered first at a baseline point. As predicted, it was found that the death threat condition had

---

[13]McMordie (1981) reported in one study that conscious fear of death is correlated not so much with degree of religiosity as with strength of belief about religion, whether it be accepting or rejecting. Thus, persons either extremely high or extremely low in religiosity were observed to have significantly less death anxiety than those in the middle range of religiosity. This is an interesting finding that awaits further exploration.

a special impact. More specifically, it turned out that those subjects who were initially high in their belief in an afterlife were significantly more likely to show increased belief in an afterlife as the result of death threat than was the case during the shock threat or neutral conditions. Osarchuk and Tatz (1973) commented with regard to this finding:

> The mechanism envisaged is one in which, when fear of death has been aroused, if the individual thinks in positive terms about a life after death, he experiences cognitions and affects incompatible with those comprising fear of death. Thus, accepting belief in afterlife results in a reinforcing fear reduction, so that the individual is likely in the future to use belief in afterlife to produce the same effect. (p. 259)

Analogous defensive phenomena involving larger value systems have been delineated in a series of studies (Greenberg et al., 1990; Rosenblatt, Greenberg, Solomon, Pyszczynski, & Lyon, 1989; Solomon, Greenberg, & Pyszczynski, 1991) that examined the impact of death anxiety on belief structures. These studies, which referred to the control of death anxiety as "terror management," started out with the assumption that Becker (1973) was correct in his statement that death "terror" is pervasive, and that a top priority of cultural "worldviews" is to provide individuals with a buffer—a way of avoiding awareness of that terror. Maintenance of individual self-esteem was also depicted as basic to terror management, because it provides reassurance that one is meeting the culture's standards of value, and therefore that one has the right to participate in the cultural order that was devised to create the illusion that humans are above the natural state of things. Rosenblatt et al. (1989) stated:

> According to terror management theory, the beliefs and values that make up an individual's cultural worldview serve the vital function of buffering the anxiety that results from awareness of human vulnerability and mortality. The theory posits that the cultural worldview espoused by any given individual is a fragile construction that needs persistent social validation if the individual is to maintain faith in it. Those who deviate from cultural standards are responded to with disdain because such behavior threatens the values that underlie the individual's source of security. Similarly, those who uphold cultural values are admired because such behavior validates the individual's values. (p. 688)

The basic experimental paradigm in the numerous studies carried out by Rosenblatt et al. (1989) and Greenberg et al. (1990) aroused death anxiety in subjects (i.e., by asking them to write descriptions of what it feels like to die) and then measured how this anxiety affects their responses to various representations or figures that either threaten or reinforce cultural values important to them. It is hypothesized in all instances that, as death anxiety is intensified, there will be greater negativity toward that which threatens one's protective cultural values. The data have demonstrated diversely that intensified death anxiety results in larger reward recommendations for a hero who upholds cultural values and harsher reactions to persons like prostitutes who violate cultural standards. Further, intensifying death anxiety results in Christians feeling more positive toward other Christians, but more negative toward Jews (cultural deviants). Increased death anxiety also results in particularly positive reactions to those who directly praise subjects' cultural worldviews and heightened negative responses to those who criticize them. Overall, the data are significantly supportive of the "terror management" hypothesis.

The personal strategies employed by individuals to control their death anxieties are only beginning to be investigated. As indicated, we do have some evidence that variables like religious faith, achievement imagery ("I can create and accomplish lasting things"), worldviews, and a repressive–denying orientation may be important for comforting self vis-à-vis intimations of mortality. Quite a number of studies have been conducted to ascertain whether conscious death anxiety can be decreased by exposing persons to various kinds of "death education" procedures, "desensitization" regimens, and specialized psychotherapeutic approaches. While there are scattered reports that such procedures dampen "death anxiety" (usually to a small degree), the majority has been unsuccessful in this respect (Lonetto & Templer, 1986). We were unable to find any substantial studies in the literature concerning attempts to apply presumably therapeutic techniques to the reduction of unconscious death anxiety.

However, we should mention two instances in which a decrease in a presumed indicator of unconscious death anxiety occurred as the result of experimental manipulations. In one study (Fisher, Wright, & Moelis, 1979), death anxiety scores, as defined by the amount of death imagery in response to inkblot stimuli, were determined for samples of college women at a baseline point and subsequently after listening to a recorded message full of images of maternal closeness, a maternal message not emphasizing closeness, or a neutral message. Only the message depicting mother closeness consistently produced a significant decline in death imagery. One is reminded of the reassuring effects of the subliminal message "Mommy and I are one," reported by Silverman, Lachmann, and Milich (1982). In another (unpublished) study, we obtained baseline measures of the amount of death imagery given by subjects (college women) to a series of inkblot stimuli and subsequently while they were listening to a collection of recorded jokes. It was found that a significant decline in death imagery occurred. Furthermore, the decline was greater than that produced by exposure to a neutral recording. Such findings provide a sample of the sorts of inputs that may help to quiet death concerns. It is noteworthy that humor seems to be an effective agent in this respect. We have suggested elsewhere (Fisher & Fisher, 1981) that actors, through their dramatic presentation of imagery that spans past, present, and future and through their ability to assume different consecutive roles, provide a comforting sense of continuity. Their implicit and explicit depictions of continuity may have important reassuring value for audiences concerning the reproductibility of time and notions of role transferability.

THE PROBLEM OF MULTIPLE FORMS AND GUISES

Defining the prevalence of death anxiety has proved to be a surprisingly frustrating task. In the process of trying to understand why this is so, we have come to see that the difficulty resides in the slippery fluidity of the concept of death anxiety and the many guises such anxiety may apparently assume. We have already pointed out in some detail that there is a distinction between conscious and unconscious death anxiety. We do not know much about the interdependency between these two spheres. As detailed, some studies find negative correlations between the two levels; others find positive or zero correlations. One factor analytic study (Richardson & Sands, 1986–1987) reported that conscious and unconscious death anxiety clearly loaded on separate factors. In any case, questions immediately arise, such as should one represent an individual's level of death anxiety as the sum of the two spheres? Or is one of the spheres of greater importance and therefore should be given a larger weighting? Is there some optimum ratio of the intensities in the two spheres that defines an adequate level of control or comfort in this area?

Even within each of the spheres there is further complexity and multiplicity. It is now known that conscious death anxiety can be factored into a number of elements. Studies have described major components typifying various questionnaire measures of conscious death concern. To illustrate, T. O. Martin (1982–1983) listed the following: general death anxiety, denial of death anxiety, fearful anticipation of death, fear of physical (painful) death, and fear of a potentially catastrophic death. Lonetto and Templer (1986) concluded, after examining an array of factor-oriented studies, that there are four basic components to conscious death anxiety:

An affective–cognitive negative concern about death

Concern about the physical changes that accompany dying and serious illness

An anxious awareness of the inevitable and "unstoppable" flow of time

Sensitivity to the pain and stress linked with chronic or terminal illness and having personal fears[14]

---

[14]To further complicate matters, there are suggestions that the factor structure for conscious death anxiety may be different in normal as compared with psychiatric samples (Lonetto & Templer, 1986).

That is, conscious fear of death not only manifests itself in a direct concern about dying but also alarm about the passage of time and sharpened preoccupation with matters of illness and pain. Incidentally, it is also true that there is significant overlap between death anxiety and a more generalized form of anxiety (e.g., Lonetto & Templer, 1986). Possibly there is interchange between these two forms, such that one may enhance the other. Increased generalized anxiety might, in some instances, be a disguised representation of intensified death anxiety.

Alexander and Constanzo (1979) introduced finer intricacy into the picture. They indicated that in an earlier work (viz., Alexander et al., 1957) a negative correlation was found between a measure of "overt" and "covert" death anxiety. One of their students, Farley (1970), also demonstrated that an inverse relationship exists between "overt" death anxiety and feelings of competence. People expressing high levels of conscious death anxiety were less secure about their "general competence" than were those with a low level of such anxiety. The Alexander et al. (1957) and the Farley (1970) studies were based on samples of college students collected during a period extending from the mid-1950s to the mid-1960s. However, in a later sample collected in the 1970s, the earlier reported findings could not be duplicated. There was not a simple inverse relation between "overt" death anxiety and feelings of self-competence. Indeed, it turned out that there was an important variable that mediated whether high "overt" death anxiety would be accompanied by low "felt competence." Alexander and Constanzo (1979) had reasoned that, because of the Vietnam war and other increased environmental threats, "individual concern with death could be conceptualized" to a greater degree than in the 1950s or 1960s as a "situationally appropriate response" (p. 736). They stated:

In our view, the tumultuous events of the late sixties and early seventies not only influenced the political process but had profound effects on psychologically relevant internal dynamics. The consequences of widespread dissent from government policies in life-threatening domains provided an avenue of expression for suppressed concerns about death. For example, opposition to the imminent threat of death from participation in a puzzling war or impinging concerns about the life-shortening consequences of industrial pollutants became as viable a political perspective as the espousal of national defense loyalties and capitalist expansion of the economy. While neither perspective alters the existential inevitability of death, the acknowledgment of those influences that could serve to foreshorten life transformed the definition of day to day death fears from manifestations of neurotic anxiety to expressions of real anxiety. Whereas neurotically labeled fear might undermine felt competence, reality-based anxieties in response to consensually identified threats are not necessarily incompatible with competency feelings. To go one step further, active attacks and overt efforts to change the influences bringing about real threats might indeed enhance one's sense of competence. (pp. 748–749)

Therefore, in their 1979 study, they not only ascertained level of "overt" death anxiety (by interview) and "felt competence" (by interview), but also evaluated (by interview) the degree of overt criticism of, or opposition to, what were considered to be governmental policies responsible for the environmental threats (e.g., Vietnam war, toxic pollution). The resulting data indicated, among other things, that if subjects had high death anxiety but also mustered clear heightened dissent with governmental "life-threatening" policies, their "felt competence" remained high. However, felt competence was low in those with high overt death anxiety who did not have a clear attitude of dissent. Alexander and Constanzo (1979) concluded:

> the expression of death concern through dissent and the link that this expressed concern provides between death fears and situational referents . . . make unnecessary an insecure self-reference. If overtly expressed death fear is linked to palpable environmental circumstances, the person need not attribute it to some weakness or dispositional fear or insecurity within himself. If, however, overt death concern has no obvious external referent, high expressions of it will be more likely to be linked to personal insecurities and thereby reflect negatively in the self-perceived competence of the person. (p. 737)

What is striking about Alexander and Constanzo's (1979) work is that it shows that the experiential impact of one's level of death anxiety can vary as a function of the degree to which that anxiety can be attributed to conditions outside of oneself. One of the destructive effects of death anxiety that was observed (viz., a diminished sense of self-competence) could apparently be minimized by tying that anxiety to a visible external referent. It is equally possible that there are myriad other mediating variables that modify how death anxiety will be experienced and the larger effects it will have upon personality functioning.

When we turn our attention to the realm of unconscious death anxiety, we find additional unexpected complexity. It would appear that what is called unconscious "death anxiety" is not a unitary entity. Various indices that purported to measure unconscious death anxiety typically showed low to zero correlations among each other (e.g., Handal, Peal, Napoli, & Austrin, 1984–1985). This may reflect a lack of validity in some of the measures, but it may also be due to the existence of multiple forms of unconscious death concern. So, it is possible that one index of unconscious death anxiety (e.g., reaction time to death words) will indicate a relatively low level, whereas another index (e.g., death themes in Thematic Apperception Test stories) that taps into another dimension of unconscious death concern might indicate the presence of a higher level. Here, too, the question arises whether the total amount of unconscious death anxiety should be represented as the sum of a series of independent modes of tapping into the unconscious realm. It may eventually be meaningful to compare ratios of various categories of unconscious death anxiety to each other.

An imaginative issue relevant to the meanings of both unconscious and conscious death anxiety has been speculatively raised by Helgeland (1984–1985). He proposed that, aside from death anxiety's intrinsic significance, it may also mirror decline or disturbance in the culture. Guided by the original formulations of Douglas (1970), to the effect that the body is frequently the medium a social group chooses to symbolize institutions and meanings, he suggested that images of body decline or death may be projective representations of feelings of decline prevailing in a societal group. He stated: "What society does and what is done to it is understood by means of analogies based on body metaphors" (p. 150). He illustrated his view by analyzing the symbolism of death that was so prevalent in the late Middle Ages. He noted a great upsurge of death imagery during this time period. Many depictions of death are to be found in the paintings, writings, and poetry of this period. Helgeland (1984–1985) described the prevalent death imagery (e.g., "explicit paintings of sword play ending in split skulls and severed limbs") as involving a "frankness" that is "startling to the contemporary mind" (p. 145). He theorized that a dramatic decline was taking place at that time in the sense and stability of the major cultural institutions. The average person "perceived the dying of the old structure and could not envision the new" (p. 158). Presumably, this dread transposed into a preoccupation with the vulnerability and deterioration of the flesh and with the ultimate somatic defeat defined by death. There is certainly a growing empirical literature attesting to the fact that the body is often a projective target for feelings and conflicts nested in the culture.[15] For example, certain forms of social stress may intensify individuals' feelings of body vulnerability (Fisher, 1986). Helgeland's (1984–1985) perspective is generally tenable in terms of what we have learned about body image dynamics. It remains to be demonstrated specifically that death anxiety is responsive to social conditions.

But pertinent to this point, some evidence exists that certain forms of psychological trauma may play a part in death anxieties, both at conscious and unconscious levels. Schwartz (1980) was able to show, in a sample of college students, that the greater their recall of having suffered separation from their parents during childhood (e.g., due to divorce, death, or physical illness of mother) the greater their death anxiety as defined by both questionnaire and by associations to words with death connotations. Therefore, negative social

---

[15]Helgeland (1984–1985) referred to ways in which feelings of instability and chaos about the culture may be projected onto representations of death. For example, he referred to "devils and demons" as being depicted with physiques that

"resemble a game of animal parts, which children might assemble at their whim, replete with teeth, horns, hair, and warts. . . . Devils with faces on shoulders, knees, and abdomens, people with tails and hoofs, black teats, vicious canines, horns from nostrils, and so forth. . . . All this is a graphic symbolism of chaos; it would be difficult to imagine a better rendering. The world has come unglued and reglued together wrongly. . . . (p. 157)

conditions that would cause families to break up or diminish the security of ties between children and their parents might inflate death anxieties (both conscious and unconscious) in the former.[16] This could be seen as a bit contradictory to the earlier mentioned fact that conscious death anxiety does not seem to be increased in persons exposed to intense life-threatening experiences (e.g., being seriously ill, very old, or on death row). But keep in mind that the Schwartz (1980) study referred to separation experiences that occurred specifically during childhood; and it may be that there is an early anlage of conscious death anxiety that is shaped by, and sensitive to, a variety of social experiences occurring at that phase in life, but which once formed persists with some stability. Note that certain observations by Kagan and Moss (1962), concerning how early childhood experiences do influence body anxiety in adulthood, are interestingly congruent with such a possibility.

INTEGRATIVE COMMENTS

One emerges with the picture that death anxiety takes many forms and is mediated in surprising ways. It is this complexity that prevents simple answers to questions about how large a part death anxiety plays in normal living and action. One cannot find direct affirmation of Becker's (1973) formulation that we are all, at the core, wracked by death anxiety and stridently preoccupied with containing it. There is a puzzling, erratic pattern to the manifestations of death anxiety as one samples the spectrum of sites at which they might potentially appear. We have already indicated that, at a public level, relatively small percentages of persons admit to or complain about fear of death. Also, relatively few persons admit to thinking about death with more than occasional frequency. We do have evidence that death anxiety can exist at levels that escape the individual's conscious awareness. We know that persons may deny even a hint of death concern and yet show clear signs of disturbance (e.g., as manifested by autonomic arousal) when exposed to stimuli with death connotations. However, the prevalence of unconscious death concern has not been shown (within the limitations of the psychological methodologies available) to be of large, really impressive proportions. In sum, our psychological techniques for measuring death anxiety in individuals do not reveal the overwhelming fascination with death that Becker (1973) and others have posited. However, let us look further.

---

[16]Indeed, it is known that there are significant positive correlations between parental death anxiety scores (as defined by questionnaire) and the equivalent scores for their children. The correlations are higher for same-gender parent–child pairs (e.g., Lonetto & Templer, 1986). Such data imply that societal conditions that increase parents' level of death concern could eventuate in the associated children experiencing analogously greater concern.

Rather contrasting impressions can be derived from other, less strictly controlled observation posts. One notes the almost universal concern with staying healthy and the considerable prevalence of hypochondriacal concerns. There are rough data (Kellner, 1986) suggesting that 30%–50% of persons residing in the United States periodically seek medical treatment for somatic "symptoms" that have no apparent organic basis. Further, an epidemic-like fascination prevails with bolstering one's body by means of drugs, exercise, diet, meditation, and what-have-you against the ravages of age and potentially fatal illnesses (Fisher, 1986). Somatic anxiety seems to be extremely high, and one can deduce with reasonable logic that death anxiety probably lurks somewhere in the background.[17] However, note that somatic anxiety is usually phrased in a fairly euphemistic language of health, hygiene, and current myths about what is "good" for the body. Direct translations into death imagery are muted.

At a larger, more cultural level, we find scholarly texts suggesting a universal preoccupation with death themes in religions and myths (e.g., Eliade, 1967, 1969). All cultures seem to have invented elaborate symbols and metaphors that "explain" the nature of death and often serve to blunt the potential threat portrayed in the concept of dying. Themes of "ascension," "death and creation," being "swallowed by the monster," the "terror of time," and the "symbolism of the water" have appeared everywhere, and they simultaneously highlight and negate the presence of death. Borkeneau (1965) has classified entire cultures by whether they are death defying or death accepting. It is known (Choron, 1963) that religions can often be distinguished with reference to their depictions of the consequences of death. For example, one of the prime differences between Judaism and Christianity is that the latter promises resurrection and a form of immortality. Choron (1963) noted: "It would be vain to seek in the Old Testament comfort and consolation for the fact of death in terms of belief in immortality," but "The New Testament proclaims the victory over death" (p. 84). It is also pertinent that anthropologists and others (Fulton, 1965; Kastenbaum & Costa, 1977) have found that all cultures devote great energy to proscribing burial rites and modes of mourning. Guiding images are provided with reference to the attributes of the dead and how to cope with the possible intrusions of the "departed" into the world of the living. There has obviously been a worldwide need to give meaning to death, and to furnish the individual with rituals for normalizing it.

Why is there such a dramatic contrast between the preoccupation with death themes at a broad societal level and the empirical data reflecting death concern in the individual? If death has figured so prominently in the symbols

---

[17]As already indicated, there are, in fact, studies demonstrating significant positive correlations between amount of conscious death anxiety and frequency with which "symptoms" of physical discomfort are experienced.

and religious themes of all cultures, why is it not analogously prominent in the stream of thought (either conscious or unconscious) of those persons who have been probed with a variety of measures? Being consciously concerned with death seems not to be common in persons who are adapting reasonably well to their environs. Relatively elevated conscious death anxiety is found primarily in those experiencing difficulties in coping. We would hypothesize that the discrepancy between societal and individual preoccupation with death themes is due to the energy invested at the societal level, which protects and buffers the individual. That is, the societal energy creates structures that shelter the individual from the onslaught of death threat. Most cultures have multiple strategies for reassuring the individual that death is under control, perhaps not fatal, and that its effects can be attenuated. In short, there is a collective mustering of illusions to camouflage the reality of dying.

The somewhat puzzling discrepancies just described among indicators of death concern are strikingly duplicated in the literature dealing with attitudes toward nuclear war. Consider the following. Surveys have shown that a large majority of persons assumes that if nuclear war were to come, their chances of survival would be close to zero. Furthermore, when pressed about their ideas of an atomic war's impact, most persons conjure up scary images of universal destruction, body mutilation, and a violently unpleasant demise (e.g., Fiske, Pratto, & Pavelchak, 1983; Solantaus, Rimpela, & Taipale, 1984). One study (Fiske et al., 1983) that asked persons living in a large American city to respond to an open-ended question about nuclear war elicited such themes as:

"Nobody left. We'll just all be blown up. The loser will be gone completely."
"It would destroy people. Everything in the world. All the beautiful things will be gone."
"Death. Destruction. Chaos. Survival. Hiroshima."
"I hope I die with everyone else. I can't see planning for it. Utter destruction, desolation, ruin." (p. 55)

However, despite such findings, one observes that the average individual does not express much overt anxiety about the threat of atomic war. There is even an absence of a significant correlation between one's degree of knowledge concerning atomic weapons and one's overt anxiety about them. Fiske et al. (1983), after one of the most thorough available reviews of the pertinent scientific literature, told us:

People commonly report quite bleak beliefs about a nuclear holocaust, which implies that they should also report some concomitant emotional reactions. When asked directly what emotions come to mind regarding a nuclear war, the typical person does report fear, terror, and worry (Fiske et al., 1983). . . . On the whole, however, most people do not think about nuclear war very often (Fiske et al., 1983; Hamilton, Chavez, & Keilin, 1986). The typical adult apparently worries seldom or relatively little about the possibility (Kramer, Kalick, & Milburn, 1983). And such emotional responses do not vary dramatically as a function of social class or overall political ideology. (p. 209)

It is true that most people do not see atomic war as a likely immediate event and in that sense can perhaps distance themselves from the whole matter. Still, the sheer reality of atomic weapons is there to see, and we have fairly good evidence that they are associated with a high probability of nasty dying.

Thus, it is of interest that Newcomb (1986) presented us with data suggesting that the nuclear threat may possibly have chronic perturbing effects. He found, in a large sample ($N = 722$) of young adults (ages 19–24), that 70% agreed or strongly agreed with the statement: "I feel frightened when I think of all the nuclear weapons in the world." Also, 48% agreed with: "The world feels like a very dangerous place because of so many nuclear weapons." Only 9% assented to the statement: "I imagine I would survive a nuclear war." Note, however, that only 38% assented to the statement: "There are times when I feel depressed thinking about the possibility of nuclear war"; and only 19% agreed with: "I imagine there will be a nuclear war in the next 10 years." In factor analyzing the responses to the Nuclear Attitudes Questionnaire, one of the factors that emerged was labeled "nuclear denial." But what is of special interest about this study is that it detected significant positive links between amount of nuclear anxiety (that included not only anxiety about atomic weapons but also atomic energy plants) and the following variables: less purpose in life, less life satisfaction, more powerlessness, more depression, and more drug use. Although Newcomb (1986) explicitly pointed out that causality cannot be deduced from such findings, he concluded: "the threat of nuclear war and accidents is significantly related to psychological distress and may disturb normal maturational development" (p. 906). Even though the potential impact of nuclear anxiety is highlighted in this study, one must keep in mind that most other reports have come up with a less-threatening picture. This could reflect a variety of factors, ranging from differences in the populations sampled to the amount of rapport and trust existing between the experimenter and the subjects who were questioned. Lifton (1967) summarized nicely the puzzlement posed by the often observed discrepancies between what atomic weapons can inflict and how people seem to respond to them. He said that we live "with the sense that we can be annihilated in a moment, along with everything we've known and loved and experienced in our existence, while at the same time we carry on our everyday activities, business as usual" (p. 619).

It might be well to review the solid data available concerning the repertoire of techniques available to the individual to maintain discipline over death anxieties. We begin with the understanding that the first line of defense is probably provided by the basic soothing myths and rituals prevalent in each society. But what other specific modes have we glimpsed in the studies reviewed in this chapter? Consider the following:

1. Let us begin with the simplest control measure (viz., the cognitive differentiation of various kinds of conscious death anxiety). As indicated earlier, factor-analytic studies (e.g., Lonetto & Templer, 1986) have shown that persons learn to distinguish or separate various aspects of their death anxiety (e.g., concern about physical changes that accompany dying vs. anxious awareness of the "unstoppable" flow of time). In so doing, individuals impose a certain amount of cognitive discipline on an area of threat and also perhaps make it possible to react at any given time to separate, narrowed aspects of the death anxiety realm rather than to one overbearing global entity.

2. We know, too, that individuals have learned how to deny conscious awareness of death concerns and to relegate them to unconscious levels of functioning. Presumably this blunts the intensity of the potential threat and discomfort of death imagery. We have seen that this repressive process may be so effective as to result in persons with fatal illnesses or who are residing on death row to experience no more, or even less, death concern than the average citizen. Incidentally, Lifton (1964) alluded to a "numbing" process that he feels occurred among Hiroshima inhabitants when they were in the midst of experiencing the horrendous slaughter produced by the atomic explosion. They were said to be immersed in death stimuli so overwhelming in nature that a protective negation (denying, repressive) of all concern about death had to be applied. Lifton (1964) reported:

> And indeed so overwhelming was this experience that many would have undoubtedly been unable to avoid psychosis were it not for an extremely widespread and effective defense mechanism which I shall refer to as "psychic closing-off." In the face of grotesque evidence of death and near-death, people—sometimes within seconds or minutes—simply ceased to feel. They had a clear sense of what was happening to them, but their emotional reactions were unconsciously turned off. . . . The unconscious process here is that of closing oneself off from death itself; the controlling inner idea, or fantasy, is "If I feel nothing, then death is not taking place." (p. 195)[18]

3. We have seen experimental evidence (Osarchuk & Tatz, 1973) that persons who have built up a firm belief in a religious concept like immortality

---

[18]Lifton (1967) also indicated that the close encounters with death experienced by the Hiroshima survivors often left them with a shattered sense of vulnerability. However, he also cited instances in which such encounters took on a heroic quality and were interpreted as indicative of the prowess to overcome death's best try.

will, under the impact of intensified death threat, increase their faith in the reality of immortal prospects. One can witness a dynamic protective system in operation. The heightened death inputs call for a defensive self-reassurance: "I have nothing to fear of death because God will undoubtedly provide a future existence for me." We may speculate that, quite analogously, when those who are religiously persuaded encounter intensified death inputs they may experience defensive reinforcement of other aspects of their religiosity that bear on an afterlife (e.g., faith that a merciful God exists, or that good deeds will be rewarded with assignment to Heaven). More vivid death reminders might, in the same vein, increase church attendance, more frequent reading of the Bible, or more strict observance of religious rituals.

It should be added that devotion to other value systems may have analogous shielding effects. The work of the terror management group (e.g., Solomon, Greenberg, & Pyszczynski, 1991) has documented well how identification with cultural values buffers death anxiety. One recalls, too, that Schulz (1978) found that individuals who display little faith in religious values may substitute faith in the value of personal achievement as protection against the negative effects of death upon self-esteem. Lifton (1964) has speculated at some length about how death anxiety may be attenuated by identifying with belief systems that variously emphasize the future survivability of nature, the ability of one's descendants to perpetuate one's ideas and intentions, and the future durability of one's "creative works" or "human influences." With regard to the last of these self-reassuring, pseudo-immortal modes, Lifton (1964) stated: "Certainly this form of immortality has particular importance for intellectuals conscious of participating in the general flow of human creativity, but applies in some measure to all human beings in their unconscious perceptions of the legacy they leave for others" (p. 204).

In a broader sense, it would appear that death anxiety can be contained by directing one's attention to ideas or beliefs that deny there is an end to life or neutralize the implications of nonexistence. It is possible that any inputs that dramatize continuity or vitality, or even simply distract, may be death diminishing. Earlier, it was mentioned that the reassuring voice of a mother figure or exposure to humor may decrease unconscious death anxiety (as measured by inkblot responses).

4. Moving on to the work of Alexander and Constanzo (1979), we find concrete indicators that the negative effects of death anxiety may be defended against by displacing such anxiety onto other emotional elements in the world. As described, Alexander and Constanzo (1979) demonstrated that if persons high in conscious death anxiety could blame their tension in this area on real life events (e.g., threatening governmental policies), they had a diminished likelihood of suffering loss of self-esteem. With this paradigm in mind, it is plausible to consider the possibility that other self-disruptive aspects of death anxiety might be warded off by linking that anxiety with the bad intentions

of important figures in one's life or the threatening salience of certain ethnic minorities, and so forth. Perhaps immersion in world excitement of any kind can provide additional foci for defensive displacement.

5. A remarkable form of defense is to convert the image of death into an attractive one. There are whole cultures that have actually done so by means of splendiferous promises concerning the nature of the afterlife. It is also not unusual to encounter instances where persons have committed suicide with an apparent lustful zeal—an end wanted and passionately pursued. As already indicated, surveys of normal populations have turned up concepts of death as sexy, the "gay deceiver," and a soothing figure. Some individuals seem to convert the threat of death into a fairly pleasant invitation. They seem to see death not simply as a more acceptable alternative to a grim, unbearable life, but rather as possessing an attractiveness of its own. Of course, religious systems have been preeminent in creating the conditions for such reversal of death's usual connotations. However, it would appear that other variables beside religiosity may be likewise effective. Little or nothing is empirically known about such variables. Whether studies of the mechanisms underlying masochism would provide some clarification remains to be seen.

6. More speculatively, we are impressed with the possibility that death anxiety may be defended against by excluding one's body from one's self-concept. There is a long tradition, both religiously and philosophically, of splitting the self into nonsomatic (soul) and somatic entities (body).[19] The nonsomatic is presumably composed of a substance that defies usual mortal time limitations. It is said to endure forever. Analogously, most persons become highly skillful in constructing self-images (statements of identity) that focus on nonbody constructs for definition. These nonbody constructs are variously welded together with such components as status indicators, roles in social networks, central values,[20] and an elaborate cognitive superstructure. Like most cognitive creations, they have a life of their own and may be only vaguely, if at all, anchored in concepts of biological stuff. We know that individuals range widely in the degree to which they include their body feelings and sensations in their self-concepts. Some are able to exclude all but slight traces of body from their self-images (Fisher, 1986). It is certainly conceivable that, for many persons, one means of coping with death concern is to maximize the nonbody, cognitive aspects of their self-identity and to exclude as much of the somatic as possible. In that way, one becomes a somewhat abstracted construct rather than a flesh-and-blood existence. An interesting analogy of this defensive process has been described elsewhere.

---

[19]There is evidence (Wulff, 1991) that every known culture has believed that the individual has a non-physical or spiritual life in addition to the physical one.

[20]Conscious death anxiety tends to be relatively low in those who adhere to abstract theoretical values (Lonetto & Templer, 1986).

Thus, several studies (Fisher, 1986) have now shown that, in persons with body defects, there is a significantly smaller correlation between self-concept and body-concept ratings than typifies persons without body defects. Basically, what this means is that those with body deviations learn to exclude their feelings about their (inferior) body from the more cognitively oriented self-concept.[21] Another way to look at this matter is to recognize that the self-concept can become a highly fictionalized thing that only vaguely reflects real existence. J. Martin (1988), Lasch (1984), and others have pointed up the degree to which we function through "fictive" representations of self. J. Martin (1988) indicated that the conditions of modern life, with its fantastic input of images from everywhere (e.g., via television), lead us more and more to identify with vivid nonself experiences—things happening "out there" rather than "in here." Insofar as "out there" is away from one's own body, it diminishes the somatic component of our pictures of self.

These individual modes for modulating death anxieties are diverse and seem to represent a fairly powerful repertoire. Moreover, there are probably other modes. We have really only begun to explore this area. If we are to expand our knowledge, we should initiate more studies than expose individuals to controlled conditions that heighten the input of death-related stimuli and then monitor not only which aspects of behavior are most impacted but also how personal attributes (e.g., personality, value orientation) mediate the impact. Another priority is to ascertain the relationships existing between the most prevalent myths and illusions concerning death in given cultures and the specific strategies used by individuals in those cultures to discipline their death concerns. For example, if religious myths about immortality are most prominent societally, are individual strategies largely of the repressive, "shutting out" variety? Or if a society highlights the widespread use of distracting pageantry and vivid inputs to placate death anxieties, does one find individuals relying heavily on displacement as a defensive mediator? We need detailed maps of the interactions of defenses viewed at larger cultural, and also individual, levels.

Although there is no question but that concern about death has been a major theme in all cultures, it is also clear that there are ingeniously numerous ways to channel and control such concern. The "choices" range from complete denial that death can occur to a lustful yearning for it. There seems to be no limit to the pliability of the defenses that can be brought to bear on what is probably a central existential dilemma.

---

[21]One wonders whether the often negative self-depreciating attitudes that have been detected as a function of being exposed to one's own mirror image (e.g., Fisher, 1986) may not, in part, be a response to the resultant increasing body awareness. As more "body" is added to the individual's view of self, there may be a corresponding heightened sense of incarnate vulnerability.

We have probed the nature of death anxiety in some depth. We have devoted so much detailed attention to this matter early in our presentation because, as already noted, the fact of inevitable mortality is cited again and again in the pertinent literature (e.g., Becker, 1973) as the prime paradox of human existence. It is fair to say that there has been a large investment of research energy to clarify the parameters of death anxiety. However, we have seen that the understanding attained of the role that such anxiety plays in personality functioning and everyday behavior remains quite incomplete. Hopefully, our analysis of the material in this chapter has pointed up some of the major questions and puzzles that remain to be explored. In essence, we need to learn more about how death concern (terror) (which can presumably be stratified at different levels of awareness) mediates one's capacity to attribute meaning to one's day-to-day actions.

4

THE PROBLEMS OF UNCERTAINTY AND INSIGNIFICANCE

UNCERTAINTY

The unpredictability of each person's trajectory represents still another potential source of life absurdity. It is true that practically anything can happen at any time, and there is really no dependable predictability for any given individual. Of course, there are reasonable probabilities that, within large populations, only certain proportions will experience specific changes, traumas, and disasters. However, the individual does not know from moment to moment what will happen next. The list of potential threats and destructive intrusions is endless: disease, loss of loved ones, injury, business cycles, neoplasm, spontaneous failure of a key physiological system, devastating earthquake—just to name a few. Each day, multitudes of persons abruptly experience the relentless uncontrollability of the world. The nature of our planet's structure and the social arrangements of its inhabitants introduce potential loss of control as a key theme.

There is widespread concern about this theme in all cultures, and it gets channeled into such diverse forms as existential anxiety, phobias, fictional and mythical images depicting life as chaotic, and a repertoire of religious countermeasures. Researchers have mirrored this concern by the frequency with which they have investigated the effects of feeling that things are unpredictable or out of control. Much has been written about this topic (e.g., Breznitz, 1983; Freud, 1959a, 1959b; Garber & Seligman, 1980; Lazarus, 1983; Lefcourt, 1982; Phares, 1976; Rotter, 1966), as it manifests itself in various guises (e.g., obsessive-compulsive behavior, posttraumatic syndrome, rigidity, openness to new experience, locus of control, learned helplessness). Of course, the concern about life's basic uncertainty has popped up again and again in philosophical debates about free will, determinism, Skinnerian conditioning, and many other equivalent issues (Immergluck, 1964). If individuals were truly aware of the uncertainty of things, would it not suffuse their images of existence with somewhat hopeless and perhaps even preposterous elements? There is a vast literature (e.g., Baum & Singer, 1980; Garber & Seligman, 1980; Lefcourt, 1967, 1982) documenting the fact that a sense of not being in control has numerous negative effects on behavior. Not feeling in control has been said to lead to such negative consequences as elevated anxiety, pessimism, depression, various kinds of physiological malfunctioning, diminished work productivity, and alienated attitudes.

The largest body of research dealing with the control issue has evolved around the theme of locus of control. This theme was originally formulated by Rotter and his associates (Rotter, Seeman, & Liverant, 1962). It refers quite simply to how much persons feel they have the ability to affect and control the events in their lives. Measurement of it is usually by questionnaires calling for choices between items such as the following:

   a. I have often found that what is going to happen will happen.
   b. Trusting to fate has never turned out as well for me as making a decision to take a definite course of action.

The more that individuals endorse the "a" type of item, the more they are considered to be external in orientation. The greater their endorsement of the "b" type, the more they are portrayed as internal in their life perspective. Presumably, external persons see life as dominated by powers beyond their own control, whereas internal persons feel they are the source of their own fate. Obviously, the questionnaire mode just described suffers from all of the problems inherent in any questionnaire technique. For example, some studies have found significant positive correlations between the motivation to make a socially desirable impression and depicting oneself as holding an internal perspective (Lefcourt, 1982).[1] Incidentally, attempts have been made to measure locus of control in projective ways[2] (e.g., de Charms, 1979; Dies, 1968) that presumably tap into more unconscious levels. It is encouraging that, in one instance, the questionnaire-derived and projective-derived indices

---

[1]There is good evidence (Lefcourt, 1982) that the locus of control variable is multidimensional. Various factor-analytic studies have identified more than one factor. However, for present purposes, locus of control will be treated as if it were simply a single, general factor.

[2]The potential value of a projective approach to feelings about control was exemplified by one study (C. B. Thomas & Duszynski, 1985). In this study, a measure derived from Rorschach images (viz., representations of "whirling" and "spinning") that can be construed as having implications for how much one feels "out of control" was predictive of psychological and somatic disturbance many years after the Rorschach images were first obtained.

turned out to be significantly positively correlated (Battle & Rotter, 1963). Unfortunately, few published studies have approached the locus of control issue by means of a projective methodology. Hence, virtually nothing can be said about the possible differences that exist between sampling locus of control at the two different levels. It is difficult to believe that some important differences do not exist. However, if one wants to explore the role of locus of control attitudes in life, one must make do with the accumulated data based on questionnaire responses.

Quite unanimously, the massed studies of locus of control tell us that persons who take an internal orientation often seem to be better off than those externally inclined. That is, to feel that you shape (whether positively or negatively) your own fate seems to bestow adaptive advantages, as compared with those who feel they are life's pawns. Consider the following. There appears to be evidence that the higher the internal orientation of individuals, the less they are depressed, the less they display a variety of psychopathological symptoms, the more energetically and effectively they attack problems, the less passively they respond to suggestions and demands of authority figures, the more altruistic their behavior, and the more efficiently they process certain kinds of information. Internals are also said to have a better sense of humor, be more creative, enjoy superior health, and deal with stress more adequately. The research literature presented a litany of the presumed advantages of feeling in control (Lefcourt, 1982; Phares, 1976).

What is this entity that we call internal locus of control? Why does it apparently mediate almost every aspect of human activity? Does it represent a talent? Is it an ability, a skill, or a collection of skills? One must keep in mind that it actually reflects a verbal statement of belief that one's life is not ruled by the forces existing outside of, and surrounding, oneself. It is a belief that "I significantly influence what happens to me." Of course, the question immediately arises as to whether an internal orientation largely reflects how effectively persons have been able to operate in the various theaters of their lives. Perhaps those who are well adjusted, who process information well, and do so many other things effectively end up with an internal conviction.

Lefcourt (1982), after reviewing much of the research literature related to locus of control, pondered the same issue:

> While some areas of uncertainty remain, there is good reason to believe, on the basis of the research reviewed, that external control orientation and abnormal personal functioning are correlated. One ambiguity is the direction of causality—does being ineffective and defensive generate a sense of helplessness; or, the converse, does helplessness generate defensiveness? In all probability the relationship is circular and perpetuated through a vicious circle, though there is little empirical data available to allow for certainty regarding this conjecture. (p. 129)

We would concur that a circular process is probably involved. But we detect clues here and there suggesting that faith in one's influence is far from a one-to-one product of one's actual effectiveness in the world and that it can, not infrequently, subsist on illusory ingredients. Apropos of this possibility, let us scan some of the work done on illusory sense of control.

ILLUSORY CONTROL

It is by now fairly well documented that persons can gain some of the advantages of feeling "in control" even when that feeling is anchored in fiction. Any number of experimental studies illustrate this point. Consider an investigation by Geer, Davison, and Gatchel (1970). Subjects in one group were first asked to participate in a series of trials in which they were called upon to "flick a reaction switch" each time they received an electric shock. The shock in each instance lasted for 6 seconds, no matter how quickly the switch was activated. During a second series, the subjects were asked to respond in the same way to a number of shocks, except they were told that the faster they responded, the smaller would be the duration of each shock. Quite arbitrarily, no matter how fast the individual responded to the onset of the shock, the duration of shock during this second series was reduced from the original 6 seconds to 3 seconds. A control group experienced an initial series of trials duplicating that of the experimental group. During the second series, the duration of each shock was similarly shortened to 3 seconds, but without instructing subjects that their speed of response to the onset of each shock had any effect on the duration. In other words, the subjects in the experimental group thought the decreased duration of shock was due to their own increased speed of response to the onset of shock, whereas the control group could not attribute the decrease of duration to their own efforts.

Measures of spontaneous galvanic skin responses (GSR) indicated a significant trend for the subjects who thought they were influencing shock duration to show fewer and smaller GSR reactions to shock onset during the second series of trials than did the subjects who were not given the impression they could personally influence shock duration. There was also a trend for the subjects who thought they were in control to rate the shocks during the second series of trials as less irritating, but the difference was not statistically significant. Thus, the individuals who believed, at a purely fictional level, that they controlled shock levels were less autonomically aroused (probably less anxious) by the shock than were those who did not have an analogous fictional sense of being in control.

Other related experiments abound in the literature. We direct you to just a few. Glass, Singer, and Friedman (1969) demonstrated that when persons are exposed to unpredictable stressful noise, they are less disturbed if they believe they have some control over it, even if they do not actually exercise such control. Kanfer and Seidner (1973) determined how long subjects could tolerate immersions of their hands in ice water while watching a series of travel slides. The tolerance proved to be significantly greater in those individuals who could move the slides along whenever they so desired, as compared with subjects who were dependent on the experimenter to manipulate the slides. Bowers (1968) asked subjects to find the correct pathway through a maze. One group was led to believe they would be shocked for certain errors, and that they could control the frequency of shock by learning to avoid specific types of responses. Another group was told that shocks would be administered randomly to help maintain alertness. Although the amount of shock administered was the same in both groups, there was significant evidence of greater tolerance for the shock in those who falsely believed they were exerting control.

Even more dramatic examples of the power of fictitious control are provided by investigations dealing with response to real-life situations. Note the following study by Anderson (1987), who tested the effects of various preoperative preparation strategies on patients undergoing cardiac surgery. One experimental group was preoperatively supplied with information about what would happen during the surgical procedures. This information included a description of all phases of the hospitalization, as well as the body sensations associated with various aspects of the treatment and recovery process. A second experimental group received the same information, as well as a series of exercises that would help postoperatively to cope with coughing and muscle stiffness. The individuals in this group were impressed that they could influentially play an "active role during recovery." The patients in the control group were given "routine hospital preparation" and were interviewed for 30 minutes about the history of their illness, how they decided to have surgery, and so forth.

The two experimental preparation procedures were found to induce a significantly greater sense of control over the physical recovery process than did the control condition. Further, the experimental procedures significantly reduced psychological distress, facilitated physical recovery as perceived by nurses, and reduced the incidence of acute postoperative hypertension. The best predictor of the benefits derived from the experimental procedures was the degree to which such procedures induced feelings of being in control. The acquisition of information, per se, was a minor ingredient of effective preparation of the patient. It did not reduce generalized anxiety unless it increased feelings of control. Incidentally, the two experimental strategies were equally effective. This study demonstrates that a technique, which created the impression (largely fictitious) that patients could control the process of recovery from surgery, made them feel psychologically better and also had a beneficial impact on potential somatic complications. Other studies have shown analogous results (e.g., Andrew, 1970; Langer, Janis, & Wolfer, 1975; Lindeman & Van Aernam, 1971; Mumford, Schlesinger, & Glass, 1982).

Another intriguing example presents itself in a report by Langer and Rodin (1976). They set up a field experiment in a nursing home for the aged. Their intent was to determine the effect of giving aged individuals the message that they had more choices and potential for taking more responsibility than they usually envisioned. One sample of patients was exposed to a talk by the hospital administrator, which focused on their right to make decisions for themselves (e.g., "you have the responsibility of caring for yourselves, of deciding whether or not you want to make this a home you can be proud of and happy in," p. 194). In addition, they were given the chance to take a plant and assume the responsibility of caring for it. The individuals in the control group were addressed by the hospital administrator and told that they had various options, but that the staff was responsible for providing these options. They were also given plants, but "the nurses will water and care for them for you" (p. 194). In short, the experimental subjects were given the message that they could take charge of themselves, and the control subjects were told to surrender control to the staff. A number of questionnaire and behavioral measures were obtained to evaluate the effects of the experimental manipulation.

Overall, the individuals who were told they were "in control" fared better. During an immediate follow-up period, they were more active, happier, more mentally alert, and more involved in activities. Eighteen months after the study was completed, they continued to show higher health and activity patterns and, quite amazingly, a significantly lower death rate (Rodin & Langer, 1977).[3] The truth is that the experimental and control groups were living under basically the same conditions. The only difference was that one group was given a largely illusory impression that it was in control, and the other group was discouraged from taking this perspective. The "you are in charge" message from the hospital administrator to the experimental subjects was basically propaganda, and the act of giving individuals a plant for which they would be responsible was, in reality, no more than a symbolic gesture. The experimental manipulation was, in fact, nothing more than a symbolic manipulation. However, the assimilation of such thinly concealed fictions produced a significant positive alteration in the feelings and behaviors of the experimental subjects, which persisted for some time and even affected the death rate.

There is little question that if persons are made to believe they are "in control," whether it be true or not, the result can be a significant enhancement of quality of life and even improvement of health. It should be added,

---

[3]The contribution of feelings of being in control to adequate somatic functioning is being documented more and more convincingly (e.g., Holroyd & Andrasek, 1978).

though, that evidence has been emerging that being "in control" can, in some special circumstances, have negative implications (Burger, 1989; Folkman, 1984; Rodin, 1986). If being "in control" means that one has to deny oneself an important form of gratification or style of life, this can have an untoward impact. For example, obese persons whose eating habits are "out of control" may regard the cost of "being in control" (viz., limiting caloric intake) to be terribly depriving and depressing. One should note, too, that being "in control" can, for some individuals, best be achieved by becoming attached to a more powerful figure in whom one has faith and who seems to guarantee the maintenance of stability (e.g., Fromm, 1941). In this case, paradoxically, one gains control by giving up one's executive privileges. In fact, there seem to be an infinite number of pathways to convincing oneself that one is in control. Every form of illusory fantasy is pressed into service to assure oneself that things can be meaningfully structured or managed. Persons may guiltfully blame themselves[4] (even when they are actually blameless) for accidents in which they incurred serious injuries in order to convince themselves that there was a specific (predictable) cause, and therefore their universe is not a chaotic affair (Folkman, 1984). These persons frequently interpret catastrophic losses and personal disablement as having positive value (e.g., testing and improving one's character) (Silver & Wortman, 1980). They endlessly reassure themselves with images of protective deities, superstitiously conceptualized forces radiating luck, a "just world," delusional systems, and so forth. More will be said later about such modes of self-protection.

INTERNAL VERSUS EXTERNAL LOCUS OF CONTROL

Let us return to the vast literature on the formal measurement of locus of control, which was originally spelled out by Rotter et al. (1962). As already indicated, most studies have suggested that persons who define themselves as having an internal locus of control (internals) may fare better than externals in coping with a formidable variety of problems and stressors. However, one must ask to what degree the distinction is based on illusory maneuvers. Are internals actually more "realistic," better adapted, and in all-around better condition than externals? As we begin to explore this matter, consider, first of all, that it has become increasingly clear that few persons are internal or external across the board. As summarized by Lefcourt (1982) and others (e.g., Phares, 1976), persons may take an internal attitude about one area of life (e.g., school achievement), but a more external attitude about some

---

[4]One study (Bulman & Wortman, 1977) actually found that persons who were recovering from severe spinal cord injuries coped better during the rehabilitation period if they blamed themselves for the original accident that resulted in the injury.

other area (e.g., health). Predictions of behavior as a function of internal versus external orientation improve consistently as the measurement of orientation is narrowed to more specific categories. It would appear that persons learn, from their life experiences, to ascribe different weights to their own degrees of internality or externality in different classes of situations. Most persons have mixed and even inconsistent views of how well they can steer their own life courses. We would suggest that there is a patchwork quality to each individual's schema about internality–externality. Each schema appears to be a function of what life has brought by way of success–failure ratios and complex self-protective strategies.

In any case, we may grant, as widely assumed in the literature, that persons do show broad inclinations to be internal or external with respect to their concepts of control. We repeat, with rare exceptions, that being an "internal" is viewed as better than being an "external." Internals have emerged as the "goods" and the externals as the "bads." This simply reflects the large number of studies in which internals turned out to be more successful than externals in all sorts of ways (e.g., Lefcourt, 1982). There is an obvious superiority (especially within the context of modern power values) in taking the position that one is in charge of one's own moves rather than being a pawn. The research literature is pervaded by explicit and implicit ideas that internality is more realistic, more adaptive, and "healthier." We do not challenge that internality often provides salient advantages in coping with life problems. But it is our impression, after broadly reviewing the available information, that externality also provides significant advantages in various contexts. Furthermore, we can see no evidence that internality is more realistic than externality. Both are probably constructed in equal measure of illusory notions.

"Pure externals" presumably feel that they, as personal agents, have relatively little to say about what happens to them. Instead, they are inclined to seek the favor of powers greater than themselves, with the hope that these powers will smile upon them. They ally themselves with luck, with forces rooted in superstition, and potent figures. "Pure internals" look basically to their own prowess; they are inclined to shun luck and similar irrational explanatory perspectives, and they are suspicious of any influence authority figures might exert on them. In each case, there is exaggeration and bias. The externals may be too preoccupied with the larger, uncontrollable aspects of existence and may underestimate how much they can increase their effectiveness by taking responsibility and looking for opportunities to apply their energies to solve problems. The internals may unrealistically reassure themselves they can influence existential factors that are usually beyond an individual's control. Obviously, there are many accidental and inevitable life-cycle variables that even the most energetic individual efforts cannot touch. The potential self-deception, illusion, and relativity that may underlie either of the extreme external–internal positions deserve documentation and special thought. We explore a number of areas of research that highlight such matters.

REALISM

The question of whether internals are more realistic than externals in their life orientation is indirectly addressed by a dispute encountered in the research literature. This dispute is concerned with which perspective is most defensive in shutting out information too threatening or upsetting, vis-à-vis one's self-esteem. To almost everyone's surprise, a series of studies suggest that internals are more defensive than externals in the way they filter threatening inputs. These studies included a report by Efron (as described by Lefcourt, 1982), which indicated that internal high school students are more likely to forget their failures than external students. Another study (Lipp, Kolstoe, James, & Randall, 1968) found that when handicapped persons are tachistoscopically shown slides portraying handicapped individuals, the extreme externals more quickly recognize the briefly exposed pictures than do the extreme internals. That is, the internals seemed to be more defensive about becoming aware of the stimuli with threatening "handicap" implications. Further, Phares, Ritchie, and Davis (1968) provided subjects with false (but apparently authoritatively accurate) and often negative descriptions of their personalities and examined their responses to such ego alarming inputs. While the responses of internals and externals did not differ in several respects, it did turn out that the externals were later able to recall significantly more of the negative (and also total number of) interpretations than the internals.

The studies just cited imply that externals are relatively more open to awareness of the negative or the unpleasant than internals. Burnes, Brown, and Keating (1971) pointed in the same direction when they reported that the pattern of correlations they observed between locus of control and various MMPI measures is such that it indicates those "who are more internal tend to deny difficulties or inadequacies" (p. 301). Tudor (1970) likewise discerned that internals scored significantly higher than externals on both the MMPI Denial scale and the MMPI K scale. Relatedly, Berrenberg (1987) discovered a significant positive relationship between an exaggerated sense of internality and elevated scores on a questionnaire measure of mania (presumably reflecting an attitude of excited overoptimism and the denial of any unpleasantness in one's life). One should mention, too, that Hersch and Scheibe (1967) found externals to be significantly less defensive, as defined by the Gough and Heilbrun (1965) Adjective Check List, than internals.

In the course of interpreting such findings (and others of a related genre),

Phares (1976) concluded: "All this suggests that, at least in some ways, externals are less disturbed. Put another way, they may be better able to handle immediately threatening material. . . ." (p. 132). Presumably, externals could do this because their externality provided a relatively better defense against the anxiety aroused by the threatening input. Phares (1976) went on to speculate that externals are more like sensitizers and internals are more like repressors. His speculation was encouraged by Houston (1972), who found that, although internals and externals do not differ in their verbally reported levels of anxiety in a stress situation, the internals show significantly more physiological response than the externals. He noted that an analogous trend was observed by Byrne (1964) for repressors to deny their anxiety verbally in stress contexts but to evidence accentuated reactions physiologically.

Lefcourt (1982) took a different position on this matter. He felt that the data just cited do not stand up well against a host of other studies (e.g., Davis & Davis, 1972; DuCette & Wolk, 1972; Phares, 1971; Phares, Wilson, & Klyver, 1971) in which externals were more upset and defensive when confronted with failure experiences. He concluded: "However, the ready acceptance of blame for failure and the choosing of options that provide clear self-evaluative feedback by internals provide eloquent refutation of an argument positing a 'need' to forget, with all the connotations of anxiety and defensiveness" (p. 118). Lefcourt (1982) mobilized data indicating that externals are more defensive than internals when dealing with certain types of failure experiences. However, he never explained why some of the previous studies pinpointed an apparent selective reluctance on the part of internals to recall or become aware of specific types of threatening material. In any case, because Lefcourt (1982) and Phares (1976) differed in their perspectives, the data involved are ambiguous to some degree. Although there is reasonable evidence (e.g., Lefcourt, 1982) that internals are more efficient (realistic) in processing a variety of information, one must entertain the possibility that this may not be true for inputs that are ego alien.

STRESS

The relativity of arguments concerning the effectiveness or protective value of being internal versus external emerges in the results we discovered in a cluster of research studies exploring responses to stress conditions. While internality seems to modulate positively one's adaptation to certain stress conditions (e.g., Lefcourt, 1982), there are suggestions that, under conditions of extreme stress (where feelings of helplessness are induced), internals may cope relatively poorly and become particularly upset. We cite a number of observations that point in this direction.

Let us begin with some illustrative laboratory based findings. Gregory,

Chartier, and Wright (1979) evaluated the performance of internals and externals in a setting designed to produce "learned helplessness." In one condition, subjects were exposed to an aversive tone and given the opportunity to escape it by pressing a button. Then, their performance on a subsequent soluble task was evaluated. In another condition, subjects were exposed to an aversive tone but had no way of escaping it. Subsequently, their performance on the soluble task was measured. Following the "escapable" condition, the internals and externals did not differ in their performance on the soluble task. However, following the "inescapable" condition, the internals performed worse than the externals.[5]

Garrett and Willoughby (1972) reported analogously that when Black children were exposed to a failure experience, the externals performed better on a subsequent conceptual task than did the internals. Indeed, observation of lower-class Black children who are chronically exposed to deprivation and stress led Epstein and Komorita (1971) to conclude:

> The implications of these results for the adaptability of the lower class Negro child may constitute a "double-edged" sword. Inability to assume personal responsibility for failure experiences may interfere with the use of negative environmental feedback for the purpose of modifying one's behavior in a more realistic, adaptive fashion. On the other hand, the defensive function served by this inability may enable the child to maintain some sense of personal integrity and self-esteem. Thus, the attribution of failure to external factors (e.g., lack, chance, or fate) may enable an aggrieved class of people to maintain a capacity for psychological resilience and survival for the short-term, but constitutes a self-defeating mechanism for long-term social adjustment. (p. 7)

At still another level, Houston (1972) discerned that when adults were subjected to the threat of receiving electric shock, internals showed a greater increase in heart rate than did externals. However, the two categories did not differ in their verbal reports of amount of anxiety experienced. Houston (1972) speculated that the internals covered up their anxiety (that registered in terms of heart rate) and behaved more defensively. However, it should be added that Blankstein (1984) considered Houston's (1972) interpretation of his data "acrobatic" and beyond the actual findings. Note, too, the conclusions of Glass and Carver (1980), who analyzed several studies on the response of coronary-prone individuals (Type As) to various stress conditions. Type As are characterized by a strong desire to maintain control over the environment and thus resemble internals in that respect. Glass and Carver (1980) uncovered data in the literature indicating that Type As cope adequately with

---

[5]In an unpublished study, Benson and Kennelly (1976) similarly found that "the performance of internals was impaired by pretreatment with insoluble problems. The performance of externals was not impaired by pretreatment with unstable problems. . . ." (as cited on p. 1990 by Gregory et al., 1979).

brief "uncontrollable" stress, but that when such stress is "prolonged" they exhibit enhanced "learned helplessness." Apparently, when there is an intense set to maintain control, the experience of prolonged uncontrollability becomes a magnified threat.

Data from more real-life contexts help to expand our perspective on the matter under discussion. Krause (1986) probed the effects of life experiences on elderly persons. He evaluated the degree to which such persons were depressed as a function of the frequency with which they had encountered stressful life events and also their degree of internality–externality. One of his major findings was that "older adults with extreme internal mastery control beliefs are especially vulnerable to the deleterious effects of negative stressful events" (p. 621). It should be added, however, that extreme internals reported experiencing overall fewer stressful events than did extreme externals. Krause (1986) concluded that: "having extreme internal mastery control orientation is a mixed blessing. Such beliefs have negative effects because they lead to ineffective coping actions (or self blame) with those stressors that cannot be avoided" (p. 621). In the same vein, Janoff-Bulman and Marshall (1982) reported that elderly persons[6] who adapted least well to the stress of placement in a nursing home were those who described themselves as previously having a high degree of control over their lives. In another real-life context, Taylor (1979) detected that individuals who are most accustomed to exerting control over their lives have the greatest difficulty in adjusting to hospitalization.[7] Reid (1984) cited several impressive studies indicating that persons with severe chronic diseases (e.g., cancer) may become less anxious over time if they adapt to their dilemma by becoming more external.

The studies cited are intended to illustrate rather than be an exhaustive review. They simply highlight data that raise the possibility that externality may, in certain important settings, provide as much or more security and stability than internality. It is really indefensible to argue in any overall sense that either internality or externality provides a superior set for coping with stress.[8] The defensive value of either probably varies as a function of such multiple variables as the intensity and duration of stress and the potential availability of a "solution."

---

[6]Although the matter remains in dispute (Skinner & Connell, 1986), there is a trend (Hale & Cochran, 1986; Lumpkin, 1986) for persons to become more external in orientation as they move into the later years of life. One may speculate that this represents an increased realism (based on extended experience) about how uncontrollable life truly is.

[7]Quite anecdotally, Kubler-Ross (1969) remarked that persons who have lived active, "controlling" lives have more difficulty adjusting to the imminent threat of death than do more passive individuals.

[8]One should mention the curious fact that some investigators claim to have evidence that alcoholics and drug addicts were internally inclined (e.g., Gozali & Sloan, 1971). However, Rohsenow and O'Leary (1978), after reviewing the pertinent literature, concluded this was not so.

RELATIVITY

The simplistic tendency to see "internal persons" as distinctly superior to "external persons" is additionally complicated by the relativity and considerable fluidity of each category. It already has been mentioned that there are multiple locus of control dimensions, and any given individual could be quite internal on one and yet manifest high externality with respect to another. Also, we do not know the degree to which an individual's externality–internality can be changed by immediate conditions. There are numerous hints in the literature that internal–external scores can be altered by environmental events and special laboratory manipulations. Lefcourt (1967) and others have shown that the performance of externals in a variety of tasks can be equal to internals by more clearly explicating situational cues as to what reinforcements are available in the task. Doherty and Baldwin (1985) claimed that women who have been followed longitudinally since the 1960s have shown significant shifts (one standard deviation) toward externality (but this has not occurred in male samples). Diamond and Shapiro (1973), R. E. Smith (1970), and Abramowitz, Ambramowitz, Robert, and Jackson (1974) have shown that significant shifts[9] toward internality can occur in persons who participate in either individual or group psychotherapy.[10] Interestingly, McClure (1991) considered that attempts to train individuals to be more internal are actually exercises in illusion, if the conditions of their lives have remained essentially unchanged.

The relativity of the internal–external distinction is further pointed up by the fact that each of these categories may have different meanings for the two sexes. For example, Hale, Hedgepeth, and Taylor (1985–1986) discovered that locus of control is correlated with self-reported psychopathology in older women, but not in older men. Palmore and Luikart (1972) had described essentially the same pattern previously. Lefcourt (1982) summarized a series of studies in which puzzling sex differences appeared. In one instance, externality was associated positively with academic achievement in a female sample, but in a male sample, internality was positively predictive of such achievement. In another instance, locus of control among male children was correlated with grade point average but not achievement test scores, whereas among female children it was associated with achievement test scores but not grades. Nowicki and Roundtree (1971) informed us that internality is positively correlated with achievement in males, but with involvement in extracurricular activities in females. Such differences and reversals between the

---

[9]Abramowitz et al. (1974) reported that externals are most likely to show shifts if exposed to a directive form of therapy, whereas internals respond more to a nondirective approach.

[10]It should be acknowledged that there are also reports of failure to alter internal–external scores by means of therapeutic-like procedures (e.g., Aronson, 1970; R. E. Smith, 1989).

genders are apparently not uncommon, and they imply that the meanings of internality and externality may, in specific contexts, differ for the two genders, even to the extent of being reversed.

Cross-cultural observations (Hui, 1982) indicated that locus of control may be quite vulnerable to cultural differences. The antecedents of a high or low locus of control score can be wholly divergent in unlike cultures. Illustratively, there are data showing that the relationship between locus of control and persuasibility as a function of source credibility is reversed in certain countries as compared with others. Thus, a highly credible source has a stronger influence on external Japanese and Americans than on internals, but the opposite pattern characterizes New Zealand, Australia, and Sweden. It is striking that externals in one culture can be so highly susceptible to the influences of a credible source and in another culture the opposite holds true. Obviously, the behavioral consequences of being internal or external are mediated by cultural definitions, and neither has a fixed universal meaning. To be internal in one culture may shape attitudes toward certain classes of persons that would be duplicated in another culture by being external.

OVERVIEW

As one learns more about the complexities of being external or internal, it becomes difficult to see one mode as superior to the other. Persons seem to improvise external or internal belief systems that will fit their life circumstances. Others have come to similar conclusions. Note the following statement by Rothbaum, Weisz, and Snyder (1982):

> Originally, external locus of control was assumed to entail a perception of uncontrollability. However, numerous research findings have disconfirmed the perceived uncontrollability assumption, and many locus of control theorists now espouse a position close to the one advocated here. According to the more recent *congruence hypothesis*, people reserve energy for activities that match the form of control they feel best able to exercise (with externals, for example, focusing on chance activities). Cherulnik and Citrin (1974) put it well: "Externals do not feel powerless, but simply pursue rewards in different avenues." (p. 404)

What one learns in the literature is that persons create an almost infinite variety of semiillusory ideas about how they influence the stream of events. Sometimes the world makes more sense if persons tell themselves they are in charge of fate; and yet sometimes they need to perceive events as beyond their personal control. Indeed, it will be recalled that persons may, in their search for signs of personal control, even blame themselves for catastrophes they could not have possibly initiated.[11] At the other extreme, persons may paradoxically find security in picturing events as uncontrollable (Burger, 1989). As Burger (1989) documented, the need to feel "not in control" may be necessitated by situations in which one fears failure and wishes to save face publicly or avoid admitting weakness to oneself. The attainment of equilibrium may, at one time, require ascribing magical control powers to self and on another occasion denying that one has any control. The contents of these orientations appear to be quite different, but, in fact, they are adaptive equivalents and probably to a similar degree rooted in arbitrary assumptions. The same self-protective paradigm may, to an as yet unexpected extent, apply to the individual's adoption of internal versus external stances.

THE ORIGINS OF LOCUS OF CONTROL ATTITUDES

What factors decide whether an individual will come to lean in an internal versus external direction? We have assembled all of the available studies that have looked at the relationships between persons' locus of control attitudes and the nature of their experiences with their mothers and fathers. In scanning this material, one quickly sees that an external orientation is encouraged by traumatic events that disrupted the original family or made life a struggle. Those persons who lost parents early in life (e.g., Duke & Lancaster, 1976; Parish & Nunn, 1983; Wiehe, 1986) are particularly likely to be external, and this is similarly true for those persons brought up in somewhat deprived socioeconomic (e.g., Lefcourt, 1982; Rotter, 1966) or low-status (Lefcourt, 1982) circumstances. There is fairly solid evidence that conditions imposing traumatic hardships on children as they grow up tend to shape them into believing they are subordinate to forces greater than themselves. Hence, they lose faith in their ability to control fate.

At another level, the collective data involving parental behavior strongly suggest that externals are particularly likely to have grown up with parents who were authoritarian, directive, and even rejecting (e.g., Chandler, Wolf, Cook, & Dugovics, 1980; Loeb, 1975; Tolor & Jalowiec, 1968). By way of contrast, internals seem to have been raised by parents who were nurturant, protective, noncritical, and even "babying" (Katkovsky, Crandall, & Good, 1967). One can interpret these findings to mean that externals are encouraged by parents who arbitrarily, in a spirit of "I am superior to you," impose values, rules, and ways of behaving. It could be said that these children are made to feel like objects to be manipulated. But internals are apparently given the

---

[11]Baum, Fleming, and Singer (1983) found that residents near the site of the Three Mile Island nuclear accident, who assumed some blame for the problems they experienced, were less stressed than residents who did not.

message by their parents that they are special individuals, that they are highly valued, and that they have a right to expect things to go well. The parents of internals seem to put their children in a protective bubble, but without the implication of confinement or uncomfortable restraint. Overall, one might conclude that the parents of externals act as if their children are unable to "make it" as individuals, whereas the parents of internals foster their children's sense of being prized for their individual specialness.

What we have just stated is actually an idealized interpretation of the data. In fact, there are studies (e.g., Crandall & Crandall, 1983; Levenson, 1973) that depicted one or the other of the parents of internals as "cool," "critical," "pushing" their children toward independence, and even resorting to an unusual amount of physical punishment (MacDonald, 1971). One study (Yates, Kennelly, & Cox, 1975) focused on how parents of internals apply punishment more "contingently" than do parents of externals. That is, presumably their children can more clearly recognize that the punishments they receive are consequent to their actions. One is left with the impression that the parents of internals may not necessarily be unusually "soft" or "easy" with their children. It would appear that, in some circumstances, they can be demanding and punishing, but not to the point that they violate their children's sense of individuality. We can, then, to some degree, trace persons' external versus internal expectations of life to the visions of the world transmitted by their parents. Thus, the parents of internals highlight the idea that the world is a place hospitable to the individual and likely to be influenced by that individual's output. However, the parents of externals encourage subordination to those of greater stature or potency.[12] Although parents apparently do play a significant role in how much control their children believe they exert over their own lives, one should keep in mind that the magnitudes of the reported correlations are quite modest; it is a certainty that other, perhaps even more important, variables contribute. Thus, Dyal (1984) documented a number of studies in which the parental correlates of locus of control vary as a function of the stage of life in which the child's locus of control is measured and also the child's gender and ethnicity.

INSIGNIFICANCE

Let us briefly consider another source of life uncertainty (viz., the possibility of simply not counting in the scheme of things). What greater absurdity can one envision than being of zero magnitude? The power of the threat of be-

---

[12]Surprisingly, the correlations between parents' and children's actual locus of control scores are generally low and inconsistent (e.g., Lefcourt, 1982; Davis & Phares, 1969). This probably reflects the influential importance of life variables beside parental attitudes in shaping an individual's external–internal perspective.

ing insignificant was dramatized in the upheavals occasioned by the introduction of the Copernican schema (Kuhn, 1976). This schema projected a worldview in which man was no longer the central figure in God's creation, but rather the occupant of a random planet barely perceptible in the total universe. Mankind was now of practically zero import in an infinite expanse. Unique centrality had vanished.

As one scans the accumulated psychological literature, it is apparent that concern about insignificance is pervasive in many populations. Research has, in multiple guises, touched on this matter. Thus, it is impressive how many areas of modern personality study are concerned, directly or indirectly, with questions about the individual's worth. The entire self-concept literature, which is of massive proportions, relates to whether persons perceive themselves as having high or low value in the context of various standards. The typical self-concept measure really asks for self-ratings on a continuum that extends, in paraphrased terms, from "I am nothing" to "I am a person of high value." Obviously, too, the explosive accumulation of writings concerning the nature of development of the self and the origins of identity reflect an intense interest in the reality of the self and its importance in the scheme of things.

A related genre is exemplified in the profusion of publications on the effects of focusing one's attention on oneself (e.g., Duval & Wicklund, 1972), as compared with nonself objects. This work clearly is concerned with the impact of increasing the centrality of self in the perceptual field. There are numerous other research areas, diversely touching on achievement, power, level of aspiration, narcissism, and competitiveness, that, in the final analysis, relate to how psychologically big or central persons perceive themselves to be. Consider further the whole line of body image research dealing with distortions in the perceived size of one's own body (Fisher, 1986). The stimulus for this work has come from observations of the apparent confusion of disturbed individuals (e.g., schizophrenics, anorexics) about their body size, and their acting out of fantasies that they are or ought to be of practically zero body proportions. The inner debate in such individuals seems to revolve about the issue of whether they are or are not somatically insignificant and, by implication, existentially so.[13]

Little or nothing has been done to tackle directly the question of how persons feel about their trifling part in the cosmos. There are some anthropological studies that have looked at such matters in the context of cross-cultural myths about man's place in nature (e.g., Barnouw, 1985). However, no reliable quantification of this type of material seems to be available. We obvi-

---

[13]Feeling small versus large has been explored by multiple studies in the context of handwriting, figure drawing size (Fisher, 1986), and the self-perception of comedians (Fisher & Fisher, 1981).

ously need research inquiries to evaluate how the average personality is left imprinted by the awareness of the Earth's insignificance.[14]

---

[14]Space travel may provide a rather unique opportunity to observe the psychological effects of being vividly confronted by the infinitude of space and the relative nothingness represented by the planet Earth. As persons go into outerspace, they cannot help but become affectively aware of the nature of the true paradigm—one in which humans lack any real centrality. There are scattered anecdotal reports from astronauts (e.g., Chaikin, 1985; Santy, 1983) that suggested that space travel does produce considerable discomfort and psychological distress, but it is difficult to disentangle how much of this distress is due to variables like sensory isolation and weightlessness, as contrasted to the impact of a new realization of one's insignificance.

5

TESTING THE BUFFERING POWER
OF RELIGIOUS IMAGERY

There is little question that all cultures, in their scramble for meaning, invest heavily in sacred images. Each society cultivates concepts of divine power and cosmological structure that hopefully will make sense of it all. The diversity of sacred images is remarkable, and yet each lays claim to unique validity. In essence, each culture asserts that its sacred constructions are true beyond all other claims to divine truth. The essential foundation for belief in the sacred is faith. Because religious concepts lie beyond the boundaries of science, they cannot be validated by ordinary means. They must be assimilated within the context of what is ordinarily referred to as the magical or supernatural.

In view of the objective of this book, we consider that it is profitable to explore how well this widespread class of religious beliefs has served to buffer individuals against life stresses. Do persons who are able to maintain religious belief systems gain adaptive advantages?

Such advantages might accrue from the reassurances provided by confronting religious vistas, but also from the fact that firm and well-defined "blueprints for action" (Shaver, Lenauer, & Sadd, 1980) are offered by religious dogma that reduce conflict and indecisiveness. It is difficult to believe that such advantages do not accrue. K. Thomas (1971) told us, in the course of his analysis of the role of magic in religion, that religious belief "offers the prospect of a supernatural means of control over man's earthly environment" (p. 25). He noted: "The history of early Christianity offers no exception to this rule. Conversions to the new religion . . . have frequently been assisted by the belief of converts that they are acquiring not just a means of other-worldly salvation, but a new and more powerful magic" (p. 25).

67

K. Thomas (1971) cited the innumerable ways in which inhabitants of medieval England relied on religious images for rescue and protection. They quite normally made use of religious rites and substances said to be imbued with sacred power to cope with daily frustrations, illnesses, and difficulties. K. Thomas (1971) indicated:

> By the early Middle Ages the ecclesiastical authorities had developed a comprehensive range of formulae designed to draw down God's practical blessing upon secular activities. The basic ritual was the benediction of salt and water for the health of the body and the expulsion of evil spirits. But the liturgical books of the time also contained rituals devised to bless houses, cattle, crops, ships, tools, armour, wells, and kilns. There were formulae for blessing men who were preparing to set off on a journey, to fight a duel, to engage in battle or to move into a new house. There were procedures for blessing the sick and for dealing with sterile animals, for driving away thunder and for making the marriage bed fruitful. Theologians did not claim that these procedures made the practical precautions of daily life superfluous, but they did undoubtedly regard them as possessing a power which was more than merely spiritual or symbolic. (p. 25)

Persons at this time were so convinced of the power of their religious attachment that they engaged in such practices as ringing church bells to cure serious physical ailments or carrying a holy shrine around a city to insulate against an approaching catastrophic fire. A friar's coat was regarded as a preservative against pestilence; the key to the church door was said to be an effective remedy against a mad dog, and the soil from the churchyard was credited with special magical power. K. Thomas (1971) made it clear that religious images provided comfort in every aspect of daily life. Religious forces could be mobilized everywhere as a protective aura or shield.

We should add at this point that the supportive power of religion may not lie simply in its shielding functions but also in the fact that it sanctions certain rich forms of imaginative fantasy. That is, it supplies a collection of sacred images and figures (e.g., God, saints, devils) that, despite their magical matrix, occupy a unique reality niche. Persons can, in sanctioned ways, play with these "real" figments and creatively press them into the service of useful illusion construction. More is said about this matter later.

Large-scale studies in more recent times document a continuing widespread devotion to religious beliefs. Dependable surveys (e.g., Spilka, Hood, & Gorsuch, 1985) indicate 94% to 98% of the U.S. population affirms a belief in God. Eighty-nine percent states it made use of private prayer. Approximately 98% of homes have at least one Bible. Seventy-five percent of the U.S. population indicates belief in an afterlife. Americans contribute over $80 billion a year to organized religion (Spilka et al., 1985). These data speak for themselves. While religious images may not be as pervasive and powerful today as they were in medieval England, they are still prominent. Incidentally, an additional sign of religion's current attraction is the growing number of religious sects that are efflorescing and flourishing. Also, note the surprising frequency of religious conversion experiences (Batson & Ventis, 1982) that often involve a sense of having made personal contact with God.

IS RELIGIOUSNESS PROTECTIVE?

A prime intent of this chapter is to find out whether religious belief provides protection against the onslaught of worldly problems. To what degree do persons who have convinced themselves they are part of a sacred sphere derive adaptive advantages from that conviction? In view of what has emerged in earlier chapters concerning the adaptive value of belief systems that camouflage life's threats, one would expect religious imagery to have an analogous buffering potential. A large empirical literature exists that touches on such potential. However, the interpretation of the findings rivals in complexity the playing of three-dimensional chess. This is due, in part, to the limited amount of agreement about how to define religiosity. Researchers have diversely based their definitions on frequency of church attendance, time devoted to religious activities, subjective conviction about the power of God, dedication to the pursuit of universal meanings, and so forth (e.g., Batson & Ventis, 1982). In addition, it has become obvious that many indices of religiousness and religious identification are linked with mediating variables such as socioeconomic status, ethnicity, and education. When interpreting the correlations of religious indices with other measures, one has to navigate the maze represented by such mediating variables. This has proved to be quite tricky. If one considers, too, that any enterprise that calls for defining adequacy of adjustment or other related "mental health" entities is beset with ambiguities, one can appreciate that it is heroic to ask whether, in terms of scientific criteria, religiousness facilitates adapting to the world.

A number of investigators have explored whether obvious indicators of religiousness (e.g., frequency of church attendance) are correlated with clinical diagnoses in the neurotic or psychotic range. Accounts of such analyses have been presented by Batson and Ventis (1982), Bergin (1983), Francis (1985), Gartner, Larson, and Allen (1991), Gorsuch (1988), Sanua (1969), Spilka et al. (1985), and others. The conclusions have ranged from positive to negative to indeterminate; ultimately, it is fruitless to pursue matters at this gross level. It makes no more sense to ask whether religiousness protects against psychopathology than it originally was to ask whether psychotherapy, as an undifferentiated entity, "works."

However, this statement does need to be tempered with respect to a few special areas. There is fairly good evidence that the more religious (as broadly defined in a variety of ways) individuals are, the less they partake[1] of alcohol and illicit drugs (e.g., Barnes & Russell, 1978; Gartner et al., 1991; Khavari & Harmon, 1982; Schlegal & Sanborn, 1979) and the less (but not by much) they tend to exhibit delinquent behavior (Gartner et al., 1991; Jensen & Erickson, 1979). One can, in a fairly simplistic way, say that religiosity is negatively related to drug use and delinquency. But little is known about the mechanisms that mediate the influence of religion in these areas.

Returning to the issue of how religiousness and "mental health" are correlated, we call your attention to meaningful findings that have emerged because of more careful differentiation with respect to the concept of "religiousness." One of the most interesting modes of differentiation was originally suggested by Allport (1950). He indicated that there is good reason to distinguish between "extrinsic" and "intrinsic" religiosity. The former refers to assuming the facade-trappings of religiosity (e.g., attending church), whereas the latter involves subjective conviction about the truth and importance of things pertaining to the divine. Allport (1966) said more specifically:

> While there are several varieties of extrinsic religious orientation, we may say they all point to a type of religion that is strictly utilitarian: useful for the self in granting safety, social standing, solace, and endorsement for one's chosen way of life. . . . By contrast, the intrinsic form of religious sentiment regards faith as a supreme value in its own right. . . . A religious sentiment of this sort floods the whole life with motivation and meaning. Religion is no longer limited to single segments of self-interest." (p. 455)

What is important here is the difference between religiousness in peripheral, largely socially stereotyped behavior and religiousness in one's central commitment to images of a God-constructed life space. One may presume that an intrinsic orientation signifies a fuller and more complete acceptance of basic religious concepts. In that sense, the intrinsic level provides a more reasonable test than does the extrinsic concerning the possible link between religiousness and "mental health" variables.

Donahue (1985) presented us with a meta-analysis of the total literature available (through 1982) dealing with the correlates of being intrinsic or extrinsic. The findings suggest that persons who are intrinsically religious are likely to be low in trait anxiety, high in feelings of "well-being," high in "social adequacy," and high in experiencing a "sense of purpose" in life. Haitsma (1986) and O'Connor and Vallerand (1989) have, in the same vein, shown that in samples of elderly persons "personal adjustment" is significantly and positively correlated with degree of intrinsic religious orientation. This positive pattern is not true of extrinsics, who, in fact, are particularly likely to

---

[1]There were even reports that religiousness is negatively correlated with the use of psychotropic drugs (Khavari & Harmon, 1982).

be dogmatic, manifest anxiety about death, and experience both high trait anxiety and magnified sensations of powerlessness.[2]

A further updating of the research pertinent to the intrinsic–extrinsic distinction emerges from a study by Bergin, Masters, and Richards (1987). College students responded to the Religious Orientation scale (which measures the intrinsic–extrinsic variable) and several measures of personality and anxiety level. Intrinsic religiousness turned out to be positively and significantly correlated with a variety of positive personality attributes (e.g., sociability, sense of well-being, intellectual efficacy)[3] and negatively correlated with anxiety. Extrinsic religiousness showed the opposite pattern of correlations. It was also reported that intrinsic individuals tended to have slightly higher scores than "other normal populations" with respect to a number of favorable personality qualities.

Ellison, Gay, and Glass (1989) reported an intricate investigation, in which multiple aspects of religious behavior were related to an index of subjective life satisfaction. A large pool of subjects representing multiple religious denominations was appraised. The data indicated a significant (although relatively small) link between the degree of religious "devotional intensity" (as measured by variables like "frequency of prayer" and "feelings of closeness to God") and general satisfaction with life. The "devotional intensity" measure appeared to overlap considerably with the notion of intrinsic religiousness. The mediating effects of membership in specific religious denominations proved to be minimal; but there was a special positive boost in satisfaction associated with membership in a fundamentalist group (Baptists). Ellison et al. (1989) considered that their review of the previous literature and their own results support the existence of a positive connection between religiousness and life satisfaction. Incidentally, they cited a meta-analysis by Witter, Stock, Okun, and Haring (1985), which concluded, on the basis of the studies available to that point in time, that religion accounts for roughly 2% to 6% of the variation in adult subjective well-being.

However, the matter becomes more complicated when one considers the work of Park, Cohen, and Herb (1990). They probed the mediating effects of intrinsic religiousness and the inclination to rely on religious modes of

---

[2]Despite these promising trends, Donahue (1985) made it clear that it may be meaningful to order subjects within a fourfold scheme that simultaneously considers whether one is high or low for intrinsic and high or low for extrinsic. Subjects can then be classified as intrinsics (simply high on intrinsic), extrinsics (simply high on extrinsic), indiscriminates (high on both), or nonreligious (low on both). Using this scheme, intrinsics and nonreligious are both less dogmatic than extrinsics and indiscrimates. The closeness of the intrinsic and nonreligious categories in this instance is duplicated in certain other cases, and it remains puzzling as to why such similarity between two apparently unlike categories should exist.

[3]McClain (1978) reported a similar pattern of correlations between an intrinsic religious orientation and personality variables.

coping upon the ability to adapt to controllable stresses (at least partially influenced by the individual) and uncontrollable stresses (occurs independent
of the individual's efforts). The ability to adapt was defined in terms of measures of depression and trait anxiety. The degree of life stress was evaluated
by the subjects (college students) reporting a variety of life experiences and
indicating how positive or negative the impact was. Data obtained in a first
study were cross-validated in a second.

Rather unique findings emerged from separate analyses of Catholic versus Protestant samples. Thus, general "religious coping" proved to be a positive buffer against the depressive effects of "controllable" life stresses in
Catholics, but not in Protestants. Further, for Protestants intrinsic religiousness demonstrated certain positive buffering effects against depression in the
context of uncontrollable negative events, but not for Catholics. The positive finding for the Protestants signified that an intrinsic orientation serves
as a life stress moderator by providing a framework of meaning, a sense of
being "stronger," and a positive view of one's coping assets. In that sense,
one can say that there probably is a connection between a mode of religiosity and the ability to buffer stress. However, the nature of the connection is
open to interpretation.[4] Does intrinsic religiosity provide comforting images
and concepts that buffer the impact of stress? Or does intrinsic religiosity actually define a life-style (e.g., moderate eating habits, low use of intoxicants,
modulation of impulsivity) that guards against the buildup of stressful contin-
gencies?[5] Or is it some combination of such variables that is involved?[6]

Aside from differentiating specific modes of religiosity, Gartner et al. (1991)

---

[4]Interpreting the correlates of intrinsic religious motivation scores is further complicated by
the dispute concerning the degree to which such scores are influenced by social desirability.
Batson and Ventis (1982) presented data suggesting that the influence of social desirability in
this respect is quite significant. However, Gorsuch (1988) concluded after an analysis of the pertinent literature, that Batson and Ventis (1982) have exaggerated and oversimplified the whole
issue.

[5]The observed positive correlations (e.g., Donahue, 1985) of an extrinsic religious orientation with indices like anxiety, rigidity, and fear of death are not easy to explain. Extrinsics presumably identify with the more external trappings of religion (e.g., going regularly to church) but
do not assign central importance to religious faith and imagery. Perhaps it is the quality of depending on "facade" that signals a deficit in being able to construct reliable belief systems. At
this point, one is left only with speculation.

[6]Jarvis and Northcott (1987) concluded from their analysis of the pertinent literature that
religiousness may decrease morbidity and mortality with respect to somatic illnesses and that
the contribution of religiousness goes beyond the health practices and social support associated
with it. However, the data are somewhat tenuous and not interpretable in a clearcut fashion.
Still, Levin and Schiller (1987) asserted, after an analysis of more than 200 studies, that those who
are religious are able to maintain better health than those who are not religious. Nevertheless,
most of the studies reviewed are so uncontrolled that they cannot be viewed with an acceptable
level of confidence. Levin and Vanderpool (1987), after dissecting the literature relevant to the
correlation between church attendance and somatic health, found no dependable relationship.

suggested that one has to differentiate particular classes of measures of malad-justment or psychopathology. After reviewing more than 200 studies on the relationship between religious commitment and psychological disturbance, they concluded that it is important to distinguish between those that define disturbance in terms of "soft-criteria" (viz., "paper-and-pencil personality tests") and those that utilize "real-life" behavioral indices (e.g., suicide, drug abuse). They indicated that religiosity is positively correlated with pathology when one relies on "soft" indicators, but is negatively correlated with "hard" be-havioral criteria. They noted that Donahue and Bergin (1983) reached a similar conclusion on the basis of a meta-analysis of the pertinent literature. Fur-ther, Gartner et al. (1991) offered the following observation:

> A pattern can also be found in those dimensions of mental health that are posi-tively and negatively associated with religion. The absence of religious com-mitment is associated with disorders of impulse control, what we call problems of "under control" (e.g., alcohol and drug use, anti-social behavior, suicide) whereas religion is associated with problems of over-control (e.g., rigidity). (p. 15)

These perspectives are novel and further underscore the intricacy of the vari-ables involved.

BUFFER TO SPECIFIC STRESSORS

Conversion Experiences

Examining correlations between religiousness and measures of "mental health" or adjustment to test the defensive efficacy of religious imagery is obviously imprecise and somewhat unsatisfactory. But in surveying the avail-able related literature, we wondered if it might be more satisfactory and more specifically definable to ascertain how well religious constructs support in-dividuals when they are confronted by acute or out-of-the-ordinary stressors.

There are data indicating that persons who undergo religious conversion experiences or who join new religious sects are often in a state of emotional crisis[7] when they do so (Ullman, 1982). The question then is whether the transition to a new religious state helps persons cope more successfully with their upset condition.

Overall, the accumulated data favor the view that the new religious in-vestment is helpful and stabilizing. Richardson (1985) reviewed the empiri-cal literature on the levels and modes of psychological adjustment of persons who join "new religions" (both in the United States and elsewhere) and con-

---

[7]Shaver et al. (1980) and Ullman (1982) provided data suggesting that religious converts may have had more unhappy childhoods than religious nonconverts.

cludes that the process is "often therapeutic." Gartner et al. (1991) concurred on the basis of their extensive review. Numerous studies of persons who have joined such religious groups as the Divine Light Mission, the Hare Krishna Temple, and the Unification Church indicate that, despite their previous upset condition, they no longer appear to be "abnormal" (e.g., Galanter & Buckley, 1978; Galanter, Rabkin, Rabkin, & Deutsch, 1979; Ness & Wintrob, 1980; Ross, 1983; Ullman, 1988). Most of these studies have used standardized psychometric measures (e.g., SCL-90-R, state and trait anxiety), and some have examined changes in adjustment over time.

Galanter (1982), a prominent researcher in this area, reported:

> In one series of controlled studies . . . my associates and I measured the psychological impact of conversion to the Divine Light Mission and the Unification Church. Structured self-reports of representative samples of members of these groups indicated considerable amelioration of emotional state (a "relief effect") upon joining; this improved state was maintained over the course of long-term membership (2 to 3 years). . . . Another area of psychopathology to be considered is that of substance abuse. There are a number of reports . . . of remission in patterns of alcohol and drug abuse, along with rapid changes in attitudes toward drugs . . . when individuals are converted to a sect. We found, for example, that in two sects both mild and heavy use of drugs declined; this applied to social intoxicants, such as alcohol and marijuana, and also to stimulants, hallucinogens, and opiates. (p. 1541)

He stated that his data indicate that joining a sect results in a "considerable moderation" of the effects of "lifestress on psychological well-being" (p. 1542).[8] Bergin (1983) reached a similar conclusion after reviewing the basic literature: "conversion and related intense religious experiences are therapeutic" (p. 178).

Following a survey of the pertinent publications, Kilbourne and Richardson (1984) pinpointed the variety of ways in which joining a religious sect improved adjustment. They enumerated: (a) elimination of illicit drug use; (b) enhanced vocational energy; (c) decreased neurotic disturbance; (d) prevention of suicide; (e) minimized anomie and moral indecision; (f) increased social responsibility; (g) greater freedom to be self-expressive; (h) decreased psychosomatic complaints; and (i) more articulated image of self. Apropos of the point about greater freedom to be self-expressive, note that Sunderberg, Latkin, Littman, and Hagan (1990) administered a personality measure (California Psychological Inventory) to a sample of men and women who were followers of the founder (Bhazwan Shree Rajneesh) of a new religious sect and reported that they had significantly elevated independence and flexibility scores.

---

[8]Quite to the contrary, Spencer (1975) found unusually high levels of psychiatric disturbance (e.g., schizophrenia) in the population of Jehovah's Witnesses residing in Western Australia.

Scattered in the literature are attempts to evaluate the impact of specific religious rituals practiced by sects for comforting their members. Illustratively, Griffith, Mahy, and Young (1986) described a fairly well-controlled study that analyzed the effects of a "mourning ritual" (a 7-day period of isolation during which individuals pray, fast, and experience dreams and visions) practiced by a West Indian Christian sect. Sixteen "mourners" were studied. The SCL-90-R (self-report symptoms inventory) was administered previous to the ritual process and again when it was completed. Most of the SCL-90-R scale score changes indicated "significant improvement." It should be added that there was no control group.[9]

There is currently no way of dissecting out from the "therapeutic effects" of identifying with new religious ideology those linked to the religious imagery itself and those derived from the support offered by the sect's social network. In that sense, the data concerning the stabilizing role of enthusiastically embracing a new religious scheme remain ambiguous. But one wonders whether the impact of any ideology can ever be reckoned independently of the real or imagined group ties with which it is identified.

Some observers have concluded that the therapeutic role of the new religions and sects represents a major alternative to the offerings of the psychotherapy establishment. Kilbourne and Richardson (1984) went so far as to consider the new religions and the psychotherapies as serious competitors in the "therapeutic marketplace." Others (e.g., Gross, 1978) explicitly declared that psychologists and psychiatrists have, in the guise of scientific seers, taken over a role once the property of the clergy. Presumably, psychologists and psychiatrists are "secular priests" who appeal to science, as contrasted to ministers who appeal to religious images.

Kilbourne and Richardson (1984) succinctly pictured the tie between the "new religions" and the psychotherapies as follows:

> Today's therapeutic culture . . . which in certain respects simply answers to the service needs of a highly industrialized society, has given birth to multiple forms of psychotherapy . . . , new religions (Moonies, Hare Krishna, Divine Light Mission, The Way, Children of God, etc.), self-growth groups (est, rolfing, primal scream, Transcendental Meditation, etc.), and self-help groups . . . that line the shelves of today's marketplace of experiences. (p. 239)

They went on to indicate that both the new religions and the psychotherapies appeal to similar constituencies (viz., members of the middle and upper classes). They pointed out that a disproportionate number of the consumers of the new religions and psychotherapies are from the more affluent classes.

---

[9]Griffith, English, and Mayfield (1980) provided a semicontrolled series of observations of the apparent therapeutic effects of "possession, prayer, and testimony" on participants from a Black church. Similar "psychotherapeutic" effects, as the result of "faith healing," were described by Pattison, Lapins, and Doerr (1973).

They suggested, too, that the same "deep structure" typifies the religious and psychotherapy approaches. Presumably, the approaches share a "special supportive, empathic, and confiding relationship between the client and therapist or adherent and religious group" (p. 240). Other commonalities are referred to: they both involve settings saturated with prominent symbols of "expertise, help, hope, and healing"; and they both provide explanatory ideologies that "render sensible the person's self-preoccupations and inexplicable feelings within a logically tight framework" (p. 240).

Kilbourne and Richardson (1984), in discussing the competition between the new religions and the psychotherapies, underscored that

> They are competing for a foothold . . . a larger share of the middle- and upper-class market. They are also competing for expansionist rights to other individuals and groups in society. . . . We can see . . . how both practices find themselves competing for clients, conceptual territory—that is, who will define reality, fantasy, health, mental illness, self, and so forth—and for guildlike status, wealth, and influence. (p. 247)

They hypothesized that this competition often motivates psychiatrists and psychologists to label members of new religious sects as deviant and sick.

These similarities between the "therapeutic" (healing) strategies used by religious sects and the standard forms of psychotherapy do seem striking. In both instances, one discerns important common elements of support, confiding relationships, and the provision of expert explanatory ideologies. However, as Whitehead (1987) pointed out, most psychotherapists would maintain that, while religious healing is based on the construction of illusion, the psychotherapeutic aim is to rid the patient of illusion. That is, while religion seeks to mobilize maximum "transference" to its creeds and to sustain such transference as long as possible, the psychotherapist brings the transference under scrutiny and enables the patient to see that it is illusory. Presumably, religion heals through illusion, whereas most psychotherapists debunk the transference.

Whitehead (1987) doubted that this apparent contrast holds true. She analyzed the stages that "converts" to a religion or to a psychotherapeutic regimen presumably pass through on their journey from initial distress to final "healing." In both instances, there is the initial positive "transference" that involves the "renunciation" of old beliefs and attitudes and the positive investment in new figures and doctrines. Eventually, said Whitehead (1987), doubt and uncertainty develop about such renunciation and new ideational investments, and many of the phenomena associated with the concept of "negative transference" appear. The psychoanalytic position is that, ultimately, the therapist explores with the patient the irrationality of both the positive and negative transferences and exposes their illusional base. Whitehead (1987) felt that a similar process occurs in many religious settings. As converts begin to doubt the things they accepted during their initial positive phase, they are given the message that their faith was not fully sincere or committed, and that they need to renew such faith on a sounder, more reliable basis (a purer, more rarified commitment). This concept of renewing faith on a sounder basis obviously is analogous to the psychoanalytic concept of deconstructing the transference.

By way of illustration, Whitehead (1987) described a similar deconstructive process with reference to Zen: "In Zen, for instance, the worlds of attachment—whether by our standards 'real,' or supernatural—are all considered illusion: *Makyo*" (p. 265). She went on to quote another observer (Kapleau, 1967):

> Other religious sects place great store by experiences which involve visions of God or hearing heavenly voices, performing miracles, receiving divine messages, or becoming purified through various rites. . . . In varying degrees those practices induce a feeling of well-being, yet from the Zen point of view, all are morbid practices devoid of true religious significance and hence only *Mayko*. (p. 265)

Whitehead (1987) ascertained that in both religious and psychoanalytic contexts, further, higher forms of renunciation are eventually called for if one is to achieve the "true," idealized state.

Coping With Aging

Another opportunity to examine the possible buffering power of religiousness, with respect to a class of stressors, presents itself in the literature on the correlations between religiosity and adaptation to the advanced aging process. There is no question that as individuals cross the threshold into "old age" they encounter special difficulties related to increased illness, decline in status, and loss of social supports. Of course, there is also the issue of increased imminence of death,[10] which we explored earlier. Actually, quite an array of researchers has wondered whether religiousness mediates the effects of "getting old."

Illustratively, studies have variously suggested that the greater the religious involvement of older persons, the higher their "morale" (Koenig, Kvale, & Ferrel, 1988), the greater their ability to adapt to residential relocation

---

[10]The relationship between religiousness and fear of death was reviewed in a previous chapter. In the one available study (Richardson et al., 1983), in which death anxiety was measured at an unconscious rather than conscious level, it was reported that those low in religiosity manifest higher levels of death anxiety. With respect to studies in which death anxiety was measured by means of questionnaires, there is a trend for death anxiety to be negatively correlated with religiousness (e.g., Thorson & Powell, 1989; Westman & Brackney, 1990).

(Zuckerman, Kasl, & Ostfeld, 1984), the more intense their "life satisfaction" (Hunsberger, 1985), the greater their "happiness" (Cutler, 1976), and the better their "adjustment" (Gartner et al., 1991; Mull, Cox, & Sullivan, 1987). Although there are a few negative studies (e.g., Steinitz, 1980), the major trend indicates a positive association between religiousness in the elderly and "doing well." Of course, one is only speculating when one attributes causality to the religious factor. However, the findings are certainly suggestive and well worth keeping in mind.[11]

THE TEXTURE OF SUPPORTIVE RELIGIOUS EXPERIENCES

At this point we would like to turn to the experiential side of religious adaptations and illusions. How do individuals conceptualize their ties to divine forces? How is the sense of communicating with God, the entertainment of mystical images, assimilated? Does opening oneself to mystical experiences produce rents in personality defenses or lead to disequilibrium? An analysis of such issues follows.

Mystical Images

Large numbers of persons report having communicated with God or forces possessed of God-like attributes. There is unending testimony to having "felt" God, having seen or heard God, and otherwise having made contact with entities not of this world and far greater than oneself. The flavor of mystical confrontation is conveyed by the following quote (Spilka et al., 1985):

> I remember the night and almost the very spot on the hilltop where my soul opened out and the inner and outer worlds rushed together. My own deep struggle was being answered by the unfathomable deep without, reaching beyond the stars. I stood alone with him, who had made me, and all the beauty, love, and sorrow of the world. I felt the union of my spirit with his. The ordinary sense of things around me faded, and for the moment nothing remained but an indescribable joy. (p. 178)

Although mystical experiences often involve religious content, they may also focus on such nonreligious themes as unity, ineffability, and spatial change. National surveys suggest that about 30% of the U.S. population feels it has

---

[11]It should be parenthetically noted that studies of degree of psychological disturbance among clergy and seminarians (Argyle & Beit-Hallahmi, 1975; Batson & Ventis, 1982; Spilka et al., 1985; Wulff, 1991) suggested a higher than average level. However, most of the studies are not well designed, and the issue must be considered far from settled.

had dramatic contacts with sacred sources. Similar percentages have been found in Great Britain. Among college students, there have been reports of as many as 66% having suddenly perceived they were "in the presence of God" (Hay & Morisy, 1978; Spilka et al., 1985).

The usual psychodynamic interpretation of such mystical experiences is that they represent strategies for coping with serious conflicts or difficulties. As is well known, Freud (1959b) considered all religious beliefs to be personal projections designed to satisfy regressive wishes. From this perspective, dramatic forms of mystical experience were regarded as signs of immaturity and even more pernicious forms of psychopathology. Presumably, they indicate lack of realism and an inappropriate form of defense. While it may very well be true that mystical experiences evolve for psychodynamic reasons, one cannot find any scientific evidence that they signal the presence of psychopathology.

The first factor that would argue against equating mystical experiences with psychopathology is their sheer prevalence in apparently normal populations. But more importantly, formal studies of persons who testify to mystical experiences have been unable to show that these persons have elevated levels of psychological disturbance (e.g., Caird, 1987; Greeley, 1975; Tobacyk & Milford, 1983). Greeley (1975), who carried out one of the most extensive of the empirical studies on mystical perceptions, concluded: "There are lots of mystics around, more than anyone ever thought. They are happy people who apparently had happy childhoods. They are neither prejudiced nor maladjusted nor narcotized. They claim to have had contact with the Ultimate and it does not seem to have hurt them. On the contrary, it seems to have helped" (p. 74). Relatedly, L. E. Thomas and Cooper (1980) administered tests of fear of death, manifest anxiety, and personal flexibility to large samples of college students who did or did not report mystical experiences. The researchers stated: "Overall, our data gives no support to the still widely held assumption in the psychological literature that persons who have intense spiritual experiences are more or less pathological types. On the contrary, . . . indices of personality flexibility (correlate positively) with spiritual experiences . . ." (p. 84).[12]

As already mentioned, the mystical does not necessarily include explicit religious content. Specific religious figures may not participate in mystical imagery. Indeed, an unusually high percentage of those who consider themselves not to be religious in a formal sense report having mystical experiences (Wulff, 1991). However, the mystical does frequently touch on themes that are basic to religious concepts. That is, mystical experiences, even though not pointedly "religious," often involve the supernatural, forces vastly superior

---

[12]Maslow (1962) similarly proposed that persons who have what he calls "peak experiences" are psychologically in a better state of integration than are "nonpeakers."

to self, and "larger meanings." From a psychological perspective, one can reasonably speculate that mystical imagery represents the creation of scenarios that feature figures and effects beyond the bounds of science and earthly standards. They portray the potentiality of "out of this world" channels for understanding and coping with life problems. In that sense, they fall into the category of many of the other forms of illusion fabrication, which we have discussed.

There have been attempts to analyze, in more specific terms, the psychological functions of mystical experiences and the conditions that trigger them. Illustratively, Proudfoot and Shaver (1975) have applied attribution theory to religious phenomena. They theorized that when persons become diffusely physiologically aroused (or disturbed) by threatening events they need to give the events meaning (to "label them"). Diffuse, unexplained arousal is exceedingly threatening and individuals urgently scan their environs to link it to something meaningful. In that context, if there is already a religious or mystical set, the arousal may be most meaningfully explained as signaling the opening of a special channel into a realm where magical solutions and assistance become available. Presumably, the burden of coping with the disturbing arousal as "my problem" is at least partially lifted and displaced to an "outside power." Previous studies (e.g., Batson & Ventis, 1982; Spilka et al., 1985) have, in fact, already demonstrated that those with a religious set are likely to give a religious twist to diffuse arousal produced by drugs or other agents. Implicitly, many of the discussions of the functions of attributions to the mystical give weight to the idea that individuals are thereby able to shift the burden from self as sufferer and agent to an outside target.

There are interesting data (e.g., Paulhus & Levitt, 1987) indicating that as affect states intensify they multiply a species of self-preoccupation and concern. Such self-focus can be quite uncomfortable. Indeed, it is well documented that self-focus has many negative experiential consequences (Fisher, 1986). The mystical may be a way out from upsetting self-preoccupation. Lifton (1968) referred to "losing oneself," via what he called the "experiential transcendent mode," as a way of escaping the turbulence linked to an awareness of death's inevitability. It is fascinating how most religions are consistently uncomfortable with the self and its somatic representation—the body. Typically, religions regard the body as bad and unclean, and want to go beyond it (Fisher, 1986; Wulff, 1991). Not unrelatedly, there are exploratory data suggesting that alcoholics may be drawn to alcohol because it minimizes awareness of one's own body (Hull, 1981).

Berger (1967) speculated about the alienating effects of shifting agency from self (i.e., from the human) to the sacred. He pointed out that an essential quality of the sacred, as represented in religious experience, is its "otherness," its apparent total difference from ordinary, profane human stuff. The sacred is perceived as determining the human; and so the active role of the human in constructing and conceptualizing the sacred disappears from view. In this sense, religion is alienating. As Berger (1967) noted, it transforms "human products into supra- or non-human facticities. The humanly made world is explained in terms that deny its human production" (p. 89). He added, "in positing the alien over against the human, religion tends to alienate the human from itself" (p. 90). He concluded that this alienation process, while having various negative consequences, serves the purpose of "sheltering" humans from multiple "terrors."

As already noted, persons who report having mystical experiences are not psychologically disturbed. They have actually been described as particularly self-assured and mature (Wuthnow, 1979), and score high on self-reports of "well-being." Greeley's (1975) extensive survey found that, of those who have had frequent "ecstatic" (mystical) experiences, a greater percentage attended college than those who never had such experiences. Thus, he concluded that "mystics are better educated" (p. 75). Perhaps mystical images are especially available to those who have a wider repertoire of response choices.

Indeed, we would like to pursue this point in greater depth. Much of the scientific literature dealing with religious phenomena explicitly or implicitly suggests that being religious involves a narrowing of perspective, a rigidifying process, an identification with biased authoritarianism.[13] Within this literature, the mystical is rarely considered to be freeing rather than confining. Zern (1984) carried out an extended analysis of over 100 societies to ascertain the relationship between religiousness (ritual and belief) and a spectrum of cultural complexity indicators. Cultural complexity was defined by the amount of writings and records in the culture, the amount of technological specialization, and the degree of social stratification. Religiousness was measured by the amount of belief in a divine entity in the culture and the frequency of religious rites. Zern (1984) found a rather large and significant positive correlation between religiousness and the "productive" complexity of each society. That is, religiousness was linked with intricacy rather than simplicity and constriction.

In a later study, Zern (1987) followed up on this finding by testing whether religiousness in individuals would prove to be an asset for "maximizing one's ability in a specific area." He demonstrated, in a sample of college students, that the greater their religiousness the greater was their capacity to make use of their intellectual potential (as measured by the discrepancy between grade point average and Scholastic Aptitude Test scores). Zern (1987) concluded that "religiousness helps maximize one's potential" (p. 894). He stated

---

[13]Although there is a fairly consistent trend for indices of religiousness to be positively correlated with authoritarianism, it is also true that those who are deeply religious (e.g., as defined by high intrinsic religiosity) are probably not authoritarian (Wulff, 1991).

that religion supplies the "motivation to learn how to develop as well as provide a model for certain kinds of skilled behavior" (p. 893). This is a rather vague finding, but is cited because the study grew out of Zern's original observation of a significant correlation between societal complexity (achievement) and societal religiousness.

The idea that religion can open up novel vistas is obscured by the fact that many religious images have been around for a long time. We are accustomed to them and usually equate them with orthodoxy. However, if one steps back and examines the true nature of religious imagery, it is obvious that it embraces a highly imaginative level of fantasy. It calls for acceptance of a sacred domain "out there," in which figures and forces unknown in the secular life space operate. This becomes easier to see if one minimizes the current Western frame of reference and scans the sacred figures in the Greek or Roman pantheon, or the exotic sacred figures conceptualized within the realm of a religion like Buddhism. What an exotic panoply emerges! What sweeps of playful constructions are revealed. With the permission afforded by a religious attitude to conjure up a whole new level of existence, persons are stimulated to rich fantasy creations. Although it is true that most religions lay down a fairly tight framework of permissible ways to picture the central actors in their sacred pantheon, there is evidence that most individuals richly extend and elaborate the stereotypes that have been presented to them.

Heller (1986) illustrated this point in this descriptions of how U.S. children who are members of different religions (viz., Catholicism, Protestantism, Judaism, Hinduism) think about God. He interviewed 40 children about how they imagined God to be. He asked them to draw pictures of God, to use play materials to act out fantasies about how God would behave in various settings, to make up stories about God, and so forth. He discovered that the children created elaborate narratives about who God is (indeed, whether male or female), what he (she) can do, and how he (she) feels. Their drawings of God were highly individualistic and often unique. Consider, too, some children's comments as they speculated about God.

One 10-year-old, in discussing where God lives, said: "It's a planet, like you need special glasses to see it. First, you need to get past the sun and then you have to have enough power to get out of the galaxy. . . . And then, and only then, you might find it" (p. 58). A girl declared: "I believe that God may have a little of both sexes. . . ." (p. 74). Several children insisted that God participates in everyday events. One said that God watches over him when he is engaged in sports and even goes swimming with him. A 12-year-old boy asserted that God is "invisible and hard to get a hold of; even though you know he has an impact on you" (p. 61).

It is parenthetically interesting that Heller (1986) discerned a gender difference in the way the boys and girls in his sample elaborated on the stereotyped God images. Boys portrayed God as distant and instrumental (rational and pragmatic), whereas girls emphasized God's potential for emotional intimacy and aesthetic appreciation. In any case, what impressed us was the free rein of ideas that prevailed in how these children pictured God. One may presume that such creativity in envisioning the sacred realm extends into adulthood. Most religious adults probably construct a variety of idiosyncratic images about the major sacred figures they "know" (Roof, 1979). In so doing, they have a large imaginative stage with unique qualities available to them. They are able to play with supernatural and magical ideas in a context where such ideas can simultaneously be regarded as "real." They have access to a place of imagined solutions and supports that offers many of the advantages of pretend play and yet with the sense that this is beyond pretense.

We would speculate that, despite the codified construction on fantasy required by many religions, there is a compensatory flexibility provided by the ability to play with religious representations. Obviously, this means that a broad repertory of well-camouflaged, illusory images can be tapped, which arm the individual with enhanced powers for self-protection. The nature of the religious and the mystical opens access to a unique fantasy domain. This point meshes well with the views of Pruyser (1983),[14] who saw religion (also the arts and physical sciences) as requiring the adroit manipulation of illusion. He noted that illusion derives from the Latin verb *ludere*, to play; when he referred to religion as illusionistic, he meant it is rooted in the play of imagination. He was convinced that the "intermediate" realm of the illusionistic is a major source of ingredients that nurture cultures.

Images of God

As indicated, persons may differ considerably in the ways they picture God. Merely knowing that individuals believe in Gods tells one little about how they think about such figures. Piazza and Glock (1979) demonstrated that differences in the content of God images have consequences for the kinds of social and political attitudes that are manifested. The attributes that one ascribes to sacred figures would be expected to influence the ways in which one makes use of fantasy self-protection. There may be more difficulty in using a grim, vengeful God as an imaginary lever than one perceived as benign and protective. What have we learned about the factors that mediate persons' concepts of sacred figures?

A fair amount of directly or indirectly pertinent information has accumulated in the anthropological literature. A series of studies (Levinson & Malone, 1980) has shown fairly consistently that, in cultures where the socialization

---

[14]Pruyser's (1983) concepts about the "illusionistic world" were derived to some degree, from Winnicott's (1971) concepts about "transitional objects" and illusory "intermediate" areas of experience that bridge between "inner" and "outer" sectors.

of children is severe and punishing, the figures conjured up at the supernatural (sacred) level are described in more unfriendly, aggressive terms than in cultures where socialization is relatively indulgent. In other words, there seems to be a connection between the way children are treated in a culture and the prevalent notions concerning the friendliness of the resident supernatural ones. It is usually assumed that the socialization factor is a causal one. Such data do, of course, agree with Freud's (1907) original theory that religious images are projections of fantasies shaped by early childhood experiences.

To test this projection theory in a more specific fashion, investigators have examined the correlations between how persons perceive their parents and the qualities they attribute to God. The design of most of the studies in this area (Birky & Ball, 1988; Deconchy, 1968; Godin & Hallez, 1965; Nelson, 1971; Nelson & Jones, 1957; Nicholson & Edwards, 1979; Strunk, 1959; Tamayo & Dugas, 1977; Vergote & Aubert, 1972; Vergote & Tamayo, 1980; Vergote, Tamayo, Pasquali, Bonaimi, Pattyn, & Custers, 1969) involved subjects rating their parents and God with an array of attributes. Generally, such studies have come up with low positive (significant) correlations between the two rating domains. Sometimes these correlations are higher for father versus God, sometimes higher for mother versus God, and sometimes higher for the average of mother plus father versus God. It also has been argued (Wulff, 1991) that whatever significant correlations do emerge in this domain are artifacts that simply reflect the commonality of parent and God figures occupying generic liked or disliked positions. In any case, a consistent, although low level, positive relationship exists between perceptions of parents and God, which is vaguely supportive of Freud's idea that parent images are an anlage for God images.[15]

After reviewing the whole matter, Grom (as described by Wulff, 1991) concluded that the following variables shape an individual's God images:

1. Parental relationships
2. Relationships with other significant persons and groups
3. Self-concept (how positively or negatively one feels about oneself)
4. Formal and informal teachings about God
5. Experiences with religious practices, ceremonies, etc.

There are some (e.g., Rizzuto, 1979) who ascribed high importance to the role of God images in the development of personality. Interestingly, Randour and Bondanza (1987) theorized that the average woman is penalized psy-

---

[15]Several studies reported a positive (but quite low) correlation between how positively persons rate themselves and how friendly or warm God is rated (e.g., Benson & Spilka, 1973; Buri & Mueller, 1987; Jolley & Taubee, 1986).

chologically because she is not able to relate her own identity to an accepted representation of God as a feminine figure. They consider that the "cultural view of God orients us to ourselves, to one another, and to the world" (p. 301).

Attraction to Religious Imagery

What determines whether individuals will be drawn to the use of religious imagery? Surprisingly, our knowledge in this area remains somewhat vague. Reviews of the pertinent literature were presented by Batson and Ventis (1982), Spilka et al. (1985), D. L. Thomas (1988), and Wulff (1991). In essence, one learns that the more religious one's parents are, the greater the likelihood that one will, in turn, be religious. The correlations tend to be in the range of 0.50–0.80. There may be mediating variables, such as the particular religious denominations of the parents, how much the parents agree with each other in their religious beliefs, and whether the child is firstborn. However, the data with respect to such variables are not entirely consistent. Furthermore, it is not clear that the impact of these variables is of large magnitude.

Religiosity may also, but probably to a quite limited extent, be influenced by whether one attends schools that provide religious instruction and whether one's peers are religiously inclined. While there is a good deal of speculation about the stages that children pass through in the course of becoming religious, detailed solid observation is in short supply.[16] The possibility of utilizing known personality correlates of religiousness to reconstruct factors that might lead one to become religious is dampened because few personality traits have consistently shown themselves to be correlated with religiousness. Indeed, aside from a tendency for the religious to display certain signs of rigidity and also paradoxically signs of special openness to influence (e.g., as defined by high suggestibility and acquiescence), few of the reports in this sector inspire much confidence.

INTEGRATIVE COMMENTS

Although there are problems in defining religiousness, we have side-stepped the matter of defining the threshold point at which imagery should be labeled "religious." When persons entertain fantasies about obvious God figures

---

[16]Elkind (1963), on the basis of his Piagetian-oriented studies of religious ideas in children, vaguely sketched out three stages:

1. Ages up to 7: global and undifferentiated notions about religion.
2. Ages 7–9: concrete characteristics of religious ideas.
3. Ages 10–12: a more abstract approach to one's religious identity.

and the other actors in the orthodox religious pantheon, one can, with assurance, classify such fantasies as having religious meaning. In a broad sense, religion embraces faith in schemas that connect the individual to a transcendental realm, to imagined figures with superior powers. We know that over the centuries such figures have been assigned every conceivable form and shape. There seem to be no limits to the range of qualities humans ascribe to divine representations. As we examine the stream of figures populating the fantasies of persons, how do we know which are religious, slightly religious, or not at all religious? If persons toy with fantasies about leprechauns that can fulfill their wishes, is there a religious element present? Are there any religious connotations when children picture Santa Claus arriving to bring them gifts because they have been good? If persons believe their lives are governed by the astrological positions of the planets from the moment of their birth, are they into a form of religious imagery? Does belief in supernatural figures, per se, signal the presence of religious ideation? What about the whole spectrum of superstition, which we know is embraced by even well-educated individuals (Tobacyk & Milford, 1983)?

Wulff (1991) referred to one of the broadest possible views of what might be considered religious: "The beliefs and practices labeled 'religious' have only one thing in common: the beliefs lack any empirical or statistical evidence, and the practices are regular, habitual, and predictable ways of meeting the unpredictable, the impossible, or the uncontrollable . . ." (p. 120). From the standpoint of such a definition, most individuals would be involved with religious imagery almost every day of their lives.[17]

A central question that we have pursued in this chapter is whether religious imagery, with its cast of sacred characters residing in an imaginary space, provides protective psychological shielding. While it would be rash to assert that this question can be answered definitively, a tentative "yes" is probably justified. As has been described, the difficulties in arriving at an answer are manifold; they involve such complications as how to define religiousness and how to control for mediating variables like socioeconomic status and education. However, one must be impressed with the consistent reports that degree of intrinsic religiosity is positively correlated (although at times quite complexly) with various indices of adjustment and well-being.

Also, persons who have conversion experiences or who join new religious sects are often initially in acute psychological distress but then regain their equilibrium in the course of their new religious loyalties. Further, data suggests that those who are religiously oriented weather the stresses of advanced aging better than those who lack religious belief. It is pertinent, too, that

---

[17]Fromm (1950) came up with an even broader definition of religion. He asserted that any "system of thought and action" maintained in a group represents a religious frame. Thus, the question is not whether specific individuals are religious, but rather what kinds of religious ideas they favor.

religiousness may buffer someone from becoming an alcoholic or a drug addict. The story is far from complete. Although one can justify the conclusion that religious imagery has protective value, little can be said about the amount of protection or the nature of mediating mechanisms. Religious images provide protection, but probably only if individuals assign them centrality and have a proper amount of trust in them.

Although religiousness is accompanied by various rigidities, it does provide permission to engage in certain forms of rich imaginative fantasy. Religious persons have a reservoir of sacred figures and symbols upon which they can draw, with magical rationales, to put spins on their experiences. They are in the advantageous position of cognitively manipulating figures associated with an unearthly and at least partially unreal dimension, yet imbued with the solidity of sacred doctrine. Because these figures inhabit a special, Alice-in-Wonderland realm, in which anything is possible, they can be cast in idiosyncratic dramas[18] that benefit the faithful. Such a "validated" reservoir of fantasy probably facilitates illusionistic strategies. A whole realm of imagination becomes almost obligatory, and even the most rigid of individuals is provided with a channel into what might otherwise arouse alarm because it is "not real." A special imaginative space can be entered without one feeling anxious about losing control. Such a plunge into the magical is guided by a profusion of religious markers and religious representatives (e.g., priests). Obviously, most cultures provide less intense but analogous opportunities for safely hooking up with imaginative figures in the context of fairy tales, stories, and Disney-like depictions. However, such figures rarely, if ever, attain the sanctioned reality of those presented in religious images.

The path to a better understanding of religious fantasy's facilitating effects may lie in a more microscopic study of how such fantasy fluctuates in various contexts. Rather than examine the rough correlational relationships that may exist between religiousness (however defined) and other variables, perhaps we should devise sensitive indicators of the occurrence of religious ideation or imagery and use them to find out how the flow of such ideation varies as specific classes of stressors are encountered and, furthermore, the repercussions of the variations upon measures of coping efficiency. In other words, there may be real advantages to studying religious imagery in laboratory settings where inputs can be substantially controlled and the flow of religious ideation, and its impact on behavior, can be quantified. Wulff (1991) cited a number of studies (e.g., dealing with the effects of Transcendental Meditation) that have attempted, with varying success, to observe religious-

---

[18]The established religions are engaged in a constant battle to filter out and control the exuberantly novel images and concepts about God that their members construct as they fancifully (mystically) explore the sacred (Spilka et al., 1985; Wulff, 1991).

like phenomena in at least quasicontrolled settings. There is no reason why we cannot study religious fantasy with research designs analogous to those we have used to probe other categories, such as achievement or aggressive or passive fantasy.

6

LEARNING HOW TO PRETEND AND MAKE THINGS UP

PRETENSE AND ILLUSION

Up to this point, we have taken it for granted that persons generally possess the capacity to deceive themselves, to slip into illusory modes. However, the ability to create a fictional scenario for oneself probably involves complex skills and maneuvers. How do people learn to pretend, to imaginatively fashion their own versions of what is happening? Our intent in this chapter is to sift through what is known about the development of make-believe skills.

A reservoir of information exists concerning children's use of pretense. Numerous observers have scanned children's repertoire of pretend behaviors (e.g., Pepler & Rubin, 1982; Singer, 1973; Smith & Franklin, 1979; Winner & Gardner, 1979). There are now investigations of such diverse topics as types of pretending; shifts in modes of pretending with age; individual, gender, and socioeconomic differences in pretend behavior; and influence of parents on children's pretending. It is remarkable how quickly children begin to learn to pretend. By the age of 12 months (perhaps earlier), they show signs of being involved in, and enjoying, make-believe (Cole & LaVoie, 1985; Fein, 1975; Sherrod & Singer, 1979; Ungerer, Zelazo, Kearsley, & O' Leary, 1981). Piaget (1962) was struck with the early appearance and vigor of pretending in his own offspring.

We have been fascinated with the literature on children's pretend strategies because it is so pertinent to the issue of illusion. Children who are caught up in pretend play may be said to be engaged in a form of illusion construction. They conjure up make-believe scenes and invent imaginative circumstances. They are usually consciously aware that their pretending differs from reality. However, at times (especially before age 5) they have been observed to be carried away to the point where they momentarily become hazy about the distinction. DiLalla and Watson (1988) described a 3-year-old child who introduces a "monster" into a pretend scene, but then becomes genuinely frightened that the "monster" will do him harm. Similar shading of the boundary between the pretend and the real is obvious when children (and also adults) watch "monster movies" and become scared. Consider, too, the blend between pretend and real that occurs when children adopt an "imaginary companion" or become highly invested in a "transitional object." "Pretend" and "illusion" may be fairly contiguous points on a continuum of the real to the unreal. Illusions obviously vary in their intensity, their fixity, and how close they are to the threshold point where they might be doubted. We would speculate that the extensive pretending in which children engage provides practice with respect to how to slip into illusion. Conscious forms of make-believe may foster skills or attitudes needed for less conscious forms. Some commentators might disagree with this point. For example, it has been argued (Sherrod & Singer, 1979) that children's pretend play actually sharpens their ability to differentiate the unreal from the real; and in that sense it might help to immunize them against the illusory.

As mentioned, a good deal of detailed observation has accumulated about children's pretend behavior. We are informed that, relatively early, infants "simulate eating, drinking, or sleeping, signaling awareness or pretense by 'knowing' smiles and sound effects that accompany the various actions" (Bretherton, O'Connell, Shore, & Bates, 1984, p. 272). Make-believe intent is exemplified in the child eating from an empty spoon or pretending to drink from a toy baby bottle. Bretherton et al. (1984) indicated that more complex forms of pretending follow, as infants extend their make-believe to include other "actors" or "receivers of action." Infants "feed" mother or a doll, "groom" mother or a doll, act as if they are reading a book, or move a toy car "with appropriate sounds of a vehicle." Their make-believe becomes increasingly intricate, as exemplified by pretending to comb their own hair or their mother's, or when the "child picks up a play screwdriver, says 'toothbrush' and makes the motions of toothbrushing" (p. 274). Children go on to such marvelous expertise as putting a doll through its paces, as if the doll were an independent agent devising actions on its own. Papousek, Papousek, and Harris (1987) indicated that "In pretend play, one object is used as if it were another, one person behaves as if she were another, and an immediate time and place are treated as if they were otherwise and elsewhere" (p. 283). Substitution of objects and persons is the keynote of pretending. The ability to substitute one object for another increases dramatically between 12 and 24 months of age. More and more, meanings of things become distinguished from their literal representations and are therefore available for imaginative rearranging.

Some investigators (e.g., Bretherton, 1984) depicted the capacity to engage in imaginative play as one manifestation of the more generalized ability to use symbols. As is well known, Bateson (1972) pointed out that children involved in pretend play frame their activities with the understanding that "these activities in which we now engage do not denote what the actions for which they stand would denote" (p. 180). His equivalent metaphor for pretend play, "This nip is not a bite," also is quoted widely. Bateson (1972) highlighted the idea that pretending involves a realm of metacommunication, the adoption of a broad attitude that what is occurring within a given frame should not be interpreted in relation to accepted reality criteria. Just beyond infancy, children achieve an amazing capacity to enter into pretend play relationships with other children (and adults), anytime and anywhere, with only a brief preparation required. Such play ranges from fanciful reenactments of everyday scripts (e.g., feeding, giving a bath) to "way-out" adventures.[1]

Incidentally, there have been observations (Lockard, 1988) that animals can engage in pretend acts which suggests they are being playful and making use of pretense with deceptive intent. For example, animals have been described as feigning disablement to mislead potential competitors. Such observations raise the question of whether pretend play may have some evolutionary or biological anlage. The matter remains speculative. However, there are certainly enough data (e.g., Bretherton, 1984) to document that socialization experiences play a crucial part in the development of play behavior in humans.

Children (and also adults) at play share a special culture based on the metacommunication "this is not real." Indeed, children evolve elaborate rules about entering, maintaining, and exiting from pretend frameworks. For example, Giffin (1984) concluded, after extensive observation of children's make-believe play, that it occurs within the context of an "illusion conservation rule." This rule stated: "When constructing make-believe play, players should negotiate transformations with the least possible acknowledgement of the play frame" (p. 88). That is, the pretend play participants are obligated to exclude references that would bring to awareness that make-believe is merely make-believe ("it's only pretend"). Giffin (1984) noted that enforcement of this rule involves a complementary series of "coordination rules." Thus pre-

---

[1]There seem to be clear individual differences in children's styles of pretend play. Bretherton (1984) documented that some children can freely pretend without the necessity of linkage with tangible objects, whereas others seem to need tangible props to proceed with their make-believe. Wolf and Grollman (1982) described individual differences in the degree to which children focus their make-believe on the social ("dramatist") versus nonsocial ("patterner"). It would be interesting to investigate whether such individual differences reflect contrasts in the kinds of unrealities and contradictions encountered by each child in its specific family or subcultural milieu.

tend play participants are expected to learn the "implicit pretend rule," which states: "When engaged in make-believe play, players should interpret statements that transform real meanings as implicit requests to pretend and should respond within the playframe" (p. 89).

Giffin (1984) also mentioned a "script adherence rule," which assumes that those engaged in pretending are linked to a "shared transactional script" and therefore "prescribes that players should only propose transformations or action plans that are consistent with the general script" (p. 90). Further elaboration of such rules designed to facilitate pretending assigns importance to an "incorporation rule," which "encourages players, to the extent of their ingenuity and the script will allow, to adapt their personal definitions of play in order to incorporate each other's proposed transformations" (p. 91). We cite this material to illustrate the elaborate apparatus that has been constructed in our culture (and probably most others) to encourage pretend behavior, particularly within a social context.

THE ORIGINS OF PRETENDING

A central question that bursts forth from the mass of data accumulated about childhood pretending relates to the functions of such pretending. Why should infants, who have been out of the womb a short time, already be experimenting with pretense? Most accounts of early development have focused on children's need to learn the nature of reality. Developmental maturity is often equated with level of realism attained. Why should young children rehearse unreal scenes when one of their prime developmental goals is to tune into reality? Some observers (e.g., Sherrod & Singer, 1979) have answered this question by proposing that playing with unreality may be an excellent means for learning the boundaries between the real and the unreal. Presumably, the process of pretending sharpens skills needed to make fine reality–unreality distinctions.[2] Indeed, Sherrod and Singer (1979) cited exploratory studies indicating that, in some circumstances, those who have acquired pretending skills are especially capable of making realistic judgments. Singer (1973) noted, too, that:

> Engaging in make-believe play, by the very fact of its quality of shifting roles, that is, shifting between direct response to reality and the introduction of elements drawn essentially from long-term memory, coupled with the necessary distinction between the toys played with and the objects imagined, all may begin to create a more differentiated sense of separation between self and environment. As Piaget (1962) has noted, the very definition of symbolic play hinges

---

[2]Golomb (1979) demonstrated that children who undergo "symbolic play training" show an improvement in "conservation performance."

on the child's ability to tell the difference between the cloth being put to sleep as a game and the real cloth. In some sense, the high-fantasy child within reasonable limits may be practicing a more acute differentiation of self and environment and may develop a heightened sense of self. (p. 222)

Other speculations abound with respect to the functions of pretend play. It has been proposed (Rubin, 1982) that such play offers opportunities to practice and master life skills, to provide catharsis for frustrations and emotions, to cultivate creativity, to release "surplus energy," and so forth. We do not have solid data for rank ordering such explanatory possibilities in terms of their potential validity. In any case, Leslie (1987) pressed an issue that we noted earlier: "If, as generally assumed, the child is just beginning to construct a system for internally representing . . . knowledge, why is this system of representation not undermined by its use in both comprehending and producing pretense?" (p. 412). In other words, can children immerse themselves in pretense without damaging their hold on the "real world" and, if so, how is this possible? If pretense is potentially damaging to reality distinctions, one must wonder why young children risk so much involvement with it. Leslie (1987) beautifully highlighted the paradox of early pretending:

> Pretending ought to strike the cognitive psychologist as a very odd sort of ability. After all, from an evolutionary point of view, there ought to be high premium on the veridicality of cognitive processes. The perceiving, thinking organism ought, as far as possible, to get things right. Yet pretense flies in the face of this fundamental principle. In pretense we deliberately distort reality. How odd then that this ability is not the sober culmination of intellectual development but instead makes its appearance playfully and precociously at the very beginning of childhood. . . . Indeed, how is it possible that young children can disregard or distort reality in any way and to any degree at all? Why does pretending not undermine their representational system and bring it crashing down?" (p. 412)[3]

It does seem a bit farfetched to reason, as some have, that practicing unrealities is a sensible means for increasing one's reality testing skills.

Leslie (1987) told us that, in fact, children's fascination with pretending is a logical derivative of the sensitivities and subtleties that frame the state of being human. He indicated that it derives from children's growing capacity to understand human cognition itself. He states:

---

[3]Leslie (1987) elaborated on this problem further:

> Pretense affects the normal reference, truth, and existence relations of the representations it uses. These relations become highly deviant. Any primary representational system affected would quickly be undermined by arbitrary meaning changes. To prevent this, pretend representations must somehow be marked off, or "quarantined," from primary representations. Indeed, so deviant are the reference, truth, and existence relations of pretend representations that it begins to seem unlikely that they are primary representations at all. (p. 415)

It is an early symptom of the human mind's ability to characterize and manipulate its own attitudes to information. Pretending oneself is thus a special case
of the ability to understand pretense in others (someone else's attitude to information). In short, pretense is an early manifestation of what has been called
theory of mind (Premack & Woodruff, 1978). (p. 416)

In essence, children learn that the "mental states" of persons who are communicating information mediate the meanings of that information.[4] They
learn to impute to themselves and others mental states that are represented
by such terms as "believe," "think," "pretend," "wonder," and "expect"; and
they become aware that each communication needs to be interpreted within the context of the communicator's mental state. Subjective intention can
suspend normal rules of truth and falsity.[5]

Leslie (1987) pointed out that, in the context of what is implied by mediating terms like "believe" and "pretend," statements become "opaque." For
example, the assertion that John Doe *believes* Paris is the capital of France
in no way bears on the truth (or falsehood) of whether Paris is the capital.
Leslie (1987) remarked: "In a mental state context one can no longer 'look
through' terms to see what they refer to in deciding issues. The mental state
term suspends normal reference relations" (p. 416). He elaborated further:
"Propositions involving mental state terms do not logically imply the truth
(or falsehood) of propositions embedded in them. Thus, 'John believes the
cat is white' says nothing about whether or not the cat really is white" (p.
416). He concluded:

Pretend representations . . . are *opaque*, even to the organism who entertains
them. They are in effect not representations of the world but representations
of representations. For this reason I shall call them—*metarepresentations*—Using
an appropriate mechanistic metaphor, one can say that the metarepresenta-
tional context *decouples* the primary expression from its normal input–output
relations. (p. 417)

Overall, one can say that children are drawn into the world of make-believe
because they discover that human meanings and portrayals can be switched
from one level to another by simply shifting one's subjective frame of refer-

---

[4]Piaget and Inhelder (1956) referred to this phenomenon as "the recognition of the universality of subjectivity."

[5]Harris, Donnelly, Guz, and Pitt-Watson (1986) asked, "How exactly do children discover
that real and apparent emotion do no coincide?" They went on to comment:

Children may frequently find themselves complying with social expectations that they should
not cry when they hurt themselves, or express disgust when they dislike their food, or express
anger when a sibling is annoying them. In all these cases, provided they can monitor their
mental state, they will be confronted by a discrepancy between what they feel and what they
express. (p. 907)

ence. Meanings can be reshaped arbitrarily by a mere change in intent or attitude. Meanings need not be anchored in "truth" but simply in a subjective paradigm. Children learn that the world is full of people who arbitrarily manipulate meanings as they subjectively please. Such manipulation is, of course, the essence of "making things up."

Pretending as Socialization

We present a derivative and yet more radical schema concerning the origins of pretend behavior. We propose that, from the outset, the process of socializing children substantially involves make-believe maneuvers. The culture comes to children with expectations that certain values and "truths" will be accepted. Until relatively recently, most of such verities were derived from religious dogma, and their truth was derived from cultural make-believe. It is probable that the majority of the verities that we seek to inculcate in young children are quite arbitrary. However, the culture seeks to convince children that such verities are indeed The Truth. We suggest that children soon sense (in perhaps largely ill-defined ways) the arbitrary nature of what is being inculcated. They may very well detect a deceptive gap between the supposed validity of what is being asserted and its actual validity. They learn that they are expected to play an elaborate game of make-believe that revolves around treating cultural values as if they were unquestionable truths. In essence, we propose that one of the most basic aspects of socialization, namely, the transmission of values, requires an elaborate and skilled exercise of make-believe on the part of children, who are the targets of the whole process.[6] They must adapt to the illusion that the culture knows what is correct and right.

Even further, we suggest that parental behavior is typically so infused with contradictions and illogical expectations that children catch repeated glimpses of the substantial elements of deception and "we are fooling you" involved. Parents usually try to convey the impression that everything they do "for their kids" has positive intent. Generally, they camouflage their demands as "reasonable." Yet universally, often in the name of absolutes, they expect absurdities from their children, such as shutting out the reality of urgent body sensations or specific body parts (e.g., sexual), feeling arbitrary disgust with reference to whole classes of potentially attractive foods that are declared to be forbidden, screening out awareness of major aspects of the environment that are culturally defined as invisible, and so forth. The literature dealing with parent–child interactions (e.g., Spinetta & Rigler, 1972) abounds with

---

[6]An interesting parallel is provided by a study of actors that we (Fisher & Fisher, 1981) completed. We found actors, who are supreme specialists in pretending and make-believe, to be highly concerned with the preservation and continuity of the culture's values.

illustrations of how parents exploit children, subject them to contradictory demands, and expect them to adapt to illogical requirements.

In fact, children have to become experts in coping with the unrealities basic to their socialization. Perhaps that is what motivates children to become experts at practicing and playing with unreal images so early. They need to master the nature of unreal constructions to thread their way through the maze of unreal expectations and rules in which they find themselves.[7] It is interesting that some observers (e.g., Chandler, 1975; Riegel, 1973) have questioned the portrayal of abstract reasoning as the ultimate in cognitive development. Chandler (1975) suggested that the "classic principle of identity, which maintains that facts or opinions should not contradict one another, is an unnecessary and peculiarly nonhuman standard of judgment" (p. 176). This perspective urges that cognitive development "depends not on abstraction, but upon a new kind of concretism in which . . . contradictory views . . . are held in . . . an 'awkward embrace' " (p. 176). In other words, the basic illogical state of affairs confronting humans requires that they be at home with "illogical" modes of integrating contradictions.

There may be still another aspect of the socialization process that accounts for children's investment in make-believe fantasy. Quite simply, parents may be highly motivated to encourage such investment because they find that it facilitates their ability to maintain control over their offspring. This statement may seem surprising because the use of imagination and fantasy is often associated with creativity, originality, and unconventional deviation. However, there are multiple research reports indicating that the ability to pretend and imagine is associated with the ability to be reflective rather than impulsive, to exercise self-control rather than seek immediate gratification. The capacity to create pretend fantasies apparently provides a buffer against immediate motoric expression of feelings and impulses. It has been observed that the more children can and do engage in pretend play, the more controlled and "law abiding" is their overt behavior (e.g., Fein, 1981; Singer, 1973). Fein (1981) noted: "Pretense provides an unusual opportunity for children to control their own emotional arousal and to maintain a level that is both comfortable and stimulating. The intrinsic motivation of pretense resides in its ability to convert external sources of motivation into an internal symbolic form" (p. 301).

Empirical data indicate that children's inclination to fantasy enhances their ability to wait patiently in a frustrating situation, their amount of friendly, sociable interaction with peers, and their expression of positive affect.[8]

---

[7]However, as documented by Chandler, Paget, and Koch (1978), it is not until 9–11 years of age that they show fairly clear understanding of the major defense mechanisms (e.g., denial, repression, displacement).

[8]Singer (1973) commented: "The high-fantasy child may appear to the outsider as relatively calm, capable of positive affect and enjoyment, and a 'good child' " (p. 220).

The inclination to fantasy is negatively correlated with aggressive play and motoric acting out (Sherrod & Singer, 1979). Interestingly, children who are particularly invested in pretend play show low egocentricity and high ability to adopt other's perspectives. Note, too, that when children are given special training in how to cultivate their fantasies, they manifest enhanced impulse control in dull situations (Fein, 1981; Saltz & Brodie, 1982). Singer (1973) indicated that the "high fantasy child" may adapt "more quickly" to the limitations and restraints imposed by the typical school classroom.

Mischel (1981) demonstrated that children's ability to delay gratification with respect to a desired object was significantly increased if they were provided with the opportunity to engage in distracting fantasy. The association between the ability to generate fantasy and to restrain one's motor responses also has been described in adults. A considerable research literature (e.g., Greenberg & Fisher, 1973; Meltzoff, Singer, & Korchin, 1952) bears on this matter. There tends to be an inverse relationship between the motor and fantasy spheres. Human movement responses to the Rorschach inkblots can be increased by imposing motoric restraints on the individual. Further, persons who are fluent in the production of Rorschach movement images are capable of significantly greater inhibition of motoric responses in various contrived laboratory settings than are those who are of limited fluency (Fisher, 1967).

Children probably learn that pretending facilitates their adjustment to the extreme demands for inhibition and restraint associated with becoming socialized. They learn that the domain of pretend is an excellent locale for parking, delaying, and side-tracking their impulses. Presumably, most parents sense the vital role of fantasy and therefore appreciate its utility. There are various ways in which parents do, in fact, encourage their children to use fantasy in a self-comforting, diverting fashion. They may even consciously persuade their children to believe certain myths that have apparent value in managing behavior. For example, many parents deliberately teach their children to believe in Santa Claus or certain moral and religious concepts, about which the parents themselves are personally skeptical. Such parents implicitly recognize that make-believe can be used to smooth the process of shepherding their children toward conformance and doing the "right thing."[9]

Moran (1987) provided illustrations of how parents use make-believe strategies to avoid conflict and confrontation with their children. He noted: "The mother's wish to avoid battles (with) the toddler . . . motivates her to use a variety of playful distractions and diversions. Entering the animistic world of the toddler by personifying the inanimate is a common example. Instead of ordering the child to eat, the mother may say that the food wants to 'go

---

[9]Bettelheim (1976) speculated that inculcating children with fairy tales provides them with paradigm images of mastering evil through the exercise of virtue and heroism.

to his tummy' " (p. 14). It is an interesting finding that children who are closer to their parents are more invested in pretend fantasy. Matas, Arend, and Sroufe (1978) observed that children who are securely attached at 18 months evidence higher levels of pretend play at 24 months than did children who were less attached at 18 months. It also has been found that children most likely to engage in pretend play have a good deal of contact with their parents[10] and come from families with minimal physical punishment and relatively little marital discord (Hetherington, Cox, & Cox, 1979; Singer, 1973). Such data suggest that make-believe is practiced most by children from families in which socialization has been relatively smooth and effective. The harmony and closeness that characterize such families may be because there is facility in using fantasy to control impulsive, erratic, or hyperaggressive acting out.[11] It is paradoxical that such families encourage various forms of spontaneity (e.g., free conversational interchange, imaginative elaboration) but seem, to a significant extent, to harness the potential for make-believe for purposes of facilitating control functions.

Pretending emerges as a skill[12] needed to cope with the fictions and pretenses inherent in culture and the socialization process. Becoming a socialized human does, in many ways, call for perspectives that are anchored in commonly agreed illusions and make-believe. Children probably cannot enter their culture unless they master the intricacies of the rules defining its pattern of unrealities. It would appear, too, that the rigid impulse controls demanded by cultures require a cognitive "compartment," where illusory images can be generated. These images dampen the need for immediate impulse expression by providing distraction and the support of pretend scenes and agendas. It is intriguing to speculate about the degree to which children are aware of the cultural make-believe game in which they participate. They may be much more aware than is apparent. However, the cultural contract with children may require their pretending that what is culturally pretended is not pretended. There may be large individual differences in the degree to which the make-believe aspects of their culture are perceived. Probably some minimal level of understanding of these aspects is necessary to cope with the impact of unrealities. But one wonders if great penetration of the cultural story line could interfere with becoming "adequately" socialized. As mentioned earlier, we see children's mastery of make-believe as the anlage

---

[10]Nicolich (1977) reported, on the basis of an intensive 1-year observation of children (ages 14–19 months), that "maternal presence" facilitates pretending.

[11]Sherrod and Singer (1979) stated: "Certain family experiential factors correlate with the fantasy-predisposition measure. Children with high-fantasy predispositions tend to be only or older children . . . and to have more educated parents who are more tolerant and encouraging of make-believe and fantasy, and they tend to be closer to one parent . . ." (p. 21).

[12]Regarding pretense as a skill contrasts with Piaget's (1962) view that make-believe is "no more than lack of coherence and still more, subjective assimilation" (p. 131).

for more elaborate forms of self-deception and illusion fabrication common among adults.

Pretending and the Relativity of It All

If pretending is, indeed, rooted in the realization that subjective attitudes shape meanings and interpretations, the question arises as to why this does not undermine average children's faith in truth. Why do children not conclude that it is all but impossible to be sure about alternate interpretations of events? Chandler (1987) concluded that such skepticism does surface prominently at adolescence. He also suggested that this "ontologically" linked doubt mirrors philosophy's recurrent concern with the nature of knowledge and truth. He indicated that as children acquire an awareness that knowledge is "person-relative," the seeds of a broad "Cartesian anxiety" are sown. He pointed out:

> Once under reflective scrutiny, knowledge inevitably begins to lose its former aura of scrupulous objectivity. So long as meanings were imagined to be features of objects rather than subjects, it was easy enough to suppose that the facts would remain the same regardless of who was in the business of collecting them. As meanings come to be understood as mental products that are actively manufactured rather than harvested as natural resources, however, the idea of absolute truth is emptied of much of the earlier significance, and the companion notion of objectivity deteriorates. . . ." (pp. 149–150)

He pinpointed adolescence as the developmental period when this process of "deterioration" is discernible. He notes: "The effect of pulling in this small thread of insight is to eventually unravel the whole epistemic fabric of middle childhood. . . . With the growing realization that all acts of knowledge acquisition are inescapably subjective . . . all prospects of closing the gap between *seems* and *is* are cut off, and all hope of obtaining absolute knowledge is irretrievably lost" (p. 150). Finally, he added:

> The price of all of this new-found uncertainty is generic doubt, not the kind of mundane, case-specific doubt of middle childhood, but a wholesale, transcendental kind of doubt that threatens to annihilate the whole of one's system of beliefs. . . . Like hobgoblins that remain a threat under the bed, no matter how often or how carefully one verifies their absence . . . , these transcendental doubts, once set in motion, tend to rattle the foundations of the entire knowing process and, if left unchecked, eventually leave no belief standing upon any other belief. (p. 150)

Chandler (1987) depicted most adolescents as having to find some mode of adaptation to such "generic doubt." He speculated that one mode is to seek out an extraordinary figure whom can be imbued with the power to know the absolute truth and to attach oneself to this "unimpeachable source." The attachment may be to religious figures or dogmas, political heroes, highly consensual peer groups, and so forth. In this way, one no longer need take responsibility "for settling doubtful matters." At the other extreme, Chandler (1987) referred to a solution in which individuals "throw in the towel" and "skeptically accept life for the irrational enterprise it has seemingly turned out to be . . ." (p. 151). He told us that those who adopt this "know-nothing stance" still need to make life decisions, and they turn to such strategies as "impulsivism (acting without thought), intuitionism (doing what affect demands), and indifferentism (tossing a coin or acting on whim)" (p. 151).[13]

To support his argument that adolescence is the time when epistemic doubt most often takes on significant proportions, Chandler (1987) cited work by Nucci (1981) to the effect that adolescents often clash with their parents over the validity of arbitrary conventions. He mentioned studies by Kuhn, Pennington, and Leadbeater (1983) and Enright, Lapsley, Franklin, and Steuck (1984), which indicated that teenagers accept that knowledge is "inherently subjective"; and referred to Marcia's (1976, 1980) observations of their indecisive concern with alternatives. However, it is not clear that such observations preclude the possibility of epistemic doubt well before adolescence. In fact, we know that adolescence is not a qualitatively unique phase, but rather represents a point on a continuum (Fisher, 1986). Psychological phenomena that manifest during adolescence have typically evolved throughout childhood. It is not unreasonable to assume that if there is a noticeable blip of epistemic doubt at adolescence, it was actually building up over the preceding years. As initially documented, notions about the relativity of truth take root during infancy and exist in tandem with what we call "pretend behavior." Clinchy and Mansfield (1985) observed that children as young as 10 are open to the idea of "nonreducible plurality" in the opinions and views that may be entertained concerning issues. Enright et al. (1984) have presented data with similar implications about children who are preadolescent.

We do not know how most children avoid serious "Cartesian anxiety" as they learn about the relativity of knowledge. We can only speculate about possible perservative strategies. One serious possibility, already mentioned, is that an early warning signal is built into the socialization process. It might

---

[13]In this context, Chandler (1975) also referred to the adolescent's defensive use of abstraction:

> An . . . almost universal method employed by adolescents in their efforts to minimize the idiosyncrasies of their world view is to simply do what persons at the formal operational level do best—think abstractly. Abstract thought, through a kind of selective attention and inattention, provides a means of circumventing a variety of potentially disruptive contradictions, and identifies similarities at the cost of obscuring differences. For all of its other much lauded attributes, abstract thinking is a powerful tool for lopping off awkward differences of opinion and imposing a kind of elegant, if somewhat syncretic consensus. (p. 175)

be paraphrased as follows: "You are discovering and will continue to find that truth is subjective (often make-believe) and you must, if you want to be an actor in our culture, pretend that the subjectivity is of small and certainly manageable dimensions." It would be too threatening to most societal structures to permit widespread awareness of the relative nature of truth. Obviously, most cultures provide an extraordinary amount of reassurance concerning the solidity of truth by means of religious, scientific, and other authoritative images. Because the "discovery" of subjectivity probably takes place in small increments over an extended period, this could facilitate a gradual desensitization process. Such desensitization might involve putting on the proper blinders and minimizing the implications of what does seep through. Even those individuals, who by virtue of exceptional intellectual skill or opportunity become clearly attuned to the relativity of knowledge, would, because of their basic need to maintain membership in the culture, probably narrow their skepticism to a primarily intellectual sector.[14] We assume that the process of learning to make-believe, which seems to be a part of all cultures, provides most individuals with the initial insight into the prevalence of unreality and the cognitive expertise in pretense needed to come to terms with this state of affairs.

THE CONTRADICTORY FUNCTIONS
OF MAKE-BELIEVE

The possibility that children's early expertise in pretending serves to stabilize their socialization and their acceptance of the mythic matrix basic to their culture stands in contrast to pretending as a means for creativity and innovation. Children who are good pretenders are likely to display above-average creativity and "divergent thinking" (Pepler, 1982). This represents quite a paradox. A force for conservatism is also a potential force for the introduc-

---

[14]Chandler (1987) described the various philosophical solutions that have been devised to cope with skepticism. He noted that the "postempirical" philosophers deny that it is necessary to have "certainty as a necessary condition for rationally guided action" (p. 143). He indicated that

post-skeptical rationalists, who see (the) objectivism–relativism axis as misleading and distorting . . . argue instead that it is possible to accept the ambiguity inherent in human experience without renouncing hope for a kind of discursive truth capable of being argumentatively validated by a common community of interpreters. . . . The capacity to form and exchange symbols, guaranteed by our common sociohistorical and linguistic traditions, also guarantees our ability to share meanings and to achieve a legitimate consensus with others. . . . According to Wittgenstein, this is accomplished not by dictating once and for all that some one version of reality is absolutely right, but rather by giving good grounds for choosing between alternative interpretations, by providing convincing reasons in support of our views, and by relying upon the force of the better practice of argument. (p. 143)

tion of novelty. This contradiction produces a persistent dilemma for the keep-
ers of the status quo. The trick is to encourage children to pretend about
the right things. Actually, much of children's pretend play does focus on, and
often rehearses, everyday themes, issues, and activities (Bretherton, 1984).
As such, it is confined to the "right" channels. However, what is pretended
is always potentially antiauthoritarian and will, in the long run, give rise to
ideas and themes that make trouble for the current structure.[15]

Although make-believe facilitates coming to terms with the major cultural myths, it may also stimulate individuality. As children experiment
with various pretense concoctions, one would expect them to be impressed
with the power they possess to fabricate what they will. They would presumably see again and again that they can, from within, create images that
bear their own unique stamp. The sense of self, the "I," should be magnified by such awareness. The self as a generator or originator would presumably be reinforced. As mentioned earlier, Singer (1973) similarly commented that make-believe play "may begin to create a more differentiated
sense of separation between self and environment" (p. 222). However, he
thought the important element in this differentiation process was that make-
believe play provides practice in shifting between "reality" and subjectively
derived elements, distinguishing between "toys played with" and "objects
imagined."

From another perspective, Chandler (1975) concluded that a genuine
differentiation of self calls for a respect for the "highly individualized" or "per-
sonalized" (of which pretend fantasy might be a central example), as contrasted with the depersonalized modes associated with formal reasoning and
logic (ala Piaget). He considered that the formal depersonalized modes are
really contemptuous of personal feelings, fantasies, and intentions. In that
sense, they are anti-individual. Interestingly, Chandler (1975) suggested that
when young people do convert to formal thinking modes this creates an
awareness of the relativity of knowledge ("plurality of alternatives") and therefore arouses a sense of being isolated within one's own unique perspective
and not able to participate in consensually perceived truths. That is, there
evolves a relativism (an objectivism) that highlights one's cognitive isolation
in the world. However, instead of reinforcing self-feelings, this position, which
is based on a "vertigo of relativity," probably undermines the credibility of
the individual's own convictions. The relativism would appear to increase

---

[15]The contrasting forces embodied in pretend play are metaphorically referred to by Erikson (1977):

> Of all the formulations of play, the briefest and the best is to be found in Plato's *Laws*. He
> sees the model of true playfulness in the need of all young creatures, animal and human, to
> leap. To truly leap, you must learn how to use the ground as a springboard, and how to land
> resiliently and safely. It *means to test* the *leeway allowed by given limits*; to *outdo and yet
> not escape gravity*. (p. 17)

self-isolation (and probably self-awareness[16]), but also reduce the credibility of just about everything, including the self. Perhaps the self is simultaneously magnified in some ways and diminished in other ways, as a function of shifting away from imaginative toward logically exacting modes.

THE PROTECTIVE VALUE OF EARLY MAKE-BELIEVE

We have discussed how make-believe helps children adapt to being participants in this cultures. We have suggested that children need to master pretense in order to assimilate the pretend images and values mandated by the culture and to learn to "park" impulses rather than express them motorically. These are largely matters of conformance. Let us probe briefly the role of make-believe in providing a protective boundary. It is fairly well established (e.g., Blatt & Wild, 1976; Fisher, 1986) that persons need to possess a boundary that is capable of providing protection against potentially intrusive forces "out there." Moran (1987) speculated, on the basis of clinical observations, that parents often engage in playful (pretend) maneuvers to cushion the impact of a potential stressor upon their children. They may render the demands of "reality" less threatening by imaginatively giving them a twist so that they seem less real or less harsh. Moran (1987) notes: "Playful parents find many inventive ways to lighten the demands which they make on the child. . . . Playful mothers may contort themselves while . . . dressing their babies. Such parents will invent playful interactions to mediate a large variety of tasks" (p. 16). He gave one concrete example of such a playful maneuver: "Pretending to drive a bus upstairs on the way to putting the child to bed" (p. 16). This actually involves blurring the border between fantasy and reality, so as to provide a buffer. In this fashion, parents teach their children the advantages to interposing the "not real" between oneself and that which looks uncomfortable or menacing in nonself territory. Children learn that transmuting events into "less real" representations provides a special kind of boundary.

The power of unreal images to reinforce one's boundaries was empirically shown in an earlier study of schizophrenic persons. It has been observed (Fisher, 1986) that, contrary to theoretical expectation, certain classes of psychotic individuals were able to maintain the sense that their boundaries (as measured by the Fisher–Cleveland Barrier score, which is based on the boundary properties ascribed to inkblot percepts) were intact. Exploratory research demonstrated that the more these individuals were able to conjure up gran-

---

[16]If self-awareness varies significantly as a function of imaginative versus logical modes, this could have a number of consequences for behavior. It is now well established (e.g., Duval & Wicklund, 1972) that degree of self-awareness (self-focus) influences accuracy of self-perception, amount of negativity one entertains toward oneself, and intensity of guilt about nonconformance.

diose images of self (no matter how unrealistic or delusional), the greater was their measured level of boundary articulation. Their unreal but self-reassuring fantasies provided significant boundary support. Analogous defensive strategies occur in nonpsychotic persons. For example, it has been shown (Fisher, 1986) that, in certain contexts, normal subjects who ingest a placebo evidence increased boundary differentiation.

Many observers (e.g., Bretherton, 1984; DiLalla & Watson, 1988; Scarlett & Wolf, 1979) have conceptualized imaginative play in boundary terms.[17] Such play requires children to establish a contoured area in which the rules of pretend apply and to distinguish this area from the "real world" realm. Children learn elaborate rules about how to step back and forth across the borders separating pretend and real. They do this day after day and accumulate unlimited amounts of practice in border crossing. Thus, they build up wisdom about the nature of boundary setting and how boundaries can be manipulated to alter one's psychological state, usually in the direction of self-comforting and supporting. One may speculate that the experience gained in crossing the border between pretend play and reality is particularly valuable in stimulating a sense of protective boundary control, because it involves a realm of special individual power. That is, children are uniquely in command when they conjure up pretend images. There are few, if any, other areas of functioning in which they can so independently shape what is happening. The entire process of moving in and out of the pretend state occurs in a context of heightened "I am in command." This, in turn, may translate into "I really know how to set up bounded protective spaces for myself." Obviously, each individual's boundary practicing strategies mimic the spirit of the culture's encapsulation of its members with common myths designed to cast existence in required shapes.

SWITCHING TO MAKE-BELIEVE

Children's expertise in switching back and forth to make-believe may lay the foundation for a variety of skills that have adaptive power throughout the life cycle. McGhee (1971), in reviewing the development of the humor response in children, made the point that appreciation of humor becomes possible only when children are able to insert discrepancies or violations of expectancies into a pretend context. He discussed experiments in which infants (around 13 months of age) consistently smile when shown pictures of a

---

[17]Huzinga (1949) referred to the bounded spatiality of pretend play as follows: "All play moves and has its being within a playground marked off beforehand, either materially or ideally, deliberately or a matter of course. . . . The arena, the card table, the magic circle, the temple, the screen, the tennis court" (p. 10).

three-headed man or a mule's head on a man's body. He commented: "The disarranged face or three-headed man . . . becomes funny only when the child realizes that what is depicted could not really occur, except at a fantasy level" (p. 333). He added:

> The . . . situation is assimilated only in a fantasy or pretend fashion, and it is the comparison of the normal criteria governing complete assimilation into a schema with the present violation of these criteria that causes the child to see the situation as funny. . . . As long as the child remains in a reality mode of assimilation, expectancy disconfirmations may generate interest, confusion, or fear, but will not lead to humor. . . . By switching to a fantasy mode of assimilation, the child is immediately able to make sense out of the stimulus and construes it as a play on reality. (p. 334)

Thus, McGhee (1971) linked the humorous (funny) perspective with the ability to switch into a mode that might be paraphrased: "I see something that does not make sense in terms of my usual 'realistic' ways of judging things, but if I pretend this is not real and play around with it in divergent ways I can see what titillating potentialities it represents." We know (e.g., Fisher & Fisher, 1981) that the ability to visualize events in the world as funny has considerable comforting and supportive value.

What other long-term adaptive modes result from children's make-believe? Little, if any, empirical data exist for probing this question. However, quite generally one wonders whether becoming knowledgeable about "turning on" the unreal does not provide the paradigm for many later defense strategies that involve "escaping," leaving the field, or somehow denying the full reality of the immediate situation. It is likely that a number of the "classical" defense mechanisms, with their focus on evading awareness of specific issues, have their roots in the escape functions of the earlier exercise of make-believe. Incidentally, we are impressed that, with the initiation of pretending, children become entangled with duality. They learn that they can look at practically every experience through both "real" and make-believe lenses. Of course, it is true that developing children come to an awareness of polarized viewpoints through a variety of mechanisms. But one may speculate that the split between real and pretend is one of the most radical they encounter; and this could therefore dramatize the puzzle of splitness and divergence in one's understanding.

7

CLASSICAL DEFENSE MECHANISMS

Any endeavor concerned with the tactics of illusion construction must scan the nature of the classical defense mechanisms. As can be seen, such mechanisms represent the everyday tactics of adaptation to all of the things in life that are fear provoking, puzzling, or not easily handled within a strictly rational or logical frame of reference.

As is well known, Sigmund Freud and other psychoanalytic pioneers (especially Anna Freud) described ways in which individuals who find life to be puzzling or difficult try to reshape their experiences into more palatable versions. Persons are said to make use of various "defense mechanisms," which permit them to edit selectively what is happening to them and to conjure up narratives that are less puzzling, less scary, and more triumphant. An internal feeling or emotion that is alien to one's ego ideal can be projected onto a bad other. A memory of villainous action on one's part can be shoved into the recesses of the repressed. One's unacceptably intense anger can be transformed so that it appears to be a diametrically opposite brand of affect. Psychoanalytic observers originally told us that the persons who came to them for treatment were constantly utilizing defense mechanisms to adjust their images of reality. However, as more and more research data have accumulated, we learn that defense mechanisms flourish in those who are troubled enough to seek therapeutic help as well as in the average citizen. It is not unusual to repress, to project, to rationalize, and to engage in all of the other varieties of defensive maneuvers.

The best evidence of the urgent need to defensively camouflage emerges when persons do scientific work. The scientific establishment starts out with the assumption that individual scientists innocently and unconsciously shape their observations so that they will match preconceived notions and hypotheses. It is accepted that, even with the best intentions, scientists will cleverly find ways to make "reality" conform to some ego-invested paradigm. That is why such procedures as "random assignment," "double blind," and statistical tests of significance are required for experimental designs. However, what is truly startling is that, even though strict, suspicious restraints are applied to investigators, they often manage to shade (for the most part without deliberate intent) their findings in their own favor. Their own psychological needs drive them to use subtle defense mechanisms, which render their data more ego-syntonic (e.g., Rosenthal, 1966). There are endless examples of such phenomena.

One example is provided in the literature concerned with the testing of the efficacy of psychotropic drugs. Consider the review by Fisher and Greenberg (1989), in which it was documented that double blind studies of the efficacy of antidepressant drugs are influenced by the expectations of the researchers conducting them. Despite all precautions, such researchers managed to pick up hints that permitted them to identify which patients were receiving the active drug and which were placebo controls. The fact that they then influenced the therapeutic outcomes in favor of the active drug was revealed in some interesting analyses. These analyses showed that, when studies are rated as to how well designed they are to exclude experimenter bias, the more lax they are, the greater is the apparent therapeutic advantage of the active drug over the placebo. If we assume that the researchers involved were consciously honest persons, it would follow that the pressure of their inner needs to shape the data in a preferred direction energized defensive operations (e.g., concealed exhortations of patients, biased ratings of patients' degree of improvement), which not only had to be executed, but simultaneously banished from self-awareness. The researchers had to maintain a sense of being objective even as they used ingenuity to cut this bit of reality to fit a wishful pattern. The more permeable the safeguards enclosing each drug trial study, the more that study was infiltrated by defensive intentions. The message that emerges is that, even under conditions of controlled rationality far exceeding those prevailing in everyday life, self-serving mechanisms that "reshape reality" to one's specifications are potentially influential.

MODAL DEFENSE MANEUVERS

There seem to be infinite ways in which persons put the right defensive spin on what is happening to them. Ihilevich and Gleser (1986) compiled a summary of the available defense mechanisms and showed that such mechanisms cluster into five categories. They demonstrated these clusters empirically, on the basis of their findings from a Defense Mechanism Inventory, which they devised, and an analysis of the literature concerned with defense mechanism phenomena. The defenses serve four functions:[1]

1. To fictionalize reality.
2. To create an illusionary sense of threat mastery.
3. To minimize anxiety.
4. To magnify self-esteem.

The following are the five fundamental clusters of defensive strategies they presented:

1. The first category involves using aggressive, inappropriate, chronic, or exaggerated ways "to master perceived external threats or mask internal conflicts which are too painful to confront consciously" (p. 18). This is labeled *turning against object*.
2. Another involves attributing unpleasant purpose or characteristics to persons, without solid justification. Such attributions become the basis for behavior toward those upon whom they have been projected. This process is called *projection*.
3. A third category embraces a spectrum of strategies often referred to with terms like *intellectualization* and *rationalization*. Events and experiences are reframed in a language that splits off associated emotions and emphasizes defensive abstractions or sophistries. Ihilevich and Gleser (1986) referred to this defense as *principalization*.
4. A fourth defense mode paradoxically involves the use of self-attack to cushion against threats or demands. Self-criticism and self-inflicted pain may be employed to atone for one's assumed badness, to win the approval of others who are perceived as demanding self-attack, to give meaning to or enhance one's apparent control over traumatic events, and to discount future blows to one's self-esteem by anticipating and, in a sense, acting them out in advance. This is labeled *turning against self*.
5. The last category broadly includes such defenses as repression, reaction formation, and denial. It refers to tactics based on shutting out or denying threats. Negative emotions are replaced by opposite, Pollyanna-like ones. The term *reversal* is applied.

Actually, the psychological literature is overflowing with descriptions of

---

[1]Ihilevich and Gleser (1986) stated: "The aim of all defense mechanisms is to establish illusory mastery over perceived threats when real mastery or accommodation are perceived as impossible" (p. 5).

cunning defensive modes.[2] These modes are diversely referred to with terms like *illusion, coping strategy,* and *self-deception.* Taylor (1989) and Lazarus (1983), who were particularly interested in normal individuals' use of illusions, suggested that there are multiple forms of defensive illusions. Taylor (1989) classified them into three broad areas:

1. Those designed to give individuals unrealistically positive views of themselves. Thus, normal subjects judge positive attributes to be overwhelmingly more typical of self than negative ones. Rather pervasively, persons see themselves as better than others.
2. Those aimed to give oneself an exaggerated sense of personal control over events. Persons frequently overestimate their control over chance-determined events.
3. Those intended to create a feeling of false optimism. Taylor and Brown (1988) noted: "Both children and adults overestimate the degree to which they will do well on future tasks . . . and they are more likely to provide such overestimates the more personally important the task is . . ." (p. 197).

Social-psychological research documents a surprising array of self-serving beliefs and myths that apparently can be pressed into the service of broad defensive strategies. Consider a few examples: Lerner published a book in 1980 with the title *The Belief in a Just World—A Fundamental Delusion.* He and others presented data indicating that it is common for persons to believe wishfully in a stable world in which the events that occur are just—a world in which deserving persons are rewarded and undeserving persons have bad outcomes. In the process of maintaining this illusory belief system, persons are inclined, quite illogically, to blame victims for misfortunes that are beyond their control. Lerner (1971) depicted this defense process:

> The observer can either decide that the world is not so just after all or go through the effort of persuading himself that the "innocent" victim actually merited his suffering. One relatively comfortable way the observer can resolve this conflict is by deciding that the victim, though innocent by deed, deserves his fate by virtue of his undesirable personal attributes. (p. 127)

A pool of clever experiments demonstrates the pervasive existence of this "just world" frame of reference. It is almost stunning to witness the extent to which persons motivated by the need for a stable, meaningful life space strain, in eminently unfair ways, to blame utterly blameless people. There

---

[2]Freud conceptualized the following categories of defense mechanisms: projection, repression, reaction-formation, regression, undoing, introjection, turning against self, reversal, and isolation.

are indications that the more undeserving of their misfortunes persons are perceived to be, the more such persons are devalued, so that "justice" can be read into their dilemmas (Lerner, 1980).

Another self-bolstering mode is referred to as the "false consensus effect." Numerous observers (e.g., Marks & Miller, 1987) have looked at this variable, which is defined as the tendency for persons to regard their own beliefs, attitudes, and judgments as relatively common and accepted by others but to assume that alternative viewpoints are uncommon and inappropriate. A variety of laboratory situations have shown that if subjects choose a course of action they overestimate how frequently others will do likewise. Marks and Miller (1987) referred to a study in which students were asked to walk around campus while wearing a sandwich board that read "repent." Those who agreed to do so thought that around 63% of their fellow students would also agree, but those who declined estimated that only about 23% would agree. Although there is evidence that multiple factors probably contribute to "false consensus," it is clear that a particularly significant one derives from the need for social support and self-esteem maintenance. By perceiving others as like oneself, the correctness of one's position is presumably bolstered.

A third example relates to certain cognitive beliefs that help to cushion uncertain outcomes. Pyszczynski (1982) outlined one such belief strategy. It surfaces in situations where persons have a low probability of obtaining a highly desirable outcome. Their adaptation to the predicament is either to derogate the outcome by judging it to have low attractiveness or to underestimate the probability of its occurrence. Research data suggest that this defensive mode more likely operates where the outcome at stake has the potential, if negative, for stirring up unpleasant emotions.

The examples of widely circulating defensive beliefs and perspectives just cited represent only a small sample of those that have been identified formally. There are studies that have diversely documented other defensive modes such as "downward comparison" (Wills, 1981), exaggerating the uniqueness of one's own skills (Marks, 1984), minimizing one's vulnerability to misfortune (Weinstein, 1980), downplaying information that contradicts one's judgments (Einhorn & Hogarth, 1978), and so forth.

ARE SOME DEFENSIVE MECHANISMS MORE MATURE THAN OTHERS?

Once it was officially discovered that the average person uses multiple defense mechanisms, some of which are mediated by less than perfect rationality, a considerable interest developed in ascertaining whether they can be classified by their effectiveness or maturity. Are some defense mechanisms more realistic, positive, or sensible than others? Can it confidently be said that the use of one defense mechanism as compared with another indicates greater or lesser rationality? Can any defense mechanism, with its apparent intent of denying or camouflaging troubling realities, contribute positively to one's adjustment or "mental health?"

Although Freud, the formal discoverer of defense mechanisms, generally took the position that they "weaken the ego," he occasionally referred to their positive, protective value (Sjoback, 1973; Vaillant, 1986). Interestingly, Freud (as well as Anna Freud) theorized that they provide developing children with a protective buffer against threats that might otherwise prove overwhelming. However, he considered their utilization beyond childhood as having largely negative implications. At times he hinted that defense mechanisms could be hierarchically classified, with denial, distortion, and projection representing the negative pole and sublimation, altruism, suppression, and humor representing the more positive (mature) pole (Vaillant, 1977). As one wades through the psychoanalytic literature, one finds all shades of opinion about the positive or negative consequences of defense mechanisms. Observers like Fenichel (1945) doubted that such mechanisms could, in the long run, be anything but "pathogenic." However, others like Lowenstein or Hartmann specifically spelled out their positive, protective potential (cited by Sjoback, 1973). More empirical researchers like Haan (1977) and Vaillant (1977) sharply distinguished mature from immature defense mechanisms and focus on the advantages of "realistic" adaptation; whereas others like Lazarus (1983) saw positive adaptive value in the illusory and even self-deceptive elements associated with the defense modes.

In 1989, Taylor, a social psychologist, published *Positive Illusions*, which included different levels of defenses that reshape reality. As indicated earlier, Taylor (1989) proposed that normal persons typically adopt illusory, defensive attitudes that unrealistically bolster their self-evaluations, increase their confidence and sense of personal control over events, and enhance their feelings of optimism. She portrayed such illusory exaggerations as being relatively limited and quite distinct from the more extreme distortions associated with the classical defense mechanisms. She focused particularly on the differences between normal illusory exaggeration and the phenomena associated with the classical "defense based on repression." Note her comment:

> Illusions are not simply particular forms of repression and denial. There are conceptual, theoretical, and empirical bases for making the distinction. Repression and denial alter reality, whereas illusions simply interpret it in the best possible light. Defense distorts the facts, leading people to hold misperceptions of internal or external reality. Through illusions, on the other hand, people make the most of bad situations by adopting a maximally positive perspective. (p. 126)

In other words, she felt that what she called illusory exaggeration was in a different class from the reality distortions associated with defense mechanisms. She defended her position by citing studies that contrast the correlates of "normal illusions" with those of a "repressive style." Thus, "repressors" are reported to differ from "normally illusory" individuals by being less physically healthy, less happy, less creative, less comfortable with self, less realistic in responding to threat, and less constructive in assimilating negative information. Taylor (1989) regarded normal illusory exaggeration as a way of attaining superior mental health. She was obviously committed to distinguishing good from bad ways of bending reality to one's psychological advantage. Her attitude paralleled the perspective that defense mechanisms fall into a superior–inferior hierarchy.

How convincing is Taylor's (1989) position? It is true that the literature she cited showed that persons who are formally defined as "repressors" do not fare as well as those who employ "normal illusions." However, the question immediately arises whether the entire range of defense mechanisms can be fairly represented by the one category labeled "repressors." The repressive mode is but one of a larger number. As Ihilevich and Gleser (1986) documented, there are other major defense mechanisms, which involve processes like intellectualization, projection, and turning hostility against self, that cannot be simplistically contained by the category "repressor." It is quite possible that persons who rely heavily on a defense mechanism like intellectualization ("principalization" in Ihilevich and Gleser's [1986] terms) cope with problems as well as those who, in Taylor's (1989) terms, utilize "normal" illusory enhancement. Indeed, the principalization mechanism has been demonstrated, in a number of empirical studies to be relatively highly effective (Ihilevich & Gleser, 1986).

One might wonder, too, whether there are not degrees of what Taylor (1989) called "normal illusory exaggeration;" and even within this normal range, there might be cutoff points beyond which the consequences are negative rather than positive. Baumeister (1989) discussed the question of an "optimal margin of illusion" at some length. He pointed out that "illusions can be harmful," particularly when they promote overestimating one's ability for and likelihood of success. He noted: "Judgments based on inflated views of self can lead to self-defeating processes" (p. 177). He cited data indicating, for example, that overoptimism can lead persons to persist unrealistically at unsolvable tasks. He referred also to studies showing that persons with inflated self-esteems are inclined to engage in "self-handicapping" strategies that provide them with a built-in excuse in case they fail at a task, but which could color their long-term adaptation negatively. In any case, the techniques available for measuring "normal illusory exaggeration" are still so simplistic and crude that it behooves one to be modest about offering scientific generalizations in this area.

Let us return to whether defense mechanisms are "pathogenic" and whether certain mechanisms are somehow superior to others. A considerable research literature pertinent to these matters is available, though it is quite a daunting task to untangle what this literature has to say.

The first issue one confronts in the array of publications relates to the diversities and validities of the techniques used to measure defense mechanism action. Defense mechanisms have been appraised by means of interviews (e.g., Vaillant, 1986), questionnaires (e.g., Plutchik, Kellerman, & Conte, 1979), projective tests (e.g., Blum, 1956; Cramer, 1979; Kline, 1987), semiprojective tests (e.g., Rosenzweig, 1945), and reviews of the longitudinal behaviors of individuals (e.g., Vaillant, 1977). Comparisons of these varied approaches have rarely, and certainly not systematically, been attempted. It is especially puzzling that a majority of the scientific studies has been based on questionnaires that call for persons to make judgments about their own defense behaviors (e.g., Bond & Vaillant, 1986; Ihilevich & Gleser, 1986). The concept of "defense mechanism" is, of course, rooted in a psychoanalytic scheme that locates, at unconscious levels, much of what presumably transpires during defense mechanism functioning. The question is whether most individuals have sufficient awareness of, or conscious insight about, their own defensive behaviors to bring valid information to their questionnaire replies. The few studies that have compared conscious and, to some degree, unconscious measures of defense mechanisms have revealed either quite low correlations (in the low to mid 20s) or none at all (e.g., Vaillant, 1986).

Heilbrun and Pepe (1985) provided us with the most sophisticated, in-depth probe into the relationship between conscious and unconscious aspects of the defense process. They created a laboratory situation in which subjects (male and female college students) were asked to judge whether a variety of adjectives were descriptive of their personalities, as contrasted to those of others. The defense modes aroused by this somewhat threatening task were measured by the ways in which subjects coped with their original judgments. For example, repression was evaluated by asking for recall of the original pool of adjectives and then determining to what degree negative adjectives, which had been applied to self, were forgotten. Projection was measured by ascertaining the ratio of unfavorable to favorable adjectives applied to others as compared with self. Other defenses (viz., rationalization, denial) were sampled with analogous strategies. Heilbrun and Pepe (1985) also had subjects rate how conscious they were of the degree to which they utilized each of the defense mechanisms. Finally, they obtained a rough self-report measure of symptoms that presumably reflected the degree to which one felt stressed.

In analyzing their data, they found no correlations between the extent to which subjects utilized a specific defense mechanism and their stated awareness of how much they employed that defense. Only in the case of repression was there a significant positive correlation between measured use of the mechanism and self-awareness of use. This correlation was .21 ($p < .05$), and only accounts for 4% of the common variance. This would suggest that the defense process, in this experimental context, was largely (but not completely) unconscious. Heilbrun and Pepe (1985) looked further to the link between subjects' awareness of their use of a specific defense mechanism and their apparent stress level. High projection without awareness was associated with relatively low stress. This was also true for high rationalization without awareness. But high repression without awareness was associated with a relatively high stress level; and subjects using denial with awareness reported relatively low stress.

Heilbrun and Pepe (1985) concluded: "Whether awareness *or* lack of awareness appears to exert an influence upon defensive behaviors depends upon the defense in question. Similarly, whether that apparent influence is associated with less stress or more stress . . . depends upon what defense is being considered" (p. 15). Overall, this study told us that conscious and unconscious measures of defense mechanisms have only tenuous overlap. It suggested, too, that degree of conscious awareness of one's use of a mechanism plays a mediating role in how successfully that mechanism will reduce stress. There were instances where awareness apparently increased stress, but there was also an instance in which it paradoxically decreased stress. Such complexity needs to be unraveled by future studies.

One must question whether measures (e.g., questionnaires) based on conscious awareness can adequately sample the defense mechanism process. On the other hand, in reviewing the multiple studies that have used the Ihilevich and Gleser (1986) Defense Mechanism Inventory, which is based on conscious choices concerning one's behavior in hypothetical situations, one finds a network of data that provide a reasonably interesting story concerning defense strategies. We have encountered this issue of conscious versus unconscious levels of response in previous chapters (e.g., with regard to the measurement of death anxiety). Actually, it is conceivable that measures of defense mechanisms based on questionnaires only peripherally tap the "true" defense modes and reflect a metanetwork of maneuvers to rationalize or give meaning to the limited awareness persons might have of how they remodel reality. When Ihilevich and Gleser (1986) reviewed most of the existing methods of measuring defense mechanisms, they concluded that all (except for the one they had devised) were seriously flawed. This points up the uncertainty prevailing in this realm.

The various defense mechanisms that have been isolated and labeled may not be as nicely demarcated as their separate names suggest. Ihilevich and Gleser (1986) and Cramer (1988) noted that the scores derived from the Defense Mechanism Inventory demonstrate fairly high correlations between turning against self and projection on the one hand, and between reversal and principalization on the other hand. Cramer (1988) stated, in the course of a review of the literature pertinent to the Defense Mechanism Inventory, that raters have considerable difficulty differentiating the test items presumably specific to either turning against others or projection.

Juni (1982) and Juni and Masling (1980) have concluded, on the basis of the available data, that the multiple dimensions of the Defense Mechanism Inventory actually represent a single continuum of the expression of aggression. The defenses at one pole (viz., turning against others and projection) are defined as facilitating the expression of aggression. The other end of the continuum (viz., reversal and principalization) is said to block or inhibit aggression. The five major defense mechanisms may be strategies that are so overlapping that it would not be sensible to arrange them in a differentiated, vertical hierarchy.

In any case, rather confusing results typify the research on the relative efficacies of the defense mechanisms. One cluster suggests the possibility of an effectiveness hierarchy, whereas another fails to do so. Vaillant (1977) and Ihilevich and Gleser (1986) presented the largest blocs of data that appear to support the hierarchy concept. Vaillant's (1977) major work, a longitudinal study of Harvard students, is cited widely. He used raters to evaluate the use of defense mechanisms in a sample of males who were first appraised at Harvard while still undergraduates and then again during subsequent years. The ratings were based on a spectrum of information that had accumulated for each individual. Vaillant (1977) categorized defenses within a multilevel schema extending from those involving "psychotic adaptation" (e.g., delusional projection) to those typical of "mature," "healthy" adults (e.g., sublimation). He reported significant positive relationships between the rated degree of maturity of defenses and various indices of social, psychological, and medical adjustment. Later, in a longitudinal study (Vaillant & Drake, 1985) of inner-city males that used a parallel methodology, a similar significant relationship was reported.

After critiquing these studies, we have serious reservations about them. Although one is assured by Vaillant (1977) that those who rated the maturity levels of the defense mechanisms were "blind" to the data defining adequacy of life adjustment, one gets contrary impressions after inspecting the experimental procedures. In the original Vaillant (1977) study of Harvard students, the raters of "maturity" based their judgments on a series of vignettes about how each individual had responded to past crises and conflicts. However, the raters also were supplied with a "one-page summary of each man's life-style" to provide an overall context for their conclusions. One such summary described in Vaillant's (1977) book is full of information that clearly leaks cues about that rated individual's ability to adapt (e.g., his carelessness in meeting obligations, his inability to attain goals, and the failure of his marriage.[3] Under the circumstances, one can hardly agree that the raters evaluated the maturity levels of the defense mechanisms "blindly."[4]

The same criticism applies to the methodology of the Vaillant and Drake (1985) longitudinal study of inner-city men. In fairness, one should note that, in a later study, Vaillant (1986) found a significant level of relationship, although quite low in magnitude, between the rated intensities of the individual's defense mechanisms and the intensities of such defenses, as defined by a questionnaire (developed by Bond, Gardner, Christian, & Sigal, 1983).[5] The questionnaire asked subjects how much they agreed with a series of statements referring to the use of, or belief in, specific defense mechanisms. Such data demonstrate that the ratings of the defense mechanisms bear some correspondence to what individuals declare about their own defenses on a questionnaire. Yet, the degree of relationship was so limited that ample room remains for the possibility that the ratings were originally contaminated by bias and therefore not acceptably objective. Haan (1977) also described a significant trend for persons in a longitudinal study, who were rated as using immature defenses, to be relatively more maladjusted than those rated as employing mature defenses. This was true even though low interrater reliabilities characterized the evaluations of several of the defenses.

Another major block of data supporting the notion of an effectiveness gradient for defense mechanisms comes from studies employing the Ihilevich and Gleser (1986) Defense Mechanism Inventory. As mentioned earlier, this questionnaire called for individuals to indicate how they think they would experience and react to a hypothetical series of stressful, frustrating situations. Numerous publications indicated that some of the defense mechanisms defined by Ihilevich and Gleser (1986) may be associated with better adjustment and mastery than are others. The so-called principalization defense (synonymous with "intellectualization" and "rationalization") is positively linked with elevated levels of self-esteem, emotional stability, ego strength, coping ability, adaptive functioning; and negatively linked with "symptom distress."

Contrastingly, the turning against self-defense is higher in psychiatric than

---

[3]It should be added that while the reported interrater reliabilities in judging maturity of defense mechanisms are overall in the 70s, they are at times very low or borderline for a number of individual defenses (e.g., sublimation and dissociation). It is noteworthy that Battista (1982) concluded, on the basis of a study of psychiatric patients, that the original maturity levels assigned by Vaillant (1977) to several of the defense mechanisms may be inaccurate.

[4]Indeed, in a later publication, Vaillant (1986) admitted, in the context of his methodology for securing judgments of the maturity levels of defense mechanisms, "There was no way of completely blinding the raters of defensive behavior from the behaviors underlying the ratings of the outcome variables" (p. 82).

[5]Data derived from this questionnaire and similar ones have, in the course of several studies (Battista, 1982; Bond, Gardner, Christian, & Sigal, 1983; Bond & Vaillant, 1986), shown that those individuals who described themselves as using immature defense mechanisms are significantly inclined to be in poorer "mental health" as measured by a variety of techniques.

nonpsychiatric populations and is positively (although not strongly) correlated with elevated levels of depression, anxiety, suicidal behavior, and diminished self-esteem. Analogous positive and negative correlates are differentially, but in largely inconsistent ways, associated with other defense mechanisms like projection, reversal, and turning against others. Overall, while principalization[6] stands out as a superior defense mechanism, the remainder of the mechanisms do not show clear, consistent differences among themselves. Surprisingly, Ihilevich and Gleser (1986) ultimately interpreted the accumulated data as unsupportive of Vaillant's (1977) idea that one defense is to be preferred to another. They felt that most investigators have found that moderate use of all defenses is the best way to attain optimal adjustment. They focused on "flexible use" of the entire array of available defenses, rather than specialization in a few presumably superior ones, as the best strategy for optimizing adaptation.

Approaching the whole issue from a different perspective, Suls and Fletcher (1985) provided a searching meta-analysis that points up the difficulties in classifying defense mechanisms as superior or inferior. They examined 43 studies in which it was possible to ascertain the mediating effects of "avoidant" versus "nonavoidant" coping strategies on the experience of a stressor. The avoidant strategies all involve focusing one's attention away from either the source of stress or from one's reactions to the stress. Of course, the nonavoidant strategies refer to just the opposite pattern. They would correspond to the supposedly more realistic defense modes. The stressors that were appraised across the 43 studies diversely involved such variables as cold pressor, childbirth, noise, threatening film, and shock. Outcome measures embraced ratings of distress, anxiety level, pulse, galvanic skin response, and pain sensations.

Suls and Fletcher's (1985) meta-analysis indicated that the avoidant and nonavoidant defense modes did not, overall, differ in effectiveness. But when the studies were separated into those that evaluated the impact of the stressor immediately and those with a longer follow-up, more complex results emerged. They stated: "Specifically, avoidance was more beneficial during the 3-day to 2-week interval after stressor onset. However, after that time, attentional (nonavoidant) strategies tended to be associated with more positive adaptation" (p. 279). The results matched a previous formulation by Lazarus (1983), which stated that persons may need to use "denial-like" tactics when initially confronting stress because the input may be "overwhelming." Presumably with time, active confrontation becomes more feasible and perhaps permits more realistic coping. The Suls and Fletcher (1985) findings

---

[6]It is ironic that whereas the Ihilevich and Gleser (1986) principalization dimension is portrayed as a superior defense mechanism, Cramer (1988) concluded, after a review of the literature, that it is among the most poorly validated.

were actually more complicated than conveyed by the brief summary provided. However, they highlighted the importance of context and matters of relativity in deciding whether one defense mode is superior to another. In a previous, wideranging review of the pertinent literature, Thompson (1981) also underscored the relativity of how effective defense modes are in mediating aversive events. For example, she pointed out that avoidant strategies decrease preoperative anxiety but result in more unfavorable postoperative attitudes; or that avoidant strategies increase tolerance to cold pressor pain but magnify anxiety during the anticipatory period.

Numerous studies are now available that document the shifting power of specific defense strategies as a function of a host of variables. Beginning at a simple level, there are gender differences with respect to which defenses are normatively most often utilized. Thus, turning against self (as defined by the Ihilevich and Gleser [1986] measure) most frequently characterizes women, whereas it is one of the least utilized by men. More specifically, we learn that a defense mechanism's effectiveness may shift in relation to such factors as age, socioeconomic level, type of stress impinging, method employed to measure the impact of the stress, individual's degree of psychological distress, perceived controllability of the stressor, and "perceived efficacy" of the defense mechanism.

Let us consider some illustrations of such mediating factors. We begin with a study that demonstrates the relativity introduced by age as a mediating variable. Dollinger and Cramer (1990) examined various defense mechanisms' effectiveness in moderating psychological disturbance in a sample of preadolescent boys. The boys had been traumatized by a tragedy (the death of one boy) that occurred as the result of lightning striking during a soccer game. Defense mechanism use was measured by objectively analyzing stories given in response to pictures in which lightning was part of the action. Among other findings, it was shown that the more individuals employed projection as a defense the less "clinically upset" they were by the lightning episode trauma. In this preadolescent group, projection served as a positive buffer. By way of contrast, Ihilevich and Gleser (1986) documented that the use of projection by adults tends to be associated with psychopathology and relatively poor adaptation.

Consider next a large-scale study by Menaghan (1982). She probed, by means of reliable interview procedures, the amount of difficulty and distress experienced by individuals in relation to their marital, parental, occupational, homemaking, and economic roles. She also determined the degree to which they used various defense mechanisms as they struggled with their problems. She ascertained that certain defense mechanisms, based on optimistic denial that facilitated adjustment in higher income and occupational categories, were significantly less successful in the lower categories. The value of such defense mechanisms depended on the economic-occupational status of the individuals involved.

Pearlin and Schooler (1978) observed in the same sample of boys that the defense mechanism's effectiveness varied as a function of the problem area to which it was applied. They stated:

> With relatively impersonal strains, such as those stemming from economic or occupational experiences, the most effective forms of coping involve the manipulation of goals and values in a way that psychologically increases the distance of the individual from the problem. On the other hand, problems arising from the relatively close interpersonal relations of parental and marital roles are best handled by coping mechanisms in which the individual remains committed to and engaged with relevant others. (p. 18)

To complicate matters further, Houston and Holmes (1974) discovered that the buffering effect of "avoidant thinking" upon threat depends on whether the measures of reaction to the threat are individuals' subjective self-reports or their physiological responses. These examples are but a few of a larger array that one can easily sift out of the pertinent literature.

The relativity of it all is highlighted, too, by the fact that a defense mode may not be what it appears to be. Felton and Revenson (1984) appraised the influence of coping strategies on adjustment to chronic illness. One of the coping strategies they measured was "information seeking"; this referred to patients doing things like looking up medical information about their illness. However, it became apparent that at times the information seeking was really a way of "diverting people's attention from pessimistic, distressing thoughts about their illness to more seemingly useful matters" (p. 351). In other words, the "information seeking" was a disguised form of denial and inattention.

One is reminded of the data presented by Rothbaum, Weisz, and Snyder (1982) indicating that very passive and even self-destructive modes of defense may be founded on the intent to control a threatening situation. For example, individuals may undermine the chances of their own success "so as to avoid rising expectations and subsequent disappointment" (p. 27). Rothbaum et al. (1982) provided a spectrum of examples of such camouflaged ways of securing "secondary control." What looks like passivity, giving up, or the absence of any defense may actually represent an organized, defensive plan. Norem and Cantor (1986) showed, in a laboratory context, how effective the apparently passive and ineffective strategies can be. Indeed, they also have demonstrated that interfering with self-destructive strategies can impact performance negatively.[7]

---

[7]Norem and Cantor (1986) noted:

> Attempts to change an apparently maladaptive or nonfunctional response set may have unexpected and undesired consequences if one ignores the potential cognitive/strategic value of that behavior. Thus, one can easily imagine an instructor who tries repeatedly to assure a student who defensively predicts he or she will perform poorly that in fact he or she will do "just fine" and there is nothing to worry about. If one considers that the encouragement provided in the experiment led to a decrease in performance, it seems clear that exhortations of the power of positive thinking may not always be particularly helpful. (p. 1216)

We are not in a position to declare that one defense mechanism is, in any general sense, "better" than another. To begin with, modesty about generalizations is demanded by the current inadequacies in our technology for measuring defense strategies. Second, the existing data can be read as contradictory and inconsistent. Finally, because the power of any particular defense mechanism depends on so many situational variables (e.g., age, type of stressor, socioeconomic status), it is unrealistic to speak in terms of any inherent or general effectiveness. We would also oppose Taylor's (1989) position that the so-called standard defense mechanisms are somehow inferior to the brands of "normal illusions" that are widely prevalent. Defense mechanisms and "normal illusions" seem to be allied modes in the larger repertory of techniques for giving life the right twist.[8]

DEVELOPMENTAL PATTERNS

Earlier we sketched in some detail how children learn to pretend. One might expect that the various defense mechanisms would anastomose the entire flesh of pretending. To what degree do children use defense mechanisms? Are there observable sequences in the timing or introduction of the various defense modes in the maturing child? Have gender differences been detected? Let us examine these questions.

By age 2, children already begin to deny socially undesirable feelings (Brody, Rozek, & Muten, 1985). There is fair agreement that as children acquire greater cognitive complexity they adopt more and more elaborate defense strategies (Schibuk, Bond, & Bouffard, 1989). Cramer (1983, 1987), in her surveys of the pertinent literature, concluded that repression, denial, and negation dominate the earliest childhood years, with projection and turning against the self following somewhat later. Then, at adolescence, the complex intellectualizing modes begin to flourish. In one of her own studies, Cramer (1987) established significant trends for three defense modes (denial, projection, and identification) to shift significantly over the age sequence represented by the following categories: preschool, elementary school, early adolescent, and late adolescent. With increasing age, denial decreased, identification increased, and projection was highest during elementary school and early adolescence.

Chandler, Paget, and Koch (1978) showed that children's understanding of defense mechanisms builds up in a gradual fashion. Six-year-olds lack an understanding of even the simplest defenses; 10-year-olds comprehend repression and denial; but only children who have arrived at the formal operational stage seem capable of grasping the nature of projection.

---

[8]The attempt to classify defense mechanisms into the more and less primitive (superior–inferior, effective–ineffective) reminds one of the endless difficulties that have arisen in assigning cultures to more and less primitive categories (e.g., Durkheim & Mauss, 1963).

Ihilevich and Gleser[9] (1986) presented a parallel picture in their summary of the age differences in scores derived from the Defense Mechanism Inventory.[10] However, despite such data, the overall findings on developmental changes in defense mechanisms are uneven and at times contradictory. Although some investigators reported sequential shifts, others found few such shifts. For example, Cramer (1983) reported (on the basis of Ihilevich and Gleser's (1986) Defense Mechanism Inventory) that children in Grades 1 and 2 differ little from those in Grades 4 and 5 with respect to choice of defense alternatives. The age groups did not differ for turning against object, projection, or reversal. There was a significant (but unpredicted) trend for younger children to use turning against self more often than the older ones. Relatedly, Gardner and Moriarty (1968) discerned no significant differences for use of various defense mechanisms among children in the age ranges of 6–9 and 13–14 years. Their measure of defense modes was based largely on the analysis of projective test (e.g., Rorschach) protocols. Interestingly, they concluded that by early adolescence individuals' defenses may have already attained an advanced stage of development.

Cramer (1983) suggested one reason that children may evolve increasingly complex defense mechanisms: because their own mounting cognitive sophistication makes it too easy for them to penetrate the deceptive elements of the simpler modes. With the maturing of cognitive powers during adolescence and beyond comes the potentiality for intellectual (principalization) camouflaging maneuvers of great depth and plexiform construction. Such intellectualization becomes one of the most powerful in the average individual's repertory. Incidentally, it bears repeating that children seem to make constructive use of defense mechanisms that have more negative connotations in the context of adult adjustment. As mentioned, Dollinger and Cramer (1990) determined that children traumatized by a disaster fare better if they utilize projection in defending against their anxiety. Reports concerning adults more often underscore the negative consequences of putting the blame "out there." The matter of developmental relativity with respect to defense mechanisms' effectiveness merits a good deal of further exploration.

Variations of the well-documented gender differences in defense mechanisms, which characterize adults, seem to appear in early adolescence. In adults,

---

[9]Ihilevich and Gleser (1986) noted:

Research findings support the notion that denial and aggression are among the earliest modes of defense to emerge in childhood. These modes of defense presumably reflect a child's early phases of cognitive development. At these stages of psychological development the child only attempts to obliterate, as it were, perceived threats. Denial functions as an internal mechanism of obliteration; aggression attempts to obliterate an external threat. (p. 79)

[10]Ihilevich and Gleser (1986) found that, across the life span, turning against others is negatively and reversal positively correlated with age. There is also a trend for principalization and turning against self to increase moderately with age.

as Ihilevich and Gleser (1986) and Cramer (1988) pointed out, there are fairly consistent trends for males to be higher than females on turning against others and projection, but lower on turning against self.[11] This pattern has been interpreted by some as indicating that males favor externalizing, whereas females lean toward internalizing defensive strategies.[12] Cramer (1979), who used the Ihilevich and Gleser (1986) Defense Mechanism Inventory to study 14- to 16-year-old boys and girls, reported a similar pattern. She determined that boys more often than girls significantly scored higher on turning against others and projection but lower on turning against self and principalization. She concluded: "Sometimes prior to early adolescent, males begin to externalize conflict, relying on projection and/or direct, overt aggression as defensive reactions. Females, on the other hand, begin to rely on defenses that internalize the conflict, primarily through directing aggression inward" (p. 477).

In a later study, Cramer (1983) compared samples of 7- to 10-year-old boys and girls, with respect to their defense modes. They were asked to indicate how they would deal with a series of video-presented vignettes of unpleasant life situations. Younger boys (age 7) gave significantly more turning against other responses than did girls, but the difference for the older subjects (age 10) was not significant. The gender differences for projection and turning against self were not significant. However, younger (but not older) girls gave significantly more reversal responses than did boys. In still another study, Cramer (1987) utilized Thematic Apperception Test stories to measure defense mechanisms in 5- to 13-year-old boys and girls. Males used projection significantly more than females. There was also a significant trend for females to utilize denial[13] (e.g., denial of reality, minimizing the negative) more than males. There were no gender differences for identification (e.g., self-esteem through affiliation). Cramer (1987) construed these results to mean that the male children relied on externalizing defenses more than did the female children.

But when Noam and Recklitis (1990) probed (with the Ihilevich and Gleser, 1986, Defense Mechanism Inventory), they discerned no gender differences in the defenses of adolescents in a psychiatric hospital (largely for conduct and anxiety disorders). They were puzzled by the lack of gender differences and vaguely attributed it to the subjects being psychiatric patients. Gardner and Moriarty (1968) ascertained defense modes from the projective protocols

---

[11]Noam and Recklitis (1990) suggested that principalization may be used more by females than males. However, Ihilevich and Gleser (1986) denied that there are consistent gender differences for principalization (or reversal).

[12]Cramer (1979) reported that there are a number of researchers who regard the scores derived from the Defense Mechanism Inventory (Ihilevich & Gleser, 1986) as falling on a single continuum that represents externalizing versus internalizing defenses.

[13]Pearlin and Schooler (1978) also found that the response repertoire of women often emphasizes "selective ignoring."

(e.g., Rorschach, Thematic Apperception Test) of boys and girls, ages 9–13. They found that the boys "tend toward greater use of isolation, reaction formation, and denial; whereas, girls tend toward greater use of repression" (p. 185). They interpreted this to be congruent with the fact that "repression is used more pervasively by females . . . ; whereas, the syndrome of isolation, reaction formation, and projection is more common in males" (p. 186).

Although the reviewed data are not smoothly consistent, they do suggest that, by early adolescence, the two genders differ in defense modes in a fashion roughly analogous to the adult pattern.

CORRELATES OF DEFENSE MECHANISMS IN THE LARGER PERSONALITY ECONOMY

We have discussed defense mechanisms in a quasidisembodied way. That is, little has been said about whether the use of specific mechanisms goes with particular personality configurations. Early psychoanalytic theorists such as Freud, Abraham (Fisher & Greenberg, 1985), and others (e.g., Shapiro, 1965) conceived of persons displaying trait-like consistency in their reliance on specific defense modes. Furthermore, they thought that certain character structures and forms of psychopathology were associated with each mode. Repressive defenses have been seen as basic to hysterical symptoms; projection tied to a paranoid orientation; intellectualization (isolation) linked to obsessive-compulsive traits and forms of psychological disturbance; and intrapunitive (turn against self) strategies contributing to depression.

Various studies provide evidence that, although there is substantial situational determination of defense modes, moderately high individual consistencies also prevail. Illustratively, Ihilevich and Gleser (1986) and Cramer (1988) reported that the Defense Mechanism Inventory is typified by test–retest coefficients in the middle to high .70s, when a 2- to 4-week period intervenes between test and retest. With respect to longer intervening periods (6 to 8 weeks), the data are more sparse, but test–retest coefficients probably fall in the low .70s or high .60s. Use of the major defense mechanisms does show some trait-like characteristics.

The greater share of the solid, cross-validated data on personality correlates of specific defense modes is based on the Ihilevich and Gleser (1986) Defense Mechanism Inventory. Most of the findings fall within four domains: perceptual style, locus of control, self-esteem, and masculinity–femininity.

Perceptual style relates to the concept of field independence–dependence as formulated by Witkin, Dyk, Faterson, Goodenough, and Karp (1962). Degree of field independence is defined by one's ability to accurately judge spatial position where only a few realistic cues are available and conflicting cues have been introduced. Rather consistent research reports (Cramer, 1988;

Ihilevich & Gleser, 1986) indicated that persons who are more skilled in making spatial judgments (field independent) are likely to score relatively high on turning against others, projection, and, perhaps, principalization. Those who are less skilled in making spatial judgments (field dependent) score higher on turning against self and reversal.

The locus of control dimension, as spelled out earlier, refers to how much one attributes contingency to one's own efforts (internal), as contrasted to forces "out there" that are independent of self (external). Much of the data is based on the Rotter (1966) questionnaire measure. Those high on internal locus of control tend to be high on principalization and reversal, whereas those externally oriented tend to be high on turning against others and projection (Ihilevich & Gleser, 1986).

Self-esteem has been linked with specific defense mechanisms in several studies (Ihilevich & Gleser, 1986). In general, higher self-esteem is linked with elevated principalization and reversal, whereas lower self-esteem is correlated with turning against self.[14]

Various indices of masculinity–femininity are significantly correlated with the defense modes. In summarizing this literature, Cramer (1988) indicated that, for both men and women, turning against self and reversal are correlated with a feminine orientation, whereas turning against others is tied to a masculine stance. For men alone, projection is correlated with masculinity.[15]

Across the four domains just reviewed, principalization seems to be fairly consistently associated with an independent, self-reliant, and self-confident attitude. The opposite pattern applies to turning against self. No consistencies are apparent for turning against self, reversal, or projection.

Here and there one finds hints that consistent use of defense mechanisms can be traced to specific socialization patterns. The pertinent reports are scattered and fragmentary. Consider a few illustrations. Block (1971) found, in the course of a longitudinal study, that women who are repressive of self ("hysterically bland") have mothers who lack verbal facility, are mentally slow, and exhibit little curiosity. Their fathers are depicted as "enervated," blocking of independence, and affectionately "seductive." Block (1971) also described "self-deceiving," self-repressive males as having mothers who are undemonstrative and lacking spirit, spontaneity, and "intellectual dash." Their fathers are portrayed as lacking spontaneity and being "domineering."

Kagan and Moss (1962) observed, in their longitudinal study, that women who "withdraw" in the face of stress display consistent passivity during child-

---

[14]Turning against others is positively linked with a tendency to be dominant and recognition-seeking. Principalization is also positively correlated with assertiveness (Ihilevich & Gleser, 1986).

[15]There are other scattered and sometimes puzzling findings, for example, linking "memory constriction" to high scores on reversal and principalization (Cramer, 1988), low dream recall to high scores on reversal (Cramer, 1988), and high self-deception to low authoritarianism (Monts, Zurcher, & Nydegger, 1977).

hood (ages 6–14). Miller and Swanson (1966) discerned heightened use of denial in adolescents whose parents were most severe, provided few explanations for their requests, and offered only occasional rewards. Haan (1977) indicated, among a variety of other observations, that "defensive girls" had defensive fathers but not defensive mothers. These diverse findings are too sparse to permit construction of an explanatory framework that would approach defense mechanisms in terms of their socialization origins. However, the fact that some significant relationships have been uncovered offers hope for future exploration in this area.

CONCLUDING THOUGHTS

The concept of "defense mechanism" has been a major point of entree into the phenomenology of illusory strategies. Although some (e.g., Taylor, 1989) separated normal illusion construction from the use of defense mechanisms, it is doubtful that such a distinction can be sustained reasonably. Defense mechanisms and illusory exaggeration are both ways of shielding oneself from unpalatable glimpses of the world. We regard the two adaptive modes as overlapping, fusing, and, in many instances, indistinguishable. How, for example, can a mild form of exaggeration of one's abilities wrapped in principalization be distinguished from the "normal" illusory pumping up of one's own self-evaluation? To make the fine distinctions that Taylor (1989) proposed goes beyond the technologies available for measuring defense mechanisms and illusory notions. There are conflicting ideas and techniques concerning how best quantitatively to tap into such domains.

One of the larger unsettled questions is whether the most important phenomena in such realms occur at conscious or unconscious levels. Can we truly determine what defense mechanisms or illusory exaggerations typify persons by asking what they consciously know (usually via a questionnaire) about them? We have already reviewed data indicating that measures based on conscious reports correlate minimally with those tuned to unconscious expressions. The original psychoanalytic theoretical model, from which the core ideas about defense mechanisms were derived, was permeated with the idea that it was all largely unconscious. Is it not paradoxical to assume that fundamentally self-deceptive strategies can be accurately accessed through the eyes of those who are supposedly successfully fooling themselves? While some investigators (e.g., Cramer, 1987; Gardner & Moriarty, 1968; Vaillant, 1977) have tuned into the unconscious side, they have been in the minority; unfortunately, in some cases, their research designs have been vulnerable to experimenter bias. The unconscious level has been neglected and, in many cases, simply ignored. However, as indicated earlier, the research findings derived from the use of questionnaires (e.g., Ihilevich & Gleser, 1986,

Defense Mechanism Inventory) have shown considerable consistency. They also have presented meaningful information about such defense mechanism matters as gender differences, psychopathological correlates, and externalizing versus internalizing expressive patterns. If the conscious level of data concerning defense mechanisms is so superficial, how is it possible for consistency and meaningfulness of this sort to emerge?

One can only speculate about this matter. Perhaps we underestimate the extent to which persons do, over an extended period of self-observation, gain an awareness of their own defense modes. They may, at any given point in time, when actively immersed in a defense effort, not be able to perceive how they are protecting and deceiving themselves; but possibly, as they repeatedly accumulate self-observations, they begin to build up some awareness of their own personal defense style. It is such accumulated knowledge that might be reflected in the meaningful patterns that have surfaced in the literature based on questionnaires.

An overlapping possibility is that when questionnaires call for individuals to introspect about their own defense modes, this constitutes a threatening probe that mobilizes coverup maneuvers designed to integrate and render, at least superficially, acceptable what one is able to glimpse of one's own defense mechanisms. If so, scores based on a questionnaire such as the Defense Mechanism Inventory would be a composite of whatever awareness persons can muster about their own defenses, plus an overlay of camouflaging tactics to keep oneself comfortable with that potentially unacceptable awareness.

For example, a woman who glimpsed that she was inclined to use turning against others to a heightened degree might disguise this tendency by exaggerating how much she utilizes some other defense mechanism (e.g., turning against self). Women may obtain elevated turning against self scores because they feel it would be unacceptable (antifeminine) to acknowledge the full extent of their use of hostility toward others (turning against others), and are therefore pulled to take defensive refuge in the feminine masochistic stereotype. Perhaps there are consistencies in such camouflaging tactics that result in Defense Mechanism Inventory scores, even in their compensatory forms, being regularly correlated with certain classes of variables (e.g., femininity, self-esteem). However, to the extent that such camouflaging processes occur, it would probably minimize the correlations of Defense Mechanism Inventory scores with validity criteria.

We conclude from the literature dealing with defense modes that the various defense mechanisms cannot be arranged reliably in a hierarchy of maturity. There is a great deal of relativity with respect to the potency of the defense mechanisms. Apparent effectiveness shifts as a function of such multiple factors as gender, age, socioeconomic status, and the nature of the stressor experienced. Effectiveness is mediated, too, by the degree to which the quandary being defended against can best be dealt with by modifying a

condition external to self or modulating one's interpretation of that condition. In some hopeless situations (e.g., terminal illness), the classically "most
mature" defenses may be worthless and the most primitive afford the best
chance of maintaining a workable psychological equilibrium. There probably are standard situations in which the classically mature defenses are particularly powerful. However, life is full of nonstandard predicaments. As some
have suggested, successful adaptation requires not simply specialization in
certain "mature defenses" but rather the capacity to call on a flexible
repertoire.

Idealized notions about what it takes to have "good mental health," which
were originally psychoanalytically inspired and advocated by investigators
like Vaillant (1977), have insisted that certain modes of cushioning reality
are better than others. Although it is true that blatantly psychotic mechanisms are universally regarded as inferior, little scientific support exists for
consistently exalting one mechanism over any of the others. "Good mental
health" cannot be defined by specialization in specific defense mechanisms.
One must acknowledge that the use of several mechanisms, especially principalization, tends to be positively correlated with various measures of good
adjustment, but these correlations are of low magnitude. The existing data
do not justify therapists advising persons in distress to rely more on certain
defense mechanisms than on others.

One is reminded of work (e.g., Norem & Cantor, 1986; Rodin, Rennert,
& Solomon, 1980) concerned with individuals who defend themselves against
the possibility of failure by downplaying their own power and predicting that
they will not do well. Such a "self-handicapping" stance certainly does not
fit the usual images of "healthy adjustment." However, this mode of defense
does help control anxiety and maintain an adequate level of performance.
Consider, too, Bulman and Wortman's (1977) report that persons who experienced severely disabling accidents coped better if they blamed themselves
(usually unrealistically) for what had happened. This form of self-attack provided a necessary (and yet obviously illogical) sense of having been somehow
responsible for, and therefore in control of, the whole catastrophic sequence.
It is remarkable how long it has taken theorists and researchers to stop treating defense mechanisms as forms of psychopathology. Only in recent years
have we realized, largely as the result of the perspicacity of social psychologists, that defense modes provide an anlage for normal, everyday living. Apparently, we all require a range of defensive buffers to modulate ever-
recurrent stresses and threats.

CHAPTER

8

HOW DO MAKE-BELIEVE AND PSYCHOPATHOLOGY INTERSECT?

As we already documented, it is difficult to label specific forms of illusion construction as less mature or more pathological than others. Our own inclination is to assume that normal pretending flows imperceptibly into what is regarded as psychopathological distortion. Indeed, we would say, as have others (e.g., Sarbin & Mancuso, 1980; Szasz, 1961), that the difference between "normal illusion" and "crazy" elaboration is often embarrassingly hazy.

To explore the intersection of make-believe and serious "reality distortion," we set several goals in this chapter. First, we analyze cogent observations bearing on the matter of differences between normal modes of illusory fabrication and those typifying persons who are considered psychopathological. How well can we distinguish psychologically "normal" from "pathological" modes? Second, we examine the relationship between the ability to conjure up illusory images and the likelihood of developing clinical levels of psychopathology. Does facility in constructing the illusory render one more or, to the contrary, less susceptible to extreme forms of personal disorganization? Last, we are interested in the possibility that various types of psychotherapeutic treatments represent systems for providing alternative, substitute forms of supportive illusion.

PROBLEMS OF IDENTIFYING AND CLASSIFYING "MENTAL ILLNESS"

Anyone who has, in the real world, attended clinical case conferences concerned with diagnosing psychiatric patients knows the uncertainty attending such decisions. It is an unusual occasion when easy agreement concerning diagnosis occurs. There are often disagreements about whether patients belong in a specific diagnostic category as compared with another, as well as whether they are psychotic or not. One's subjective impression is that the criteria for pinpointing "mental illness" are operationally difficult to apply. A fair amount of empirical evidence supportive of this point is available. There is a spate of publications concerning the reliability (and validity) of psychiatric diagnostic schemes. While only a few continue to extol the reliability of diagnoses, as they were spelled out prior to the more recent formulation of the *Diagnostic and Statistical Manual of Mental Disorders* (*DSM*) classification system, stout defenders of the various versions of the *DSM* rules abound (e.g., American Psychiatric Association, 1980; Spitzer, Endicott, & Robins, 1978).

But others (e.g., Eysenck, Wakefield, & Friedman, 1983; Hanada & Takahashi, 1983; Lieberman & Baker, 1985) have published telling critiques that raise serious doubts about the true reliabilities of *DSM* classificatory judgments. Eysenck et al. (1983) declared: "The fact that the categories of the scheme (in *DSM-III*) can be diagnosed only in a manner which results in unacceptable low reliabilities . . . is only one of many indications of the weakness of current psychiatric theorizing . . ." (p. 189). Kutchins and Kirk (1986) have, after an exhaustive analysis of the pertinent data, concluded that the official interrater reliabilities of *DSM-III* were spuriously inflated and are, in actuality, generally below acceptable scientific standards. If they are correct, the ambitious and intensive attempt by the American Psychiatric Association (1980) to fashion a dependable psychiatric diagnostic system has floundered.

The very validity of the *DSM* classificatory system also has been attacked. Investigators have questioned whether there are any consistent independent categories of symptom clusters that correspond to the *DSM* diagnoses. Further, the point has been made that the *DSM* categories have no significant consequences for such variables as prognosis, optimum modes of treatment, or etiology (e.g., Colby & Spar, 1983; Sarbin & Mancuso, 1980). If such is true, this would strengthen skepticism about the *DSM* enterprise. Bentall, Jackson, and Pilgrim (1988) have convincingly argued that "schizophrenia" cannot be scientifically justified as a valid diagnostic entity. There are champions of both the negative and positive poles of the dispute over whether psychiatric diagnoses are sensible and reliable. It is impressive that, after so many years of research, such polarized differences of opinion can still exist. This suggests that the underlying "facts" are ambiguous and unstable; and this, in turn, implies that the process of "psychiatrically sorting" what is abnormal from normal involves a good deal of uncertainty. While the blatantly psychotic can, in many instances, be differentiated from the normal range, most other diagnostic decisions are problematic.

The uncertainty and awkwardness of psychiatric diagnosis arise, in part, from the illogical assumption that the pathological and nonpathological are dichotomous. The patient is typically classified as either schizophrenic or not,

as either delusional or not. The pathological and nonpathological are deemed
to be qualitatively distinct. However, solid data indicate that continuum rather
than dichotomy best describes the relationship of the normal to the psychopathological (e.g., Eysenck et al., 1983; Strauss, 1969). It is often difficult
to decide whether an idea is delusional or not. Indeed, even judging whether
an apparent hallucination is really a hallucination may be problematic at times.
Strauss (1969) indicated, in his study of psychiatric patients, that raters had
difficulty deciding, in one third of the descriptive reports, whether there was
a "definite delusion" present. Raters showed similar difficulty distinguishing
"questionable" from "definite" hallucinations. Strauss (1969) offered some examples of the ambiguities encountered. If an individual declares "The Devil
seems to be trying to get me to do bad things," the possibility that this is
a delusional notion will depend, in part, on how religious one judges the individual to be. If a seriously depressed woman reiterates that she is responsible for someone's death, how is this to be distinguished from the normal guilt
of someone who fought with a parent just before that parent's fatal heart
attack? If one believes one can foretell the future, is this a greater distortion
that if one believes zodiac signs can predict fate?

Several studies (e.g., Chadwick & Lowe, 1990; Hole, Rush, & Beck, 1979)
showed that persons with blatantly delusional ideas may vary, from day to
day, in their certainty about these ideas. Delusions are not an all-or-none
phenomenon. They are multidimensional (Kendler, Glazer, & Morgenstern,
1983). They may simultaneously vary in conviction, degree of intrusion into
the individual's behavior, intensity with which they are centrally preoccupy-
ing, bizarreness, and structural "internal consistency." Such dimensions, which
are descriptive of specific delusions, have rather low intercorrelations (e.g.,
Brett-Jones, Garety, & Hemsley, 1987). Several researchers (e.g., Chadwick
& Lowe, 1990; Hole et al., 1979) dramatized the fluidity of delusions by confronting individuals with factual contradictions in their delusional ideas. This
resulted in modifications and even renunciation (incidentally, with no apparent resultant "symptom replacement"). The concept that delusions are fixed
and immovable probably reflects previous observations, which have been
narrowly confined to long-term chronic patients. Chadwick and Lowe (1990)
suggested that, all too frequently, delusions persist because the individuals
involved do not make serious efforts to check their validity against the immediately available evidence. However, they noted: "that failure to test a
belief is a charge that could equally well be leveled at the non-clinical population" (p. 231). That is, the maintenance of delusional ideas involves mechanisms not terribly unlike those that foster the rigidity of normal belief systems.

Even the most extreme psychopathological modes are not simple all-
or-none phenomena. This is paralleled by the frequent occurrence of what
is stereotypically regarded as psychopathological in apparently well-adjusted
normal persons. More and more studies find that if normal persons are ap-

propriately questioned, they will reveal a surprising acquaintance with experiences that were once thought to be linked with psychosis. For example,
Posey and Losch (1983–1984) distributed a questionnaire on hallucinatory
experiences to 374 college students. The questionnaire presented 14 different examples of auditory hallucinations and inquired whether the subjects thought any were applicable to themselves. Seventy-one percent of
the sample reported at least some brief auditory hallucinations in wake-
ful situations. Note the following personal confessions by various individuals in the sample: "I had a big test, but had stayed up late studying. I
was tired and didn't want to get up. The voice said: 'You know you'll feel
worse if you stay in bed' " (p. 102); "Sometimes when I do something wrong,
or am about to do something wrong, or am not doing something I'm supposed to do, I can hear a sweet voice from my mother telling me to do
it or not to do it" (p. 106); "I'm scared of driving at night and I sometimes
hear something or someone telling me to slow down and take it easy"
(p. 105).

Five percent of the sample said they had had extreme experiences[1] that
paralleled the following: "Almost every morning while I do my homework,
I have a pleasant conversation with my dead grandmother. I talk to her and
quite regularly hear a voice actually alive" (p. 105).

Eleven percent agreed that they had had an experience analogous to the
following example: "I have heard God's voice . . . not that he made me know
in my heart . . . but as a real voice" (p. 104).

Slade and Bentall (1988) described the accumulated literature on normals
having psychoticlike experiences.[2] They were impressed by the number of
reports indicating presumably abnormal hallucinations occurring in normal
individuals. They stated: "It seems clear . . . that many more people . . . have
the capacity to hallucinate than a strictly medical model implies should be
the case" (p. 76). They also reviewed the literature indicating the considerable effectiveness of various induced attitudes (e.g., hypnosis) in motivating normal individuals to have unreal experiences that attain hallucinatory
intensity. Even a simple suggestion has been shown, in some instances, to
stimulate imaginative imagery that seems "real." It is noted, too, that when
normal subjects are exposed to sensory isolation, some may eventually report
vivid hallucinations that disappear as soon as they emerge from the isolation
condition.[3]

---

[1]Andrade, Srinath, and Andrade (1989) reported that hallucinations occur in psychiatric patients in nonpsychotic states.

[2]Fisher (1989) presented the surprising observation that psychopathological modes can, in
the appropriate circumstances, become a model for normal social behavior.

[3]Heilbrun and Brown (1978) described an experiment that demonstrated that normal subjects in a laboratory situation designed to encourage delusional forms of thought did, in fact,
evidence certain delusionlike modes when asked to "fabricate ideation."

Several observers reported that there is, within the normal adaptive range, a subset of persons labeled "fantasy prone personalities." These persons are strongly motivated to engage in fantasy for extended periods, to have psychic and "out-of-body" experiences, and to vividly hallucinate objects. The "fantasy prone" revel in the imaginative and the unreal and boldly open themselves to "deviant" perceptions. Rhue and Lynn (1987) intensively studied a sample of such individuals (college students) and concluded that they "did not appear to have manifest problems in reality testing" (p. 135). The "fantasy prone," who have such fascination with the perceptually unreal, could not be distinguished from a normal control group, either with respect to their academic grades or the judged reality levels of their responses to the Rorschach inkblots.

Overall, there is excellent evidence that normal, well-adjusted persons can and do have perceptual experiences that were once thought to characterize only the deranged. They are capable of opening themselves to "distortions of reality." There is a substantial shared border region between the normal and the psychopathological. Incidentally, the relatively good adjustment of the "fantasy prone" reminds one of earlier cited (e.g., Caird, 1987) findings, in which persons who reported mystical and religious experiences of unusual intensity (often hallucinatory in quality) were not deviant as defined by various psychometric measures of adjustment.

The problem of distinguishing psychologically "normal" from "pathological" modes is further dramatized when one takes a cross-cultural perspective. Indeed, even within the subcultures of any Western industrial nation, there are fairly radical variations in what is regarded as psychologically normal. Consider the apparent degree of deviance of glossolalia when perceived in the context of a Southern fundamentalist gathering, as compared with a staid New England Episcopalian congregation. There is debate as to whether there are forms of disturbance that are unique to certain cultures (e.g., Oltmanns & Maher, 1988; Westermeyer, 1985); some (e.g., Westermeyer, 1987) are convinced that, even though cultural differences can be demonstrated, there is still commonality to the major psychopathological syndromes as they appear across cultures. Basically, moderate agreement exists that cultures put characteristic twists on the contents of delusional ideas (Ndetei & Vadher, 1984; Oltmanns & Maher, 1988) and elicit specific "psychopathological" syndromes (e.g., Maylasian *latah*, Chinese *koro*) that are somewhat singular but not unique (Westermeyer, 1987).

Interpretations of hallucinations' pathogenicity are known to vary sharply in different cultures. In some groups, hallucinating does not have negative connotations and, in fact, is sought by a variety of methods (e.g., drugs, sleep deprivation). To hallucinate is regarded not as an abnormality, but rather as a means of achieving certain aims (e.g., self-knowledge). In contrast, most Western cultures regard hallucinating as scary, abnormal, to be avoided, and a prominent sign of "craziness." To hallucinate is to signal mental deviance. However, as Al-Issa (1977) noted: "In less rational cultures where the distinction between reality and fantasy is more flexible, individuals are encouraged to observe their hallucinations, imagery, and other private events. Since these experiences are positively valued in relation to individual and group daily activities, they tend to be frequently noticed and communicated to others . . . the experience (of hallucinating) is not anxiety-arousing or disturbing to the individual" (p. 577). Psychiatrists from technically developed countries show relatively poor reliability in their diagnostic judgments about psychiatric patients from developing countries (Oltmanns & Maher, 1988). This may be due to their poor understanding of, and lack of tolerance for, ideas and concepts (e.g., sorcery, ghosts, animistic forces in nature) prevalent in such locales.

As mentioned, a cultural relativistic perspective alerts one to the possibility that, in certain contexts within a given culture, an apparently deviant mode of behavior is pathological but less so in other contexts. Swartz (1985) presented an interesting analysis of anorexia nervosa that touches on this point. She noted that anorectiform symptoms are unusually common in women who seek careers that involve self-display, such as modeling and ballet dancing. She suggested that, because the symptoms are more normative in this sense, they would have less pathological significance than when they occurred in women who are not in body-focused occupations. One might expect there to be different dynamic factors underlying the etiology of anorectiform symptoms in the one category, as compared with the other. It is easy to think of other analogous subcultural relativities. For example, does delinquent behavior signal the same degree of disturbance when it occurs in an individual reared in a neighborhood where delinquent acts are common as it does in someone whose subculture does not tolerate delinquent acts? We already noted that the expression of ideas about being in personal contact with God may indicate quite different degrees of disturbance in the fervently religious, as compared with nonbelievers.

The several themes touched on above convey the essential problems that exist in differentiating the normal from the psychopathological. There is a good deal of uncertainty in applying diagnostic categories, with respect to validity and reliability. Not only does psychiatric deviance fall on a fluid, shifting continuum, but normality also embraces variations that look like what is often labeled as abnormal. The relativity of judgments about psychopathology is particularly highlighted when one takes a cross-cultural perspective. As one wades through the enormous literature on the nature of the boundaries between what is psychologically normal versus abnormal, one is hard pressed to find much consensus. Every possible position has been formulated and defended; and in the end one sees a surprising amount of vagueness and confusion.

DOES MAKE-BELIEVE BUFFER
OR INTENSIFY PSYCHOPATHOLOGY?

In an earlier chapter, we surveyed information indicating that depressed persons may have arrived at their disturbed state because they were somehow unable to conjure up the positive optimistic illusions that typify and defend the nondepressed. As described, the depressed are, in certain ways, more realistic than the nondepressed in their judgments. They see things more darkly, but this apparently reflects their sometimes greater accuracy. We do not mean to imply that depression is solely or primarily due to a lesser ability to be illusorily optimistic, but only that this lesser ability is significantly contributory. In any case, the research concerning "depressive realism" indicated that optimistic make-believe can have a buffering, antipsychopathological function.

As previously noted, Taylor (1989) integrated the "depressive realism" findings with data from a number of other areas and boldly argued that adequate mental health requires "positive illusions" and "creative self-deception." She stated: "The healthy mind is a self-deceptive one" (p. xi). In discussing the treatment of serious depression, she declared that the best strategy is not to make the depressed more realistic but to help them construct "cognitive illusions so that they can think more positively about themselves, the world, and the future, employing the mildly inflated biases that normal people characteristically use" (p. 220).[4] She systematically perused a number of the major mental health criteria (e.g., happiness, productivity, creativity) and documented that they are fostered by the presence of "positive illusions." The empirical data she mustered for her position are quite impressive. However, we already commented on the dilemma she encountered when she tried to draw a strict line between the kinds of illusions that are mildly positive and supportive of mental health and other illusion-producing "defense mechanisms," which are presumably more primitive and rigid and therefore have negative effects on mental health. We are skeptical, considering the present state of knowledge about the defensive value of illusion, that one can confidently differentiate "good" from "bad" illusory strategies.

One of the most direct affirmations of illusion's positive role in countering psychological disturbance comes from the work of Sackeim and his associates (e.g., Sackeim, 1983; Sackeim & Gur, 1978, 1979). They constructed an instrument (The Self-Deception Questionnaire) to detect individual differences in the inclination to engage in self-deceptive strategies. This questionnaire

---

[4]Taylor's (1989) underlying conviction about the illusory nature of adaptation is splendidly conveyed by a quote from George Vaillant, which she placed at the head of one of her book's subsections: "Cannot (mental) health merely be a form of madness that goes unrecognized because it happens to be a good adaptation to reality?" (p. 244).

consists of items, the positive endorsements of which were considered to be universally true but psychologically threatening. Two examples of such items are as follows: "Do you ever feel guilty?" and "Have you ever made a fool of yourself?" When applied to a sample of college students who had also responded to several measures of psychopathology (Beck Depression Inventory, Eysenck Personality Inventory, Manifest Symptom Questionnaire), it was found that the greater the self-deception scores, the smaller the psychopathology scores (for all three indices of psychological disturbance). In 1979, Sackeim and Gur thought the best explanation for these findings was that the more "self-deceived" show a response bias by concealing their reports of psychopathology. But, in a later context, Sackeim (1983) changed his mind and came to regard such self-deceptive modes as important, positive defenses. He said (1983), with regard to the earlier "response bias" interpretation: "The possibility looms large that these findings do not reflect simply a report bias. In normal samples, people who typically utilize self-deception to a relatively greater degree actually may be subject to less depressed affect, anxiety, worry, obsessional thoughts, and other symptomatology than others who less typically distort" (p. 150). He cautiously added: "We would entertain the view that in at least some populations, or across some range, degree of self-deception and use of other distortive mechanisms . . . are positively associated with psychological health" (p. 140).

Sackeim (1983) highlighted the disparity between self-deception as a buffer against psychological disturbance and the classical psychoanalytic position that mental health is optimized only in those who banish distortion and face "reality" without reservation.[5] Presumably, greater self-knowledge leads to better adjustment. Within this psychoanalytic theoretical frame, happiness is inverse to the frequency of use of repressive and distorting defense mechanisms. Sackeim (1983) pointed out that this perspective assumes that "all defensive operations involve instinctual renunciation" (p. 121) and ignores the fact that distortion may be used to gratify impulses. It does not reckon with the alternative that "self-deception may, at times, result in greater possibilities of happiness than accurate self-representation" (pp. 121–122). Sackeim (1983) went so far as to suggest:

> When self-deceptions are not fear based but only pleasure oriented, their undoing in the course of therapy can only result in a reduction in the possibilities for happiness of the patient. Indeed, stating the converse, it is conceivable that some psychological disorders may result from an inability to use self-deception strategies to promote the experience of pleasure. Effective therapy might entail helping patients acquire self-deceptive strategies so as to maintain an adequate level of self-esteem or mood. (p. 122)

---

[5]Sackeim (1983) quoted Freud as follows: "Finally, we must not forget that the relationship between analyst and patient is based on a love of truth, that is, on the acknowledgment of reality, and it precludes any kind of sham or deception" (p. 121).

Study of the use of comforting beliefs to preserve oneself in the face of disturbance of serious proportions is just beginning. Some interesting explorations have been attempted in the area of suicide. Linehan, Goodstein, Nielsen, and Chiles (1983) constructed The Reasons for Living Inventory, which lists a variety of reasons for not committing suicide. Subjects are asked to rate each for its importance as a current rationale for not committing suicide. One of the major categories of beliefs (survival and coping beliefs) consists largely of optimistic statements concerning the future (e.g., "I believe everything has a way of working out for the best," "No matter how badly I feel, I know that it will not last"). Such statements obviously represent wishful forecasts. Individuals who had contemplated or actually attempted suicide were particularly well differentiated by their lack of endorsement of the "I know all will be well" sentiments. Linehan et al. (1983) concluded that one way to reduce the incidence of suicide would be to get suicidal persons to believe and attach importance to an array of wishful, optimistic assertions.

Cole (1989) used The Reasons for Living Inventory to study the mediating role of survival-coping beliefs in the suicide potential of male juvenile delinquents. Measures of depression and hopelessness also were administered. The degree of endorsement of the optimistic "survival coping" beliefs was negatively related to past suicidal ideation and past suicide attempts. Further, it was a better predictor than degree of depression or hopelessness of self-reported likelihood of a future suicide attempt. Cole (1989) asserted that an important buffer against suicide for adolescents is a

> personal fable, a common belief among adolescents that they are special, unusually capable and fortunate individuals and that accidents or catastrophes that could befall others will not happen to them. . . . In many respects the Survival and Coping Beliefs scale of the Reasons for Living Inventory . . . taps into this personal fable . . . failure to adopt such a fable or belief about oneself may increase one's susceptibility to suicidal contemplations. (p. 253)

These two studies provided more evidence that illusory beliefs ("fables") may help to ward off more extreme forms of disturbed behavior.[6]

In preceding discussions, the function of make-believe and illusion in mediating psychopathology was cast in the metaphor of "buffer." It appeared that make-believe softens the impact of threat and stress. One might say that illu-

---

[6]Incidentally, one could view the large literature on alexithymia as indirectly supportive of the value of fantasy constructions in defending against pathological modes. A number of studies (e.g., Karasau & Steinmuller, 1978) has shown that persons with limited ability to engage in fantasy or imaginative activity are particularly likely to develop psychosomatic symptoms (presumably in stressful situations). One may theorize that facility in constructing fantasy is one index of ability to pretend (to build the illusory), and where this facility is diminished there will be enhanced likelihood of organismic dysfunction as difficult circumstances are encountered.

sion provides a protective boundary (shield) against that which is intrusively disruptive. The idea of a protective boundary intrigued Freud (1961) in his original formulation of the "stimulus barrier" (*Reizschutz*). He conjectured that persons are suspended in a world full of powerful stimuli, which would be overwhelming if there were not a "protective shield" (Gediman, 1971). He depicted "traumatic neuroses," such as develop as the result of war experiences, as reflecting the failure of the *Reizschutz*. He was quite vague about the nature of this *Reizschutz*, but it was an appealing concept and other psychoanalysts (e.g., Bellak, 1963; Benjamin, 1961; Winnicott, 1958) have used it in various guises.

Attempts have been made to measure individual variations in boundary functioning and to ascertain how such variations affect behavior. Fisher (1986) has shown empirically that persons differ in the degree to which they feel they possess a protective boundary capable of warding off bodily intrusion. Those whose boundaries are most secure are particularly likely to behave autonomously, to cope efficiently with stress, and to relate comfortably to other persons. Some findings by Fisher (1970) on the possible relationship between illusion and boundary maintenance should be mentioned. He conducted a study in which boundary definiteness (indicative of protective power) was measured by means of the Barrier score. This score is derived from responses to inkblot stimuli. It is determined objectively by counting the number of response images in which the peripheries of percepts are assigned protective and containing qualities (e.g., "man in armor," "person in a tent"). The Barrier score has been shown, in a program of investigations by Fisher (1970, 1986), to have adequate objectivity, test–retest reliability, and validity. It was the intent of the study to clarify the possible use of illusory strategies by persons diagnosed as schizophrenics to bolster their boundaries.

Particular attention was focused on the "paranoid schizophrenic" who maintains a sense of boundary shielding quite equivalent to that found in normal, well-functioning individuals. Fisher (1970) considered that "paranoids" did so by constructing a unique fictional centrality for self that dramatized their importance and significance. He reasoned:

> One of the prime distinctions of the paranoid is that he has reconstructed the world in such a way as to give himself a position which is of central importance by virtue of either straightforward grandiose exaggeration of his power or exaggerated fantasies regarding the unique concentration of evil forces arrayed against him. The paranoid, as contrasted to the non-paranoid, has constructed a good "cover story" which gives him a sense of significance and prominence even in the midst of his disorganization. . . . Boundedness would be associated with a sense of self-significance, no matter how bizarre the assumptions underlying it. (pp. 275–276)

It was therefore predicted that, in a hospitalized sample of individuals diagnosed as schizophrenic, the Barrier score would be positively related to experienced degree of self-importance and amount of paranoia. Both male and female schizophrenic samples were studied. The Holtzman inkblots elicited responses that could be scored for boundary imagery. Each patient was also rated for grandiose expansiveness and paranoid projection by means of the Lorr, Klett, and McNair's (1963) Inpatient Multidimensional Psychiatric Scale. Analysis of the data did not indicate a significant correlation between boundary definiteness and paranoid projection in either the male or female schizophrenics. However, there were meaningful positive correlations between boundary definiteness and grandiose expansiveness in the female ($p < .05$) and male ($p < .10$) samples. In 1970, when originally discussing the significance of these findings, Fisher noted: "It is thought provoking to consider that boundary differentiation can perhaps be maintained on the basis of assumptions and modes of thought which are illogical and even bizarre" (p. 178). That is, the greater the schizophrenic's ability to muster illusory grandiosity the greater the ability to support a sense of being adequately shielded entities. This study is only suggestive, but it provides support for illusory ideas helping disturbed persons to maintain a sense of viable individuality.

It is conceivable that one of the major problems for those classified as psychopathological is that they lack the ability to muster the effective defensive illusions necessary to neutralize the world's pervasive threat qualities. Perhaps the average psychiatric patient does not learn to use the repertoire of "normal" illusion adequately and is ultimately driven by failures in containing anxiety to devise illusory compensatory devices that blatantly clash with cultural role expectations. There are hints that such a formulation may not be unreasonable. For example, MacLeod, Mathews, and Tata's (1986) study involved a sample of persons diagnosed with "generalized anxiety disorder" and another sample of normal controls. These subjects were asked to respond to threatening and nonthreatening stimuli (words) presented on a computer screen. They were asked to identify the words that were projected in various spatial positions. Analyses of different aspects of their response latencies were undertaken.

Essentially, the disturbed individuals focused their attention toward the emotionally threatening stimuli, whereas the normal subjects shifted their attention away from such stimuli. The disturbed patients were "open" to the discomforting inputs, whereas the normals shielded themselves from the threatening material. In another parallel study, Mathews, May, Mogg, and Eysenck (1990) used analogous techniques to show that subjects diagnosed with "generalized anxiety disorder" were more likely than normal controls "to adopt what we would term a vigilant perceptual mode, facilitating the pick-up of potential threat cues" (p. 172). In both of these studies, the individuals who were diagnosed as psychiatric patients did evidence a particularly "open" attitude toward what is threatening "out there." Further, the MacLeod et al. (1986) findings actually demonstrated a "closing-up" or shutting-out stance by the normal subjects vis-à-vis threatening inputs.

It is striking that debates have waxed and waned for some time as to whether those diagnosed as schizophrenics exhibit a defect in their ability to filter inputs. Not infrequently, schizophrenic individuals have anecdotally testified that the onset of their acute disturbance was marked by apparent changes in the vividness of stimuli. Freedman and Chapman (1973) interviewed schizophrenics and controls and reported that the former were significantly more likely to have experienced an increase in auditory (but not visual) intensity. About half of the schizophrenics said they had increased difficulty in "screening" (i.e., in controlling attention for selective and inhibitory purposes). In the 1970s, Silverman (1972) reviewed the existing literature on "stimulus intensity modulation" in various classes of psychiatric patients and concluded that some "central filtering mechanism" had gone awry in the schizophrenic. Reductions in responsiveness represented a compensatory adjustment to the experience of being flooded with stimulation. In 1978, Rubens and Lapidus decided, on the basis of their review of the literature as well as their own research, that "central to schizophrenic pathology is a severe deficit in the individual's ability to modulate his/her basic responsivity to stimulation . . ." (p. 210).

Since that time, a large literature has accumulated concerning whether there is a true attentional malfunction in schizophrenic persons, and, if so, the exact nature of such a malfunction. In an appraisal published in 1989, Nagamoto, Adler, Waldo, and Freedman referred to past literature that suggested schizophrenics are "flooded" by an overabundance of sensory stimulation. They stated: "A variety of clinical and psychometric data suggest that schizophrenics lack the sensory gating mechanisms" (p. 549) for controlling this "flooding" process. Other contemporary analyses of the pertinent literature point in a similar direction. Holzman (1987) told us: "Chronic schizophrenic patients show diminished variation and shorter latencies of early components of somatosensory brain related potentials, which reflect stimulus registration, and investigators have interpreted the findings as indicating impaired modulation of stimulus input, which allows too much information to reach higher brain centers" (p. 49). Various degrees of concurrence with this perspective are offered by a number of investigators (e.g., Bernstein, 1987; Freedman et al., 1987; Geyer & Braff, 1987; Nuechterlein & Dawson, 1984).

However, there is still a diversity of views about the basic defect or defects underlying the attentional malfunctions of schizophrenics (Mirsky & Duncan, 1986). One is probably justified, however, in saying that it is a reasonable possibility that so-called schizophrenics have a problem in being too open to, and less capable of selectively filtering, inputs.[7] Perhaps those with the potential of being labeled schizophrenic would fare better if they were more skillful at constructing illusory shields for themselves. Moderate protective illusions early in life might preserve them from radical imaginative distortions they defensively utilize when they begin to become more seriously disorganized.[8] Incidentally, there are a number of studies (e.g., Gottschalk, Haer, & Bates, 1972; Haer, 1970; Lipowski, 1975; Zentall & Zentall, 1983) documenting that "sensory overload," the inability to maintain selective control over what one admits to awareness, has disorganizing effects on both schizophrenic and normal individuals.

A few comments are in order also about what is referred to as the post-traumatic stress disorder. This "disorder" involves symptoms that develop in individuals after exposure to a psychologically traumatic event that is largely outside the range of usual human experience. Persons who have been exposed to such traumas as war, rape, or a serious accident may subsequently exhibit, for extended periods, signs of disturbance. This disturbance may variously take the form of elevated anxiety, intrusive reexperiencing of the trauma, reduced responsiveness to the outside world, feelings of detachment, and so forth. Not infrequently, the symptoms are quite disabling. The posttraumatic pattern has puzzled many observers, including Freud. It has been difficult to conceptualize why the disturbed response to the trauma continues to persist long after the threat is no longer present. Further, it has been puzzling why individuals, who seemed quite normal and well integrated previous to the trauma, evidence such intense upset. Some empirical studies (e.g., Foy, Sipprelle, Rueger, & Carroll, 1984) doubted whether persons' attributes prior to a trauma can predict their likelihood of being seriously disrupted by it. The immediate, blatant intensity of the trauma seems to be of salient consequence. The trauma apparently breaks through the individual's usual defensive filters and cracks previously comforting attitudes about existence. Janoff-Bulman (1985) analyzed, in some detail, how a trauma shatters world assumptions and proposed that the trauma disrupts previous rosy images about one's personal invulnerability and the meaningfulness of events. The sheer alien quality of the traumatic input results in the world being "out of

---

[7]It is interesting that Fisher (1986) reported that schizophrenics' ability to maintain adequate boundaries is positively correlated with the degree to which they apparently utilize techniques for dampening certain sensory inputs.

[8]Becker (1973) put the entire matter quite dramatically:

> In order to function normally, man has to achieve from the beginning a serious constriction of the world and himself. We can say that the essence of normality is the *refusal of reality*. What we call neuroses enters precisely at this point: Some people have more trouble with their lies than others. The world is too much with them and the techniques that they have developed for holding it at bay and cutting it down to size finally begin to choke the person himself. This is neurosis in a nutshell: the miscarriage of clumsy lies about reality. (p. 178)

whack." In a more obvious "pure" form, this breakdown in the filtering (Reiz-schutz) process may parallel what occurs, although in a more anfractuous fashion, in the conventional forms of psychopathology.

PSYCHOLOGICAL THERAPIES AND MAKE-BELIEVE

Anyone acquainted with the elusive placebo is primed to give serious attention to the potential contribution of illusion to therapeutic effects. A rich literature (e.g., White, Tursky, & Schwartz, 1985) tells us that psychologically disturbed individuals may show dramatic improvement after ingesting a substance that they imagine has therapeutic potency, but that in fact is inert. Multiple documented instances can be cited in which inactive placebos, framed only by the power that one's capacity to make-believe transmits to them, are able to "cure" serious symptomatology, both of the psychological and somatic variety. There is no longer any dispute about the potency of the placebo. In fact, its pervasive power has become a serious nuisance to those testing new psychotropic (and other) drugs who want to separate the "biological" from the "psychological" components of "drug effects" (Fisher & Greenberg, 1989).

Much already has been written about the somewhat chimerical and pretend elements that feed into psychotherapeutic efficacy. Wide-ranging analyses of these elements are offered by Frank (1961) and Torrey (1986). They pointed out that many of the practices basic to formal Western psychotherapies, and also the less formal healing ceremonies of nonindustrial cultures, are rooted in illusory displays. They indicated that, despite the apparently greater scientific aura of the formal psychotherapies, they are equivalently dependent on fostering certain beliefs and expectations. It is their view that such therapies achieve a significant part of their effects by convincing the "sick" ones that the therapist (shaman, healer, witch doctor) is a person who possesses incredible prowess, is in touch with a level of power (either religiously or scientifically defined) that is unique and ordinarily unavailable, and can portray the future as promising and renewing. The entire process is said to be founded on the illusory exaggeration of the healing power inherent in the encounter. It is depicted, too, as a magical magnification of the healer. Elaborating further, Frank (1961) noted:

> Another source of the patient's faith is the ideology of the healer or sect, which offers him a rationale, however absurd, for making sense of his illness and the treatment procedure, and places the healer in the position of transmitter or controller of impressive healing forces. In this he is analogous to the shaman. Often these forces are called supernatural, but the healer may pose as a scientist who has discovered new and potent scientific principles of healing, thus

surrounding himself with the aura that anything labeled scientific inspires in members of modern western societies. (pp. 73–74)

Although the psychotherapies are rooted in forms and modes that have a strong illusory substrate, it is simultaneously true that they often focus on themes that run counter to many of the culture's protective illusions. As Rieff (1966) described in detail, the modern psychotherapies variously question devotion to religion, the credibility of repressive defense mechanisms, and the entire rationale of submission to moral authority. Rieff (1966) suggested that psychoanalysis became widely accepted because it promised to liberate persons from introjected "shoulds" and "oughts." He noted that psychoanalytic doctrine urges every man to "become something of a genius about himself" (p. 32) and less in need of being attached to the culture. Freud envisioned psychoanalysis as morally neutral and Rieff (1966) pointed out that, whereas Freud was concerned with releasing persons from "old beliefs," he did not help them to find new ones. Rieff (1966) referred to Freud as embarking on the "moral disarmament of Western man" (p. 38). He said Freud was imbued with the idea of an independent "psychological man," the "sane self in a mad world, the integrated personality" (p. 40); and he indicated that Freud believed in the myth that persons can "live with no higher purpose than that of a durable sense of well-being" (p. 40). He added that Jung disagreed with this position and believed that it is not repression that troubles us the most now, but rather the difficulty of finding meaning in life. He continued: "The normality of disillusion and a controlling sense of resignation, which was the most for which Freud hoped, appeared to Jung the beginning rather than the end of therapy" (p. 43). Like so many phenomena, the psychodynamic psychotherapies are, to a rarely suspected degree, based on a polarity: rooted in a protective faith in the therapist on the one hand, but denigrating of many protective cultural (religious, moral) faiths on the other hand.

Psychoanalysis, one of the most complex forms of Western psychotherapy, is centrally structured around encouraging and analyzing the "transference." The transference refers to the presumed inclination of patients to project qualities onto the therapist that are unrealistic repetitions of how they feel about their parental figures. Patients are encouraged (by means of "transference interpretations") to maximize their presumably unreal fictions about the therapist, thereby providing the therapist with the opportunity to dramatize how discrepant and distorted they are. Gill (1979) asserted that Freud advocated that "the transference should be encouraged to expand as much as possible within the analytic situation" (p. 268). Although the ultimate goal of this process is to rid patients of their fictions, this is paradoxically operationalized by first encouraging them to cultivate their unreal images during therapy encounters. The therapist chooses to incite a florid expansion of illusory fantasies, albeit with the understanding that they will eventually be corrected. In fact, the aim of straightening out transference illusions is not easily accomplished. There is little, if any, empirical evidence that the cultivation of such illusions is necessary for therapeutic effectiveness. The incitement of transference illusion within the psychoanalytic paradigm may be one more example of the inclination to introduce an illusory frame, a space for make-believe, that seems to tempt most therapeutic enterprises.

It Is not surprising the some therapies explicitly advocate the use of make-believe to advance therapeutic ends. Certain notions underlying widely practiced "supportive therapies" might be paraphrased: "When patients have viewpoints or practices that help them to adapt, encourage their use even if they are not logical or conventionally realistic." Also, the desensitization therapies rely on patients to pretend repetitively that they are capable of coping with specific circumstances that are threatening to them. Consider, too, that the concepts promulgated by Milton Erikson (Beahrs, 1986) and other adherents of hypnosis-oriented therapies start out, of course, with the presumption that the patient needs to be put into the hypnotic state, which is probably a pretended role (Lynn, Rhue, & Weekes, 1990), to derive therapeutic benefits. In addition, they have patients hypnotically reexperience past traumatic events in order to reconstruct them with a more optimistic twist. The patient can thus pretend that things turned out more advantageously and presumably take heart (perhaps gain new perspectives) from the transformation. There are psychodrama therapy strategies of a parallel character.

Probably the boldest therapeutic formulation, based on the manipulation of illusion, derives from attribution theory. One of attribution therapy's basic goals is to convince individuals that there are "normal" explanations for their behaviors, which they consider to be abnormal and which, because of their presumed abnormality, arouse alarm, loss of self-esteem, and feelings of loss of control. Attribution therapy also aims to persuade individuals that disturbance experienced as intrinsic to self (and therefore as a defect in self) is actually caused by some "safe" extrinsic agent and is therefore less threatening. In brief, the attribution approach is to attack damaging dispositional interpretations and supply less damaging ones. Valins and Nisbett (1971) referred to an application of attribution therapy in which a patient who was worried about being a homosexual was led to reinterpret his apparent signs of homosexuality as being manifestations of another species of anxiety; this resulted in a significant improvement in his clinical condition. They noted: "His unsatisfactory sexual experiences were explained as not being the result of inadequate heterosexual interest, but a 'normal' consequence of anxiety about possible inadequate performances" (p. 3). In another instance, Johnson, Ross, and Mastria (1977) depicted a patient with a delusional system concerned that "he was having intercourse with a fantasied 'warm form' " (p. 422). He was treated (within the attribution paradigm) by being told that he was "normal," that his problem was "real," and that his belief in the existence of the "warm form" was due to a buildup of sexual tensions as a result of abstinence and "inadvertent" masturbation. Thus, his delusional fantasy was reinterpreted so as to render it "normal." Following this procedure, he was said to demonstrate rather dramatic clinical improvement.

Valins and Nisbett (1971) also suggested that "behavioral changes produced by therapeutic drugs may be maximized by persuading individuals that some aspects of the changes are due to themselves rather than being solely the result of the drug" (p. 11). It is obvious that "attribution therapy" is quite willing to implant illusory explanations and schemas as a way of reassuring and healing. Although some (e.g., Johnson et al., 1977) warn against the flagrant use of deception in attribution therapy strategies, much of the pertinent experimental and case material cited in the literature (e.g., Davison, Tsujimoto, & Glaros, 1973; Ross, Rodin, & Zimbardo, 1969) leans on the use of pretense and manipulation of at least semiillusory notions.

The approval of illusory formulations in psychotherapeutic practice is implicit in the statements of those who opt for a "narrative truth" approach to psychoanalytic interpretation. This approach was asserted straightforwardly by Spence (1982). He argued that, as therapists listen to their patients during multiple sessions, they do not really acquire the data necessary to establish the "historical truth" of the patients' lives. He declared that, because of such factors as the fallibility of the patients' memories, the vagueness of words, and the countertransference bias of the therapist, one cannot reconstruct what really happened to account for the patients' present difficulties. He seriously questioned Freud's comparison of the analyst to an archaeologist who puts the fragments together so as to ascertain the "historical truth." He noted that historical truth, or what "really happened," is probably beyond reach. Rather, he proposed that therapists must integrate the highly complex information they obtain from the patients' past and immediate verbalizations with their own intuitions about such information to arrive at a "narrative" or story that makes sense.

Basically, Spence (1982) said therapists should creatively pull together what is happening in a therapy session, offer interpretations that are "aesthetically" meaningful, and provide patients with new ideas that will help to advance. the flow of the therapy. He stated:

> The analyst . . . commits himself to a belief in his hypothesis and is inclined to use it in a pragmatic fashion. He is less committed to a belief in its truth value—either because he has no clear way of knowing whether or not it actually occurred or because he is proposing something that has no clear correspondence with an event in the patient's life . . . we can hardly ask questions about its historical truth. The more appropriate question concerns what might be called its artistic truth, its significance as a kind of creative endeavor, a putting together of known facts about the patient in a new form that carries a high probability of something happening in the analytic space. (p. 275)

With regard to the proper nature of psychoanalytic interpretations, he added: "They are designed to produce results rather than document the past; they are designed primarily to bring about a change in belief. . . . Once we conceive of interpretations as artistic creations that have the potential for producing an aesthetic response, we are . . . even less interested in the truth of the particular parts" (p. 276).

This "narrative" approach to informing patients about what has and is occurring in their lives focuses on the utility of what is communicated rather than what is considered to be its elusive validity (truth). Therapists try to be as honest to their observations as possible, but ultimately are more concerned with the effect of the interpretation than its actuality. Thus, therapists are given permission to construct that which is therapeutically advantageous, and there is little assurance that what they construct will not consist of illusory images and ideas. Indeed, even if the interpretation is composed of illusory elements, that is quite alright, as long as it proves to have heuristic power. Incidentally, Spence (1982) suggested that Freud, in his later years, was beginning to come around to a similar point of view.

It is inescapable that the various psychotherapies communicate their own special versions of the nature of things. In a paper titled "Integrating Visions of Reality," Andrews (1989) elaborated on ideas previously formulated by Messer and Winskur (1980) and Schafer (1976) that depicted the various "psychotherapeutic schools" as based on different cognitive structures representing specific visions of reality. He indicated that there are a limited number of such "visions" (e.g., romantic, ironic, tragic, comic), and that the various psychotherapies are, in a sense, each selling a different brand. For example, the "romantic vision" (triumph of good over evil) is linked with humanistic psychotherapy forms, such as Carl Rogers' client-centered approach. The "comic vision" (conflict can be eliminated by effective action and the power of positive thinking) is tied to behavior therapy. Andrews (1989) even asserted that the various "reality visions" reflect the personalities of those who originated them. He suggested that Rogers, who developed client-centered therapy, chose the "romantic vision" because he is affiliative, nondominating, and inclined toward "nonjudgmental caringness." Further, he speculated that Arnold Lazarus and Joseph Wolpe shaped the "comic" world view of behavior therapy because they are dominance-oriented and relatively restrained in their degree of love orientation.

In other words, the specific reality vision of a therapy can be traced to the personal needs of its originator, and each derived perspective is transmitted to those who come seeking that brand of therapy. Andrews (1989) regarded each world vision as having as much validity as any other. There are multiple valid realities, and presumably each therapy arbitrarily (based on its originator's personality) seeks to convert the patient to that "reality." Research reports (e.g., Meltzoff & Kornreich, 1970) indicate that persons who improve the most during psychotherapy also show increased similarity of their values to those of their therapists. That is, the patient's improvement may depend on how close an identification with the therapist can be attained. Incidentally, patients and therapists are selectively inclined to seek out each other on the basis of similarity in world views (Fisher & Greenberg, 1985).

Andrews (1989) urged therapists to be flexible and prepared to draw on a spectrum of world views as the needs of the patient dictate. However, he offered no data to demonstrate that therapists who can shift world views do better than those who adhere to one or a few. What emerges most vividly from his essay is the arbitrary nature of the visions or schemas offered by each therapeutic school. Ultimately, if one speaks of multiple visions of reality, this implies that they are all, to some degree, imbued with make-believe elements.

INTEGRATIVE COMMENTS

In this chapter, we have shown that the apparent precision of psychiatric diagnostic schemes has been exaggerated. Present capabilities for distinguishing the full spectrum from normal to abnormal are not very satisfactory. Delusions and hallucinations are frequently difficult to specify reliably. Also, there is much more so-called abnormal behavior prevalent in "normal" persons than is acknowledged within current "mental illness" paradigms. The borderline between normal illusion and delusion is hazier than the establishment might like to admit. In a way, this parallels our observation that the various defense mechanisms cannot reliably be differentiated into "mature" and "immature." At times, the presumably least mature way of coping can be the most effective in adapting to certain types of stress, and the theoretically most "mature" defense does not work.

In line with the literature demonstrating that illusory distortion has protective value, we questioned whether persons who develop florid "psychiatric symptoms" may have had insufficient opportunity to acquire adequate skills for pretending or conjuring up the illusory screen that buffers the painful sharpness of life events. Paradoxically, those who get into the most psychological trouble, by stretching their fantasies to the extreme, may be those who have not mastered the art of manipulating fantasy creatively and optimistically. The goal of the various psychotherapies to reverse psychological disturbance relies heavily on illusory exaggeration of the powers of the therapist and ultimately with providing a more sanguine version of what "reality" is all about. New, probably equivalently arbitrary, images of reality are supplied to replace older ones that are no longer sufficiently encapsulating.

All of the puzzles and questions that exist with respect to the defensive value of illusory images are sharpened when one examines serious psychopathology. One is immediately challenged to distinguish the protectively adaptive illusion from the presumably paranoid projection, or the comforting and supportive religious dogma from the psychotic world construction. As described, this is not easily done and may never be possible in a meaningful, reliable fashion. It is likely that the ambiguity is intrinsic to the psychological organization of human personalities. Imaginative constructions and reconstructions of experience are neverending and can ebb and flow extremely.

The most dramatic verification of the real-life ambiguity of distinctions between "sane" and "insane" has come from Rosenhan (1973). He explored what would happen to normal persons who gained entrance to mental hospitals by pretending to have certain symptoms. There were 12 incidents in which individuals without "psychiatric impairment" presented a fictitious complaint (an auditory hallucination that said "empty," "thud," or "dull") at a psychiatric facility. This unusual complaint was deliberately selected because of its atypicality. In all instances, the pseudopatients were admitted to the hospital on the basis of the presenting "symptom." Eleven were formally diagnosed as "paranoid schizophrenic," and one as "manic-depressive psychosis." Upon discharge, all were labeled as either "schizophrenia" or "manic-depressive," "improved." In a second phase of this investigation, Rosenhan (1973) agreed to send a pseudopatient to one of the hospitals to see if the diagnosticians could detect him. Rosenhan (1973) did not, of course, indicate when that "patient" would arrive at the hospital. During a given period, 193 patients were admitted to the hospital. Twenty-one percent were labeled as pseudopatients by at least one hospital staff member, and 12% were diagnosed as pseudopatients by at least one psychiatrist on the staff. Actually, none of Rosenhan's (1973) confederates sought admission to the hospital. Rosenhan (1973) concluded: "We now know that we cannot distinguish insanity from sanity" (p. 257). This conclusion may be exaggerated, but should not be dismissed too glibly.

We have said rather consistently that the construction of illusions facilitates coping with persistent absurdities. Therefore, we were taken with the view expressed by some (e.g., Barchilon, 1973) that the deviant modes of psychiatric patients, which so often seem ridiculous, are intended by their very ridiculousness to convey the message "I am behaving in an absurd way because I experience life as absurd." There may be an element of satire in many displays of psychiatric symptoms. This is often revealed in the clownish behavior of those who are in the midst of a full-blown manic episode. Freud (1959) speculated that certain symptom expressions, such as the exaggerated ritualistic repetitions of the obsessive-compulsive, may be forms of mockery. He suggested, too, that caricaturing is particularly prominent in "delusional disorders." Arieti (1950) provided illustrations of analogous symptom-stated mockery and absurdity. Daniels (1973) observed: "The madman often appears to share many attributes of the clown" (p. 468). Fisher and Fisher (1981) have actually documented that many children whose clown-like behavior gets them into trouble (and ultimately referral to "mental health" professionals) are mirroring back their senseless (ridiculous) transactions with their parents.

There are endless absurdities that humans encounter in their day-to-day existence. They not only cope with their awareness of the inevitability of death and their realization of their nothingness in the universe, but also the neverending contradictions in the behaviors of those who socialized them and those with whom they live intimately. Ellis (1987) wrote a paper titled, "The Impossibility of Achieving Consistently Good Mental Health." In this paper, he expressed his puzzlement about the difficulty of curing persons of their psychological disturbances; and even when this is achieved to enable them to maintain their state of improvement. He indicated that the rational-emotive therapy that he developed assumes that "people largely disturb themselves by thinking in a self-defeating, illogical, and unrealistic manner" (p. 364) and can best be helped by showing them the irrationality of their ways. However, he has become somewhat disillusioned over the years, because so many of the people he treats are resistive to achieving or holding onto their apparent recovery. Therefore, he concluded that there is a basic "biological" inclination for humans to "think irrationally," which dooms them to poor "mental health." Like Freud and most mental health experts, he focused on the individual's irrationality as the major source of what is called psychological disturbance. He did not once, in the paper cited above, entertain the possibility that the prevalence and persistence of "psychopathology" are due to the incurable absurdities that humans cannot escape. This is not to deny that there is irrationality built into modal psychological functioning, but the irrationality may be a relatively small contributing element compared with the basic absurdities. Indeed, one can speculate that it is the human ability to manipulate perceptions and feelings "irrationally," which permits survival in the midst of so much strangeness.

What are some semipractical implications of the information we have scanned in this chapter? First of all, we underscore how limited is our solid stock of knowledge about psychopathology. There is a need for modesty in that area, and perhaps it should be communicated honestly to persons who come seeking "treatment." Should those who present themselves as "patients" be shown the hazy line between normal and abnormal? Should they be appraised of the basic uncertainty of our apparently superprecise diagnostic schemes? Awareness of the relativity of normal and abnormal might be helpful to those who, because of their "symptoms," feel they inexorably fall into a "mentally ill" category. The diagnostic process is not only unreliable, it also seems to have limited validity. Further, there is a more natural variation in each individual's "symptomatology" and considerably more spontaneous "recovery" than usually acknowledged.

Next, less emphasis should be placed on using therapeutic techniques to make patients more "rational." There is an overblown faith in the value of transmitting "insight" to persons who are psychologically upset or of getting them to be more logical. We now know there are all kinds of "unrealistic" illusions that have considerable protective value, and one ought to be conservatively cautious about trying to undermine them. Generally, a dramatic revision is in order concerning the supposed fundamental role of irrationality in producing psychopathology. Life in most settings is full of difficulties, contradictions, and blatant absurdities that are so stressfully persistent that no amount of rationality could neutralize them. Much of what is called psychopathology is simply unavoidable shuddering at the dilemmas of the human setting. Incidentally, the treatment establishment is in a rather insecure position to preach rationality to "patients," when one considers the amount of irrationality basic to the power and influence of the psychotherapies. In fact, as described by Fisher and Greenberg (1989), the "biological" treatments for psychopathology also share significantly in such irrationality. One wonders whether more scientific creativity should not be invested in devising effective ways to teach persons how to utilize irrationality for their protective advantage. Perhaps instruction should be provided on how to construct reliable myths and find ways to improve the technology for delivering reassuring subliminal messages like "Mommy and I are one," which Silverman et al. (1989) reported to be so capable of psychologically placating individuals who are seriously troubled. The roots of so many defenses are entangled in make-believe. Humans have sharpened their skills at make-believe since practically Day 1, but they may not take sufficient advantage of that latent reservoir of self-buffering.

The paper by Andrews (1989; cited earlier), which depicts each school of psychotherapy as representing a specific version of reality, highlights the concept that psychotherapists are fundamentally intent on inculcating their world visions in their "patients." The elaborate discussions of "countertransference" in the psychoanalytic literature pretend that the biases of therapists can, with the proper safeguards, be practically banished. The elimination of any therapist's bias, in its broadest sense, might, in fact, require considerable deindividuation of that individual—the partial deconstruction of that unique individuality. Moreover, there is the tangential possibility that a significant element of what is therapeutic in psychotherapy relationships is the very fact that the therapists have their own "biased" world views, which they manage, directly or indirectly (but not exploitatively), to communicate with confidence to their "patients." As Frank (1961) and Torrey (1986) have dramatized, therapeutic prowess derives, at least in part, from therapists projecting images that portray them as special, powerful, and capable of delivering uniquely potent beliefs. The energy profusely dedicated to rid psychotherapy of therapist "bias" may, in principle, be antitherapeutic.

9

CONJURING UP A SELF

In this chapter, we inspect the "self" as a structure that is ingeniously worked and reworked by individuals as part of their repertoire of defensive make-believe tactics. We propose, as have others, that the self is an arbitrary creation, a simulacrum that can be stuffed with fictive elements. In probing this matter, we have dutifully trekked through the farrago of papers, chapters, and books on the nature of the self. Never has a concept been so diligently probed and stretched. Even if one considers only statements presented by individuals with scientific credentials, the range of ideas about what the self is and does is marvelous to behold. Although there is a widespread assumption that some sort of cognitive (self) structure exists, which defines who one is and guides one's behavior, only limited agreement exists beyond that point. There are fundamental disagreements about whether the self is a stable "core" structure or more transient and malleable in character (e.g., Gergen, 1982; Swann, 1983). Extensive discussions can be found on whether one should speak of the self or multiple selves (e.g., James, 1910; Markus & Nurius, 1986). Some saw the self as constructed primarily to ward off anxiety (Becker, 1973; Sullivan, 1953). Others focused on its information-processing functions (Markus & Sentis, 1982). Real differences exist as to how much of the self is consciously known versus resident at unconscious levels (e.g., Epstein, 1983). One also finds debates about whether self-strategies are directed to self-consistency or self-enhancement (Greenwald, 1982; Markus & Wurf, 1987; Swann, 1983), whether self-perception is unique or a special case of person-perception (Olson & Hafer, 1990), and so forth.

Although empirical studies have compiled a good deal of information about the self-realm, a haziness still prevails as to how to organize and conceptualize such information. The experts who have studied the self-phenomenon for a number of decades are fairly puzzled about the nature of the entity. An interesting parallel to this puzzlement is found in the popular preoccupation of Western cultures about finding oneself ("What is the nature of this thing I call Myself?"). Analogously, the arts are pervaded with themes of defining self, discovering one's true identify, and related forms of disorientation. In the book with the provocative title, *Who Am I This Time?*, J. Martin (1988) presented a variety of material that dramatizes the unsubstantiality of self-structures in the 20th century. He particularly analyzed the way in which fictive characters presented in television programs have been incorporated in the identities of average persons. He stated:

> To a large extent, the gods, spirits, monsters, or saints and intercessors of traditional society have been replaced in contemporary society by a conglomeration of beings we have never seen and never will see. Yet we are encouraged to believe we do have some relationships with them. These include public persons; actors and actresses, especially those in soap operas, situation comedies. . . . (p. 217)

He theorized that such fictive images become important components of the average self and "we see people leading lives as if they were characters in romance, adventure, mystery, drama, comedy, tragedy, myths, novels, and advertising" (p. 220). He added: "our society is composed according to the belief that the self is fictive, society is theater, and events have no meaning beyond their performances" (p. 229). Relatedly, Cushman (1990) took a somber perspective concerning the fictive state of the self in his paper with the ominous title, "Why the Self Is Empty." He portrayed the contemporary self as having lost its anchor in traditional values and become the "empty self," which is "soothed and made cohesive by becoming 'filled up' with food, consumer products, and celebrities" (p. 599). Incidentally, he asserted that psychotherapy and advertising have become the two professions most responsible for "healing" the "empty self." His basic sense of relativity concerning the shape of the self led him to say: "There is no universal transhistorical self, only local selves . . ." (p. 599).

RELATIVITY OF SELF

Although currently there is much anxiety and uncertainty about self-definition, it is probably accurate that most persons regard their self-perceptions as representing a universal type. That is, they probably assume that their basic mode of experiencing self is inherent in the human condition. However, Baumeister (1987) assembled some surprising information that portrays the possibility that the nature of the normative self is transformed across historical

periods as attitudes toward individuality shift. He has analyzed experts' observations about various phases of historical development and modal types
of literary content in America, England, and France from the 11th through
the 20th centuries. He concluded that the construction of the self is a product
of the specific conditions prevailing in any given historical time frame. Illustratively, he indicated that, during the late-medieval period (11th through
15th centuries), awareness of selfhood was "crude by modern standards" and
there seemed to be little introspection or "experienced inner struggles" (p.
165). Baumeister (1987) commented on a "remarkable scarcity" of autobiog-
raphy during this period of minimizing self. Also, the literature of the 11th
and 12th centuries had barely begun to present figures in dramatic works
who had individual interpretations of what was happening. The self was apparently not elaborated on at that point in history. Individuals were actually
defined in terms of their fixed positions in the public hierarchy, the "Great
Chain of Being."

Baumeister (1987) proceeded to spell out, in sequence, the subsequent increasing differentiation of an individualized self during the "early modern"
era (16th through 18th centuries); the development among the Puritans of
intense self-consciousness and the concept of self as an inner versus exterior
manifestation (with the accompanying sense of the potential for self-
deception); the rise of the Romantic notion of the individual self struggling
for freedom against society (in the later 18th and early 19th centuries); and
the eventual efflorescence of the 20th-century self with its unique focus on
the need for celebrity, self-actualization, and centrality of personality. The
modern self is depicted as qualitatively different from the medieval self. Baumeister (1987) pointed out: "The inner nature of selfhood, which is regarded
as axiomatic by much modern psychological thought, seems to have become
a common conception first in the 16th century" (p. 165). It is explicit in Baumeister's (1987) analysis that the self is an arbitrary construction reflecting
the specialized world view of each particular time frame. Not only is the content of the self-concept considered to vary as a function of the era, but also
the degree to which selfhood, as such, is cogent in the individual's stream
of awareness.

Therefore, it should come as no surprise that anthropologists have compiled material that highlights the arbitrary structure of the self-concept within each culture. An excellent example is provided by Smith (1981), who
presented a variety of data concerning the Maori culture. It is noted that Maori
individuals are identified with the group to a degree far exceeding such identification in Western societies. A Maori person can only be a person within
the kin group. Outside of this kin context, there is no identity. Persons in
the Maori culture consider their experiences to be extraneous to their individual control. They do not feel responsible for their own emotions, which they
picture as being externally imposed. J. Smith (1981) noted:

> Among the Maori . . . it would appear that generally it was not the "self" which
> encompassed the experience, but experience which encompassed the "self."
> The Maori individual was an amalgam of various independent organs of ex-
> perience, and it would appear . . . that to a significant extent these organs each
> reacted to external stimuli independent of the self. . . . Because the self was
> not in control of experience, a man's experience was not felt to be integral to
> him; it happened *in* him but not *of* him. A Maori individual was not so much
> the experiencer of his experience as the observer of it. (p. 152)

Thus, the self is regarded as playing a subsidiary role in the experience of
the world; and, in addition, Maori persons are freed from moral responsibility for what occurs within them. J. Smith (1981) suggested that if the self in
Western societies is the "driver" of the car, it is, in Maori culture, simply a
"passenger" in one's body.

J. Martin (1988) cited a similar reduction of the self among the Wintu Indi-
ans of Northern California. There are documented reports that the Wintu did
not recognize the self as a "separate entity." They apparently had difficulty
conjuring up an image of a separate self. Further, Fogelson (1982) reviewed
a variety of anthropological observations that highlight unique concepts of
self and person among groups like the Ojibwa; and Straus (1982) provided
a detailed analysis of the specialized self-concepts of the Cheyenne. Triandis, McCusker, and Hui (1990) have shown in their research that cultures may
contrast in the degree to which they inculcate "individualism" versus "collectivism" elements into the self-concept.

Groups like the Wintu and the Maori clarify that the particular conditions
of a culture may forbid the perception of a self that even roughly parallels
the self-structure Western culture takes for granted. The pressures and vicissitudes typifying the Maori or the Wintu seem to call for the creation of a
unique minimized species of self. There is great latitude as to the kind of self-
structure a culture can require its participants to fashion. A culture can de-
mand a self of practically zero magnitude or one, at the other extreme, of
the overblown dimensions common in the 20th-century West.

The influence of the social context on the construction of self is especially
evident when one takes a cross-cultural perspective. However, it is also visible within the relatively narrow range of contexts that exists in any one specific culture. Several experiments by Gergen (1982) illustrated how easily
self-feelings can be manipulated by simple, social rearrangements. In one
study, he exposed college women to an interview by an attractive female
who unmistakably demonstrated her agreement whenever they made positive statements about self but registered disagreement with all their negative self-references. In this context, the women experienced increasingly
positive feelings about self. In an additional study, women encountered
"another person" who acted out the role of someone highly egotistical and
optimistic. A second group of women encountered "another person" who

was extremely self-critical and presented herself as "miserable." Subjects who experienced the egotistical optimist shifted toward describing themselves very positively and minimized their weaknesses. Those who interacted with the "miserable" woman became sharply more critical of themselves.

Although Gergen (1982) recognized that such changes in self-concept are largely transitory, he also noted that there are other studies implying that shifts in very basic attitudes toward self may be triggered by brief social inputs. He referred to a study by Bramel (1963), in which males were given fabricated "scientific information" that led them to entertain doubts about their heterosexual orientation. Such doubts about a basic aspect of self-definition were instigated in less than 30 minutes. Other investigators have shown that self-representations are influenced by multiple factors such as mood states, attentional focus, and self-presentational intent (Brown & Smart, 1991). Although self-attitudes seem to be somewhat malleable in laboratory settings, they are stable in naturalistic situations where individuals have greater freedom to employ a spectrum of defenses (Markus & Wurf, 1987; Swann, 1987). It is probably true that certain global aspects of the average Western self-structure are fairly stable, whereas other specific self-images can fluctuate considerably (Olson & Hafer, 1990).

The full potential plasticity of the self is perhaps best dramatized in certain extreme states. Consider the so-called "multiple personality" phenomenon. There are, of course, many reports (e.g., Kihlstrom, 1984) that psychologically disturbed persons may behave as if they are not unitary but rather multiple selves. They may present themselves as having one identity, then shift into another quite different version, and so forth.[1] Such multiple selves may be diametrically opposed in their attributes and, in some cases, may be almost too numerous to count. Strikingly, the various individual selves may appear to lack an awareness of each other. Analogous radical changes in self have frequently been described in schizophrenic individuals (Fisher, 1986) who may report being transformed into grandiose celebrity identities. There are even more radical alterations in self that occur in the brain injured. For example, anosognosias may result in individuals actually denying the existence of one half of their body territory. Fifty percent of the body self has simply disappeared (Fisher, 1986) from personal view. Consider, too, the transsexuals (Fisher, 1989) who disown the current self because it misrepresents their "true" gender, and who proceed to arrange for a surgical reconstruction of a revised model of self. These instances reveal what radi-

---

[1]Hints of the "multiple personality" phenomenon are afforded, too, by the "hidden observer" postulated by Hilgard (1977) in relation to hypnosis and also the "self-deception" strategies described by Sackeim (1983).

cal "choices" are actually available for self-definitions. We tune in also on a potentially amazing fluidity in the self-concept. We see how arbitrary are the modal self-forms to which we are accustomed. The normative Western self may be a highly cultivated, carefully and selectively grown cultural product.

HOW "ACCURATE" IS THE SELF-CONCEPT?

Gergen (1982) focused on the arbitrary social construction of the self. He stated: "There is no objective person to be known, discovered, explored, or understood" (p. 142). He suggested that persons possess an array of potential self-accounts that are pressed into use as needed in various social contexts. Indeed, he concluded that "so long as the individual can gain social agreement in describing him or herself in a particular manner, this description is rendered legitimate" (p. 144). In fact, there are data in the literature demonstrating only limited correspondence between the qualities persons attribute to themselves and so-called objective ratings of such qualities. First of all, note that there are only low level correlations between persons' ratings of their own appearances and ratings made by others (Fisher, 1986). Obviously, my concept of my appearance is a significant facet of my self-concept.

Shrauger and Schoenman (1979) undertook a systematic analysis of all the existent studies on the relationship between how persons perceive themselves and how others perceive them. They located about 50 pertinent investigations that involved such diverse domains as self-esteem, self-acceptance, health, job performance, leadership, physical beauty, and dominance. No consistent correlations were detected between persons' self-perceptions and how they were actually judged by others. That is, individuals' self-perceptions were inaccurate when matched against how others viewed them. Shrauger and Schoenman's (1979) conclusion of little correlation between one's perception of self-attributes and others' actual judgments of these attributes has been supported by later studies (e.g., Felson, 1989; Schafer & Keith, 1985). Shrauger and Schoenman (1979) also reported, not surprisingly, that there are fairly consistent positive correlations between one's ratings of one's self-qualities and one's ratings of others' perceptions of such qualities. Felson (1989) found a similar pattern of relationships mediated and modified by a number of complex variables. In any case, there is a defensive quality reflected in the fact that one's self-perceptions do not correspond to the consensual perceptions of others, but, amazing to behold, do agree with one's private ideas of how others see oneself. Such findings obviously suggest that a self-serving system exists for conserving one's private images of oneself.

PRESERVING A PREFERRED VERSION OF SELF

In fact, a major segment of the scientific literature concerned with the self does, directly or indirectly, study the matter of how self-structures are conserved. Actually, the tactics employed to defend the self have already been reviewed in the earlier chapter on defense mechanisms. When persons employ mechanisms like projection and principalization, they are obviously intent on protecting psychological territory integral to what is usually defined as the self. Numerous observers (e.g., Greenwald, 1980; M. W. Martin, 1985; Sackeim, 1983; Steele, 1988) have commented on the intensity with which persons highlight the self, assign it a privileged position in the experiential field, and stave off infringements of its existing form. Many complex strategies are employed to maintain a preferred self, somewhat irrespective of whether that self-definition matches customary "reality" criteria. In a possibly exaggerated tone, one can say that most persons are determined to possess certain self-qualities and will, if necessary, sustain their beliefs with pretense.

Greenwald (1980) pictured most dramatically the extent to which individuals manipulate and distort information to bolster their self-concepts. He indicated that persons are engaged in a constant process of revising history so that it will be congruent with preferred notions of the self. He humorously noted that if historians were as careless and arbitrary with their renditions of history as persons are with respect to their personal histories, they would be evicted from campus and denounced for their faulty scholarship. In supporting their favorite self-portraits, persons selectively forget key memories of themselves and hold onto others. Indeed, they give priority to processing self-information and alertly try to stay on top of self-relevant inputs (Markus, 1980). That is, they show a special, defensively valuable quickness in assimilating data with self-implications. But most of all, there is resistance to information that is not sympathetic to the prevailing self-schema. For example, persons are more likely to be aware of their assets than their liabilities and to attribute success to self but failure to outside circumstances. Other analogous defensively distorting maneuvers are well documented (Markus, 1980; Markus & Wurf, 1987). Even when stimuli that are threatening to self register at an unconscious level, elaborate mechanisms exist for coping with and taming them (Sackeim, 1983).

Persons are experts at excusing themselves. This excuse-making expertise is reviewed in detail by M. W. Martin (1985). When describing previous work in this area, he referred to two major types of self-excusing: One ("reframing performance strategy") aims to dismiss apparent failure by "inappropriate" justification of what has been done, whereas a second ("transformed responsibility strategy") calls for acknowledging failure but minimizing responsibility for it (e.g., due to temporary or "not really like me" mistakes). M. W. Martin (1985) noted, too, that a favorite form of self-excusing revolves around drinking alcohol, which permits rationalization of failure by attribution to one's intoxicated state. He pointed out a second level of self-deception involved in heavy use of alcohol, namely, simultaneously denying that one is making such heavy use. He quoted a statement from Albert Camus, which conveys the essence of excuse-making: "Each of us insists on being innocent at all cost, even if he has to accuse the whole human race and heaven itself" (p. 30).

While most research has focused on the intraindividual mechanisms (e.g., selective memory) for affirming one's preferred ideas about oneself, a new line of work highlights interpersonal strategies commonly employed for such affirmation. A good deal of this work reflects the efforts of Swann and his associates (e.g., Swann & Hill, 1982). They hypothesized that one of the prime ways to stabilize one's self-concept is to seek out and create social interactions that will provide self-corroborating experiences. Swann and Read (1981) stated formally: "In the course of their social relationships, there is a systematic tendency for people to solicit feedback that verifies and confirms their self-conceptions" (p. 1125). They continued:

> During their social encounters, individuals may actively bring their interaction partners' interactions evaluations into harmony with their self-conceptions. To wit, the man who conceives himself to be intimidating may sustain this conception by behaving in ways that induce others to grovel in his presence; the woman who views herself as unlovable may validate this conception by acting in ways that foster rejection by her would-be lovers. (p. 1120)

A variety of ingenious experiments have been constructed to explore this perspective. Let us, by way of illustration, consider the following:

Swann and Read's (1981) study sought to demonstrate that individuals will attempt, in the course of their interactions with others, to elicit responses that will confirm their own self-conceptions. The basic design called for pairs of individuals (each composed of a male and a female) to participate (in a laboratory setting) in "getting acquainted" conversations. Prior to the conversations, the males were asked to rate themselves with respect to how likable or unlikable they considered themselves to be. Also prior to the conversations, some of the males were led to believe that the females who were to be their partners had a favorable impression of them, and some were led to the opposite belief. The conversations of the various pairs were tape-recorded, and judges tabulated how frequently each male complimented the female.

It was found that males who liked themselves elicited more favorable reactions from their partners than did the males who did not like themselves. What was particularly striking was that such favorable responses were more likely to occur when the self-liking male thought his partner entertained a negative impression of him. Apparently, the belief that the female partner did not share his perception of himself as likable acted as an extra incentive for the male to use his social skills to persuade that female to shift her perception of him in a direction more congruent with his own. Interestingly, there was also an analogous trend for the males who thought of themselves as *not* likable to elicit an extra degree of "you are not likable" reaction from females who they assumed had a *positive* impression of them. That is, in both instances the male brought a presumably incongruous view of him by another (whether more negative or more positive) more in line with his own view. More is said shortly about the motivation of those who feel negatively toward self and find it self-stabilizing to recruit others to adopt the same perspective. Incidentally, analysis of the tapes of the conversations between each male–female pair suggested that the males used praise and compliments as strategies for persuading their partners to be more supportive of their self-concepts.

In other phases of their research concerned with self-affirmation in social interactions, Swann (1981) has found that persons are more likely to seek social feedback when they believe it will confirm their self-conceptions. Indeed, when recalling social feedback, persons preferentially highlight content congruent with their self-images (Swann & Read, 1981). The Swann et al. research (Swann & Hill, 1982) has clearly shown that although self-discrepant inputs produce alterations in self-concept in situations where there is little opportunity to pursue refuting maneuvers, little change occurs if one has access to ways of behaviorally discrediting such inputs. Interestingly, Swann and Predmore (1985) reported data suggesting that persons seek out as their social intimates "individuals who see them as they see themselves" (p. 1615). Swann (1987) declared: "Most of us spend most of our time with individuals who have implicitly or explicitly agreed to honor the identities we have negotiated with them" (p. 1042). Even further, persons are inclined to overestimate the degree to which the appraisals of their friends match their self-images (Swann, 1987). These findings indicate that finely tuned techniques have evolved for manipulating one's social relationships and one's perception of these relationships to prove that one's self-image (whatever it may be) is true and stable.

As already noted, persons energetically seek self-verification of self-traits that are even negative or unpleasant. It will be recalled, for example, that in the Swann and Read (1981) study, males who disliked self and who engaged in conversation with females they thought considered them likable tried to persuade these females not to see them as likable but rather as unlikable. In other words, the males wanted the females to adopt a stance more congruent with the males' negative self-views. Seeking after verification of one's negative self-attributes has been documented by numerous studies (e.g., Swann, Griffin, Predmore, & Gaines, 1987; Swann, Pelham, & Krull, 1989). Self-verification is often sought even though it results in negative and unpleasant affective states. Paradoxically, although it may be a satisfying experience to validate a negative aspect of self, it is also, to varying degrees, painful and depressing.

This phenomenon has led to an extended dispute in the literature as to whether self-defensive strategies are primarily aimed at self-verification or self-enhancement. As described earlier, a variety of findings indicate that persons magnify self-enhancement and minimize self-derogation. Studies have piled up on both sides of the self-verification versus self-enhancement dispute. Swann et al. (1987) proposed that both processes are prominent in self-protective tactics. They reviewed experiments suggesting that self-verification is linked with cognitive systems, whereas self-enhancement is associated with affective systems. They theorized that there is considerable independence of cognitive and affective systems, therefore individuals may simultaneously strugle for self-verification and self-enhancement, even when the effects of each are opposite in character. The cognitively driven focus on self-verification is not necessarily more rational or realistic than self-enhancement intent. What is being self-verified are ideas about self that are arbitrary inventions (based on local socialization practices). Consider, too, that self-verification may be a circuitous form of self-enhancement in the context of Western values, which assign high virtue to cognitive consistency and experiencing logical support for one's attributions.

In scanning the techniques employed to bolster one's preferred self, one can see that they often involve a conscientious monitoring of all cues pertaining to the self. That is, individuals guard the self by being especially alert to all that has self-reference. This alertness has been diversely demonstrated by selective superior memory for self-referring words, preferential attitudes toward the letters in one's name, selective attention to statements with self-connotations, overperception of self as a target, and so forth (Fenigstein, 1984; Markus & Wurf, 1987). To protect the preferred self, it is assigned special prominence in the psychological field.

However, a considerable literature (e.g., Duval & Wicklund, 1972; Fisher, 1986; Wicklund, 1975) indicated that when focus on the self is intensified, increased self-criticism, self-dissatisfaction, and even depressed affect often result. Beyond a certain threshold, self-accentuation has negative repercussions on self-perception. Others (e.g., Markus & Wurf, 1987) have commented on the potential incongruity between the need for self-focus to provide defense of the preferred self and the negative impact of intensified self-awareness on the favorability of one's self-concept. One might assume that persons have learned how to balance these opposing vectors. Baumeister (1990) discussed in detail the methods widely pressed into service for diminishing self-focus, "deconstructing" the self, and avoiding painful self-images. These methods may provide antidotes to the everpresent tendency to be hyper-alert to self. However, it may be true that equilibrating self-awareness is so tricky that the self-defense system keeps getting jarred.

OVERVIEW

This chapter has spelled out how the self-concept participates in the make-believe tactics required to adapt to the quirky state of things. The information we put forth persuasively suggests that self-concepts are arbitrary constructions. Rather radically diverse forms of the self have prevailed at different historical periods. Further, anthropological observations indicate that specific cultures can somewhat shape unique forms of the self. Indeed, the full range of uniquely different potential selves becomes evident in individuals who are brain damaged or report "multiple personality" experiences. The self emerges gradually as the newborn child matures and is not clearly identifiable in most instances until the age of 20–24 months (Fisher, 1986). Children do not modally recognize their own mirror images until they are almost 2 years old. The development and maintenance of a self-structure apparently involve an anfractuous process and require a good deal of energy and dedication. Individuals struggle during adolescence and later to define their major self-aspects, often in a rather wishful and arbitrary fashion. It has been shown empirically that the degree of correspondence between persons' judgments of their self-attributes and the judgments of other persons concerning such attributes is low and inconsistent.

Having formulated preferred self-definitions, individuals learn to employ an armamentarium of strategies to defend and stabilize them. They selectively tune into what is supportive, shut out incongruent inputs, foster social relationships with those who will acknowledge their special self-definitions, direct special reparative efforts to changing the viewpoints of those who challenge their preferred self-concept, and so forth. Such defensive strategies permit considerable stabilization of self-attitudes. However, these strategies, which take so many forms, are not always mutually supportive. Self-enhancement and self-verification tactics may conflict. Self-verification modes sometimes have quite the opposite effects of self-enhancing ones. Relatedly, the special focus on self required to be alertly protective of preferred self-images may also have opposed negative repercussions as a consequence of the self-criticalness induced by heightened self-awareness.

Despite the elaborate repertoire of techniques persons acquire for guarding their self-structures, they seem to be forever experiencing doubt and insecurity in this area. The world literature bristles with terms like "alienation," "marginality," "ego diffusion," "identity conflict," and "ambivalent self." We persistently hear about adolescent and mid-life identity crises (e.g., Baumeister, Shapiro, & Tice, 1985). The tension between individuation and deindividuation is unending (Maslach, 1974). The problems of self-definition are enormously complicated, too, by the vicissitudes of persons' close relationships, which call them to keep including in, and ejecting from, their self-structures those who are their intimates.

Aron, Aron, Tudor, and Nelson's (1991) experiments have demonstrated that those who are close to persons do gain entrance, to some degree, into their self-concepts. In one study, they asked subjects to rate a series of trait adjectives for their descriptiveness of themselves, their spouses, and a well-known entertainment figure. Then, after an intermediate distraction task, they were requested to react to these adjectives in terms of whether they applied to self or not. The time required to render each decision was measured. It was predicted that the longest latencies would occur for words that originally indicated a good deal of difference in their presumed descriptiveness of self as compared with their spouses. The reasoning was that the more their spouses had been incorporated into their self-space, the greater would be the overlap of "spouse" and "self" cognitive structures. Therefore, whenever instances of self-spouse difference arose, the difficulty would be greater in deciding whether the applicable adjectives were "me" or "not me." That is, the fact that others who had overlapping identities with the person (being to some degree part of their self-cognitive structures) were, in a specific judgmental context, registering as different from them would introduce confusion into their self-systems; and thereby prolong their decision time insofar as it involved that system. The data obtained significantly supported the basic hypothesis that intimates become fused into persons' self-representations. The self would appear, in part, to have constituents isomorphic with the attributes of those close to that self.

It would appear, as James (1910) originally theorized, that the self is not a unitary entity, but rather a composite of many elements. There are conscious and unconscious components, harmonious and inharmonious parts, positive and negative constituents, elements residing within and without the body, communicating and noncommunicating components, and much more that has not been identified. The average self appears to be a compound, not always a compatible collage. This view differs from the widely accepted Western ideal of the self as a finely unified and clearly bounded entity capable of functioning "on its own." Cushman (1991) referred to this as the "mythologizing of the monadic self" (p. 218).

The themes of monadic self and self-autonomy are highly valued in Western circles and have stimulated a spate of research on topics like self-esteem, ego-strength, and boundary articulation. Much of the work by Witkin and his group (1962), which dealt with field independence versus dependence, illustrated this line of research. Other illustrations were provided by the achievement motive research (e.g., McClelland, Atkinson, Clark, & Lowell, 1953), the social psychological studies of reactance (Brehm, 1966), the numerous projects on yielding and suggestibility (Maccoby & Jacklin, 1974), and the considerable explorations of dissociation (Bowers & Meichenbaum, 1984) and automaticity (Fischer & Pipp, 1984; Underwood, 1982). Much of these works were inspired by pro and con positions concerning the reality of the construct of a strong unified self.

The most blatant revelation of the widespread tension and confusion typifying the construction of the self-concept is the almost universal human aversion to including one's body in the self. As reviewed elsewhere (Fisher, 1986), the body has, in most locales, been treated as a disreputable object. The emphasis, especially in Western cultures, has been to build one's identity on images cleansed of body stuff. In most cultural contexts, the body exemplifies sexuality, anality, and sheer biological existence with all of its connotations of fragility and death. Some early Christians were so offended by the sexual significance of the body that they castrated themselves (Fisher, 1986). Thus, the paradox exists that many persons remain awkwardly uncomfortable with their bodies, which is the most obvious and palpable representation of self-existence. They typically seek to minimize the role of their bodies in their self-concepts. It is interesting that researchers have documented that, with increasing age, persons give less and less space to body representations in their self-concepts (McGuire & McGuire, 1982). The self becomes further and further defined in terms of the abstract, the socially symbolized, and the non-corporeal. The basic dilemma is that the body is the foundation, the anlage, of self. The incessant squirming to avoid recognition of this stark fact means that most self-concepts have sizable lacunae that are covered with tricky socially contrived patches. Self-definition is all too often mythologized by the need to limit the role of the body in such definition.

10

Somatic Consequences
of Illusions

If one goes beyond Cartesian notions, it is evident that, even though we label certain ideas as illusory, they exist in central nervous system tissue and therefore have physiological consequences. No one questions that fantasies and images influence the somatic realm. One only has to consider the commonplace example of how merely thinking about food initiates salivation and gastric mobility. However, despite the obvious connection between fantasy and bodily processes, little attention has been devoted directly to how illusion registers physiologically. True, there have been scattered studies of the impact of illusory ideas implanted by means of hypnosis upon sensory, motor, and autonomic functions (e.g., Kihlstrom, 1985; McGlashan, Evans, & Orne, 1969), and they documented significant effects. Also, various studies have pointed up the potential power of imagination to target specific channels of physiological response (e.g., Cacioppo & Petty, 1983). Becoming anxious about an imagined ("unreal") threat has physiological consequences quite analogous to those evoked by a "real" threat. While it may be apparent that illusory images reverberate in body terms, it is worthwhile to provide some detailed illustrations of such reverberation. Indeed, it can be suggested that ideational paradigms constructed of the illusory stuff of fantasy may shape unique modes of physiological representation.

The best examples of illusion's role in body response come from instances in which individuals are asked to take into their bodies substances to which they falsely ascribe potent properties. Let us begin with a really surprising report by Briddell et al. (1978). They were interested in exploring the effects of cognitive and pharmacological factors, linked with alcohol consumption, on sexual arousal to sexual stimuli differing in amount of deviance. Forty-eight male college students were randomly assigned to four conditions: (a) told they would receive alcohol but given a placebo, (b) told they would receive alcohol and actually received alcohol, (c) told they would not receive alcohol and given a placebo, and (d) told they would not receive alcohol and actually received it. Each subject then listened to three separate audiotapes: (a) an account of mutually enjoyable sexual intercourse between a male and female, (b) a description of a male raping a female, and (c) a depiction of a male sadistically hurting a female, but with no sexual intent. The various narratives were counterbalanced. Penile tumescence was recorded with a penile plethysmograph. Subjects signaled when they attained full penile erection during each of the narratives. They also rated their subjective arousal to each narrative.

One striking finding to emerge was that the subjects who *believed* they had received alcohol achieved greater penile tumescence than those who did not believe. Whether subjects had actually ingested alcohol did not affect tumescence. More strikingly, the expectancy effect on tumescence of believing one had ingested alcohol reached statistical significance only in the rape and sadistic conditions. Among those who were convinced they had consumed alcohol, the number who reached full erection during the rape condition was as great as during the heterosexual intercourse condition. However, among those who really consumed alcohol, the number who reached full erection was significantly greater during the heterosexual intercourse than during the rape condition.

Interestingly, the subjective ratings of arousal that the men made following each tape recording were higher as a function of the expectancy that alcohol had been consumed. Although the ratings were positively correlated with degree of tumescence in each condition (viz., 0.57 heterosexual intercourse, 0.42 rape, 0.31 sadistic aggression), the degree of correlation decreased progressively from the mutually agreeable intercourse condition to the extreme violence condition. Apparently, "alcohol illusion" enhanced sexual response physiologically during the deviant narratives, but this did not register in a conscious awareness of increased arousal.

In summary, note that the *belief* that one had consumed alcohol increased penile tumescence, but the actual consumption of alcohol did not. Further, the impact of belief was greater during the deviant conditions (e.g., rape) than during the normal heterosexual intercourse narrative. Also, correlations between tumescence and subjective ratings of arousal were moderately high for the normal intercourse narrative, but declined a good deal for the deviant narratives. There was an increasing disconnection between the subjective and physiological levels of arousal along the continuum from approved to disapproved sexual action.

This study witnessed that the false belief (illusion) that one has imbibed alcohol increases physiologically defined sexual arousal. Even more, the increase during the disreputable condition is relatively greater with respect to the physiological as compared with the subjective level. The belief that one has ingested alcohol has a releasing effect on certain sectors of the systems concerned with controlling sexual responsiveness. One might paraphrase the perspective of those who believed they consumed alcohol: "I have taken something into my body that has effects I cannot control. I am less responsible for my feelings and responses. I don't have to inhibit my sexual excitement. I have alcoholic permission to 'let go' sexually." It should be affirmed that other studies (e.g., Hull & Bond, 1986) also have presented data supportive of an illusory supposition that being under the influence of alcohol can modulate penile tumescence. The supposition apparently gains entry to a complex regulatory system and modifies it in selective ways.

PLACEBO PHENOMENA

More dramatic examples of how ingesting substances with illusory properties can affect body systems are proveded by placebo phenomena. There is a Large and varied literature documenting the startling prowess of the placebo. If the proper expectancies are created, a capsule containing an inert substance can produce bodily effects that are difficult and sometimes impossible to distinguish from those evoked by active pharmacological agents. Placebos have been shown, in various degrees, to relieve acute pain, coughs, headaches, diabetes, ulcers, arthritis, seasickness, multiple sclerosis, and many other sources of discomfort (Evans, 1985; Jospe, 1978; Wickramasekera, 1985). In diverse contexts, placebos have exhibited such potentials as the inhibition of gastric acids or the effects of ipecac and have been able to reduce adrenalcortical activity and serum lipoproteins (Evans, 1985). A series of studies suggests that placebos are consistently about 55% to 60% as effective in their analgesic effects as are active analgesic agents, against which they are compared. A review of 11 double-blind studies demonstrated that 36% of pain patients attained at least 50% relief from pain after ingesting a placebo (Evans, 1985).

An unending array of placebos' dramatic effects on physiological systems could be cited. Especially impressive is the fact that persons who are given placebos may subsequently develop genuine toxic reactions. Placebos have been implicated in such "side effects" as headaches, nausea, constipation, skin rashes, and others of serious intensity (Ross & Buckalew, 1985). In fact, placebos can initiate significant illness. Note that placebos' therapeutic power is particularly dramatic in children and can probably be enhanced in adults by specific factors like anxiety, transference attitudes, and personality inclination. Placebos' therapeutic power may show dose effects and even produce withdrawal symptoms (Jospe, 1978).

Placebolike expectancies seem to potentiate, attenuate, or negate the impact of truly active drugs. Lyerly, Ross, Krugman, and Clyde (1964) described a study in which the effects of amphetamine varied as a function of experimental instructions. The same active drug could be experienced either as a stimulant or a depressant, depending on implanted expectancies. Relatedly, antipsychotic drugs can be attenuated with respect to their therapeutic effects by presenting them as placebos (Evans, 1985). Obviously, it is difficult to specify clear boundaries between the powers of active drugs and those of inactive substances imbued with illusory activity. Indeed, the history of research dealing with psychoactive drugs is a persistent tale of frustration about the inability to get rid of placebo static. The imaginatively charged up "sugar pill" has never ceased to amaze investigators.

BUFFERING DEATH

The ultimate demonstration of the physiological repercussions of illusion is provided by reports on the delay of death consequent upon acquiring certain supportive ideas. One of the most impressive reports in this respect was cited earlier. It will be recalled that Langer and Rodin (1976) devised a special program for aged individuals living in a nursing home. They were interested in the effects of giving such individuals the feeling that they had more choices and potential for taking responsibility than they usually assumed to be available. One sample of individuals was addressed by the hospital administrator, who emphasized their right to make decisions for themselves (e.g., "you have the responsibility of caring for yourselves, of deciding whether or not you want to make this a home you can be proud of and happy in" [p. 194]). Further, this sample was offered the choice of adopting a plant and caring for it. A control group was told by the hospital administrator that although it had options, the hospital staff was ultimately responsible for what happened. This group was also given plants, but were told "the nurses will water and care for them for you" (p. 194). That is, those in the experimental group were offered an image of self-responsibility and those in the control group were advised to give up power to the staff. The impact of these contrasting sets was monitored by means of questionnaires and behavioral measures.

Generally speaking, those who were given the message "You are in control" fared better. At follow-up 18 months later, the "in control" sample had a significantly lower death rate than the "not in control" sample. The basic difference between the two categories was that one was given a largely illusory impression of having power over what was happening and the other was made to feel "I have little influence." Actually, the experimental manipulation was primarily symbolic. A thinly concealed fiction was sufficient to buffer physiological vulnerability to death.

There is a considerable, largely anecdotal, literature full of presumed illustrations of how beliefs can directly induce death. Thus, the anthropological literature described the so-called "voodoo death" phenomenon, which is said to occur in individuals who believe they have been "bewitched" (Hahn, 1985). Taylor (1989) sketched a number of reports concerning persons who appeared to die suddenly as the result of events that made them feel catastrophically not in control. Alexander, Chandler, Langer, Newman, and Davies (1989) reported a well-designed study, in which the use of transcendental meditation (a mode of fantasy and faith) significantly reduced the death rate in aged persons. A fair quantity of scientific data has accumulated indicating that beliefs of how much one is in control of life mediate vulnerability to disease, response to surgery, immune system functioning, and many related processes (e.g., Allred & Smith, 1989; Antonovsky, 1979; Langer, 1983; McClelland, 1989; Scheier & Carver, 1987; Scheier et al., 1989). Impressive data (Rodin & Salovey, 1989) also indicate that being of an optimistic frame of mind makes persons less somatically vulnerable to stress.

Most cultures have cultivated the use of inspirational imagery to heal people. This has been true both in the East and the West (Sheikh & Sheikh, 1989), and was common both in ancient and more recent times. Sheikh, Kunzendorf, and Sheikh (1989) indicated that the Hindu/Buddhist tradition has particularly emphasized imagery techniques for healing. Exercises focusing on certain inspirational imagery themes are considered to have the power to cure bodily pathology. The disciples of Mary Baker Eddy promulgated a similar perspective. One also finds advocates of procedures for curing serious illnesses like cancer by means of optimistic imagery. Sheikh et al. (1989) noted: "The client may be asked to image a malfunctioning organ becoming normal . . ." (p. 490). This mode will presumably set things right. There are even claims that images of "white blood cells attacking germs' stimulate greater immune responses. In addition, Sheikh et al. (1989) provided a spectrum of examples of how Christianity has utilized inspirational images to cure persons' illnesses. There is no question that there is widespread faith in the value of images (largely of a pretend nature) to improve bodily functioning. Peterson and Bossio (1991) presented a range of impressive research data that does, indeed, document the association of good health with an optimistic outlook. Incidentally, Pennebaker (1990) demonstrated that simply "confiding in" others (communicating one's concerns and "secrets") has healing health effects (including facilitation of the immune system).

SHAPING PHYSIOLOGICAL SYSTEMS

Fantasy and make-believe can shape and reshape the appearance of things. Variables such as inflated optimism, religious faith, and convictions about one's efficacy can introduce particular perspectives about the nature of the world. Illusory images also can have physiological repercussions. Indeed, one could speculate that illusory notions can be transmuted into special, perhaps isomorphically analogous, physiological representations. Consider, for example, the individual who may, for some psychological reason, develop a classical hysterical conversion symptom like "glove anesthesia." Such an individual experiences a loss of sensation in a circumscribed anatomical area, which would be defined by the wearing of a glove. This pattern of sensory loss does not fit accepted schemas of sensory nerve distribution. Rather, it reflects the concept of "My hand, but no other part of me, is numb." We are not aware of any recognized versions of sensory processes that match the "glove anesthesia" phenomenon. Numerous other analogous "arbitrary" forms of anesthesia and motor paralysis are described in the literature on conversion hysteria (e.g., Watson & Buranen, 1979). In some, as yet unexplained, fashion, the central nervous system is able to mobilize a selective, localized form of inhibition, perhaps as a means of symbolic coping or communication. It would appear that central nervous system functioning may be sufficiently flexible to permit novel categories of arousal and inhibition keyed to specific psychological images. The "novel categories" involve arbitrarily defined spatial areas of the body that do not fit accepted maps of body innervation or distribution of sensory sensitivity.

Freud (1953) originally raised the possibility of unconventional physiological paradigms when he formulated his theory of conversion hysteria. He apparently believed that if persons, for psychodynamic reasons, develop certain defensive notions about their body, there may be consequent construction of matching physiological paradigms. Illustratively, he theorized that if conflict about sexual wishes is projected onto an arbitrary body area symbolically equated with sexual expression, that area may isomorphically become hypo- or hyperactivated. Freud's (1953) formulation envisioned body areas sharing physiological commonalities as a function of common psychological meanings ascribed to them. Thus, he speculated that the various body openings (e.g., mouth, anus) might be analogically assigned a parallel significance and therefore be activated by certain classes of stimuli. Such speculation has not yet been scientifically tested.

However, one study may be cited that is provisionally encouraging. This study (Fisher & Greenberg, 1979), obtained from normal men and women, reported pain and somatic discomfort experienced in a wide range of body areas. One of the aims of the study was to ascertain if there are correlations between somatic symptomatology and psychological attitudes relating to one's preference for social closeness versus distance when interacting with other persons. The psychological parameter was measured by asking subjects to judge (in a darkened room) how far a luminous rod should be set from them so as to designate a "comfortable distance for others to sit from you when you are engaged in a conversation." Initial exploratory data had suggested that attitudes about closeness–distance are linked with certain kinds of somatic discomfort. However, what was really novel was that the category of somatic discomfort did not pertain to disturbance at any one individual body site, but rather to the aggregate of disturbance in all body openings (e.g., oral, anal, urinary). It was only by using scores based on the *total* of somatic discomfort at various body opening sites that a relationship with closeness–distance appeared to exist. In any case, the original exploratory observation of a link between discomfort in body openings and tension about how close to be to others was confirmed in a formal study of male and female samples. It was found that judgments of the proper distance to set a luminous rod (to define comfortable social distance) proved to be correlated significantly with total body opening discomfort scores. The further the comfortable social distance was set, the greater were the number of body opening symptoms reported.

This was true in both the male and female samples. Scores based on various combinations of discomforts in other categories of body parts were *not* correlated with closeness–distance attitudes. The speculative framework offered for the significant findings was based on the psychoanalytic idea that body openings serve as channels for individuals' transactions with the world. That is, they symbolically represent the process of interchange between self and what is "out there." It was theorized that those who are reluctant to get close to others are "susceptible to body opening symptoms as an expression of . . . persistent unresolved needs for more commerce and psychological contact with others" (p. 425). Presumably, such unresolved needs "induce a compensatory chronic, and perhaps shifting, activation of various body opening areas. The unfulfilled wishes for interchange might . . . initiate arousal first in one body opening, then in another, and so forth" (p. 425). The soundness of this explanation remains to be seen. But the primary point is that multiple, apparently disparate, body openings seem to be integrated into a somatic symptom system mirroring a shared psychological theme. It would be more convincing, however, if direct physiological measures (e.g., temperature) from various body openings displayed the same systemlike behavior vis-à-vis the closeness–distance psychological measure.[1]

COMMENTS

In this chapter, we have tried to point out that beliefs, even if labeled "illusory," exist in tissue and have physiological consequences. Such consequences

---

[1]A number of studies (Fisher, 1986) suggested that the muscle and skin layers of the body show coordinated physiological response patterns as part of their participation in what is psychologically experienced as the protective self-boundary region.

are not mere epiphenomena. They can involve any system of the body and even be of life-and-death proportions. The physiological power of illusion is probably best depicted by the multiple effects of placebos. No active drug has yet been observed that is as pervasively "active" as the "sugar pill" imbued with faith and charged up with the authority of the healer. Indeed, it is a fair statement that we still do not know the full extent to which the power of active drugs is reinforced by placebolike fancies (Fisher & Greenberg, 1989).

The fact is that cognitive factors play a significant role in the entire physiological realm subsumed under the term *physical* health. Seeman (1989), after reviewing data in this area, stated: "Finally, we cannot ignore the mounting evidence that if there is one dominant subsystem in its impact on health, it is the cognitive subsystem. Study after study . . . reported the commanding role of self-definition, self-perception, and sense of control in the maintenance and enhancement of health" (p. 1108). Whatever ideas and theories persons fabricate about their environs will probably have a detectable influence on their susceptibility to somatic pathology.

We also have raised speculatively the question of whether certain psychological paradigms, particularly if they involve ideas about one's body, can recruit corresponding specialized physiological systems that are not conventionally conceptualized as existing. Regardless of whether images are illusory or not, they may have the power to shape novel physiological response patterns. As already noted, the arbitrary loss of sensory sensitivity (e.g., glove anesthesia) seen in certain instances of conversion hysteria is illustrative of such a possibility. The whole matter would appear to be deserving of serious research exploration.

11

LARGER PERSPECTIVES

OVERVIEW

We are now in a position to attempt some broader integrations and extrapolations of the material presented in the preceding chapters. Let us begin by reviewing the major points that have emerged. A central idea that was developed is that persons learn that being human means experiencing sharp contradictions and catastrophes. Illness, death, loss, and adaption to meaningless demands are unavoidable. Such inescapable conditions pose an ever-present threat and probably stimulate neutralization efforts based on adopting wishful, optimistic notions. It is presumed that existence is manageable only if self-deceptive and pretense-based fictions are cultivated, which reassuringly dampen the intensity of what is only too obviously lurking "out there." Death anxiety has been particularly singled out (e.g., Becker, 1973) as a fact of human biological fate that, in its raw unblunted form, would make a mockery of existence for humans who are so uniquely and exquisitely self-aware.

Much of the reviewed material is a testimony to the fantastic ingenuity persons have shown in constructing strategies to filter out death, loss of control, and insignificance. The array of "defense mechanisms" and illusion-building modes fervently pressed into service is remarkable. To maintain a sense that the world is a reasonable place, average, quite normal persons are diversely required to deny what they know, to invent make-believe rationalizations, to ascribe optimistic meanings to blatantly tragic events, and to populate the universe with a pantheon of magical figures. There is little evidence that the illusion-construction strategies pressed into service can be reasonably differentiated in terms of their levels of "maturity." What is supposedly an immature "defense mechanism" in one context may provide an optimum buffer in another. Aside from grossly psychotic management of experience, one cannot reliably label specific forms of defense as inferior to others. Practically "anything goes" when it comes to shielding self against the major existential negatives.

The importance of make-believe in adaptation is reflected in the skills that even very young children exhibit in their pretend play. In the first few years of life, a splendid repertoire of expertise in make-believe is visible. As already described, young children quickly master the concept of "let's pretend" and devote much energy and time to practicing it. Apparently, they grasp the need for pretend skills in coping with life as they experience it. They sense the prevalence of pretense and also are encouraged by their life-tested (trauma-aware) parents to become good at make-believe. Not only do pretend skills facilitate their maintenance of equilibrium in a sea of cultural fictions, but they also provide children with fantasy equivalents for action, which make it easier for their parents to impose forms of discipline that regulate acting out.

Illusion's effectiveness as a buffer is highlighted by the fact that depression and unhappiness are more likely to plague those who are "too realistic." It is well documented that persons who are not depressed tend, in a number of contexts, to be "unrealistically" optimistic. One may paradoxically speculate that psychopathology is, in many instances, not due to being "too imaginative" but rather to "not being imaginative enough." Those who "break down" psychologically may not have sufficiently mastered the pretend techniques required for neutralizing the larger things that go wrong. We already have discussed the overlap between adaptive illusion and so-called psychopathology. It is not easy to distinguish the two, because one gradually shades into the other. We have noted the drifting border between the two realms and, indeed, the largely arbitrary (not very reliable) standards used to judge whether an individual is psychologically deviant (a "psychiatric patient"). The fact is that significant segments of the so-called normal population make use of adaptive strategies and myths that are considered, within the medical model of psychiatry, to be grossly abnormal. Large numbers of normal individuals entertain magical ideas, toy with fantasies of "mind reading," believe in the power of supernatural entities, and even periodically listen to "voices."

Illusory based strategies seem to pervade the process of adaptation. They have been shown to participate in the regulation of mood, many forms of attribution, the shaping of the self-concept, the management of death-anxiety, the construction of self- and body-boundaries, world views, and even patterns of physiological response. Ortega y Gassett (1957) depicted this state of affairs with simple vividness:

Take stock of those around you and you will . . . hear them talk in precise terms about themselves and their surroundings, which would seem to point to them having ideas on the matter. But start to analyze those ideas and you will find that they hardly reflect in any way the reality to which they appear to refer, and if you go deeper you will discover that there is not even an attempt to adjust the ideas to this reality. Quite the contrary: through these notions the individual is trying to cut off any personal vision of reality, of his own very life. For life is at the start a chaos in which one is lost. The individual suspects this, but he is frightened at finding himself face to face with this terrible reality, and tries to cover it over with a curtain of fantasy, where everything is clear. It does not worry him that his "ideas" are not true, he uses them as trenches for the defense of his existence, as scarecrows to frighten away reality. (pp. 156–157)

Most persons probably have a latent uneasy awareness of the inexorable dilemmas characterizing the human cycle. Consequently, they seek ways to convince themselves that such dilemmas are only quasi-real and end up being chronically fascinated with the potentialities of pretense and make-believe. Indeed, cultures everywhere are obsessively concerned with sampling intimations that all is not what it appears to be. There is widespread playful toying with the possibility that what is being experienced can be turned upside down. The urge to reshape things is highlighted by the radical religious mythologies generated universally. Almost all religions declare that behind the apparent stream of events is a vast, complex control system monitored and energized by powerful figures. Religious schemas declare the hopeful potential for supernatural (magical) intervention. Such religious images can provide individuals with psychological shielding.

Awareness of persons' loyalties to illusory images has been progressively heightened by the increased communication among diverse cultures. As each culture becomes more aware of the "strange" and "different" practices of the other, the relativity of such practices seeps through. The arbitrary "I believe therefore it is true" character of basic cultural views comes more and more into view. Obviously, the sciences have energized dramatically the stripping away process and have induced a suspicion, even in the uneducated, that we are all too easily drawn to undocumented fictions. However, it is astounding that, even in the midst of our increased formal commitment to scientific fact, there is little evidence that the personal use of illusion as an adaptive strategy has decreased. It is not even clear that the most highly educated individuals have significantly reduced the role of illusory images in their adaptive moves. Indeed, as the "hard" sciences accumulate stupendous quantities of data, one detects that the humanities and the "softer" social sciences are accepting the idea that "reality" is a vague concept, and that it is often impossible to penetrate beyond the individual's own self-steeped version of

what is happening. The appeal of this perspective, which accepts the inevitability of illusory schema, is witnessed by the burgeoning interest in such ad-
vocacies as hermeneutic analysis of behavior (Gergen, 1982), life as narrative
and psychotherapy as narrative construction (Spence, 1982), and the utilization of "mild illusion" to bolster "mental health" (Taylor, 1989). Even in the
"hard" sciences, one hears (e.g., Kuhn, 1962; Overton, 1984) that each theory is a temporary construct that facilitates research efforts until it wears
out and the next theory is introduced to replace it.

STRATEGIC ADVANTAGES
OF ILLUSORY CONSTRUCTS

We have already reiterated, to the point of saturation, that illusory ideas serve
as buffers against trauma, meaninglessness, and well-known tragic endings.
However, we would like to explore, in more detail, other potential profits
of self-rescue based on make-believe. But first, let us caution that the definition of an "illusory idea" is inexact. Such an idea is presumably one that depicts
a state of affairs that cannot be logically or rationally confirmed. This is obviously an ideal definition that cannot be applied easily. In the heat of life's
complexities, it is often difficult to identify what is truly "rational." Obviously there are all shades of the rational-illusory continuum. Loosely speaking,
even extreme paranoid delusions have been found to contain certain valid
elements. One has to keep in mind, too, that scientific findings have repeatedly transformed what is apparent truth.

A number of observers have looked at the strategic gains derived from
illusory reshaping (e.g., Elster, 1983; Goleman, 1985; MacDonald, 1988; Martin, 1985; Taylor, 1989; Tiger, 1979). One frequently mentioned advantage
has to do with pragmatic readiness for action. It has been stated that an ap-
proximate, even somewhat inaccurate, formulation of a situation (a depiction not anchored in careful logical analysis) can have adaptive value because
it enables quick response. Note what Krebs, Denton, and Higgins (1988) said
about this point:

> In the face of infinite complexity, a purely "rational" course of action would
> be to suspend belief, to hold conclusions in abeyance until there is adequate
> evidence. But this would be highly maladaptive in many circumstances. Ad-
> ages such as "he who hesitates is lost" and "the early bird gets the worm" im-
> ply it is adaptive to act on best guesses. Early humans who waited until they
> fully understood the behavior of potential mates before making their move would
> have been no more fit than the modern individual who sits at home alone, look-
> ing at the telephone. In evolutionary currency, the adaptive value of knowledge
> lies primarily in the behavior to which it gives rise. Individuals who don't try
> don't succeed. Individuals who take a quick reading of a situation, reach a work-

ing conclusion, then act will fare better in many circumstances than those who engage in extended rational analyses.

Recent advances in the study of human inference have shown that we rarely use formal rules of inference in everyday life . . . people use heuristics when making judgments in their everyday lives . . . the three principles typically emphasized in models of rationality (invariance, consistency, internal coherence are *not* a guiding part of our mental system, and rational models have hindered rather than helped our understanding of human behavior. (pp. 124–125)

Krebs et al. (1988) suggested that inaccurate approximations are often superior, in many situations, to carefully thought through and minutely accurate formulations. This is because, in the heat of battle, they lead to immediate "functional conclusions," and, in the course of time, to an effective surplus of "hits" over "misses." The whole process of stereotyping persons, which produces radically simplified and often quite illusory versions of them, has been analogously regarded by some as necessary if there is to be any effective action in social situations. Krebs et al. (1988) concluded: "It is not the validity of beliefs that counts in natural selection, it is the adaptiveness of behaviors to which they give rise" (p. 126). Within this context, they believed: "From an evolutionary perspective, knowing the truth (valid ideas, logical inferences, accurate memories) may be *mal*adaptive. *In*valid beliefs, *mis*conceptions, and *self-delusions* may be more fitness-enhancing . . ." (p. 126).

Even when certain illusions prove to be detrimental to individuals, they may be beneficial to the wider group. The proper functioning of a culture may require persons to undertake roles that would be too unattractive if not enhanced by make-believe strategies. Nisbett and Ross (1980) illustrated this point:

> The social benefits of individually erroneous subjective probabilities may be great even when the individuals pay a high price for the error. We probably would have few novelists, actors, or scientists if all potential aspirants to these careers took action based on a normatively justifiable probability of success. We also might have few new products, new medical procedures, new political movements, or new scientific theories. (p. 27)

It has been said (Elster, 1983) that the capitalist system works so well because it persuades potential entrepreneurs to believe in an unrealistically high likelihood of economic success. In so doing, it stimulates extraordinary risk-taking and effort. The argument has been made, too, that simple improvements in social conditions call for an enormous output of effort. If persons were realistically aware of this magnitude, they would rarely launch uplifting projects. On the other side of the coin, it may be that certain forms of behavior with negative consequences for the culture are better controlled by imbuing them with heightened amounts of negativity. For example, the lethal dangers of drug addiction may be painted in hues of disproportionate intensity (Elster, 1983). Similarly, there is a long history of picturing certain sexual behaviors, which might be disruptive of conventional social arrangements, as catastrophically destructive to health and even sanity.

Various observers (e. g., Krebs et al., 1988) agreed that illusory ideas help persons to "keep going." There are so many frustrations and cyclic ups and downs that individuals need a halo of sustaining beliefs. The ability to persevere through tough phases of life may require such fantasy repairs. Krebs et al. (1988) even suggested that, although certain persistent beliefs may be false in their inception, they can initiate self-fulfilling prophesies that ultimately are validating. The paraphrase of this attitude would be "If you believe something intently enough you can make it come true."

As noted earlier, Swann (1981) showed that when persons develop a specific concept of self, even if permeated with illusory elements, they often seek out others who can be manipulated to provide confirmation of the concept. They, in turn, may be expected to support the quasifictional self-presumptions of the others. There is a mutual tolerance, such that "If you support my not terribly realistic notions, I will support yours." Krebs et al. (1988) commented:

> As we negotiate everyday social exchanges, we often are aware of the other's tendency to fool themselves, but it isn't in our interest to call them on it; we only sour occasions and lose friends. But many of our delusions are shared delusions; they are part of our culture; we are socialized to believe them; and that is adaptive. Shared beliefs foster group cohesiveness, and are self-serving ("We are the chosen people"). (pp. 132–133)

Elster (1983) introduced the novel notion that an illusory idea may be "useful" or even conducive to the truth by virtue of its capacity to neutralize some other illusory idea. Presumably, individuals might be caught up with a fiction that motivates maladaptive responses, but another fiction might be embraced that would have the net effect of canceling the first and thereby decreasing such responses. We have conjured up a few examples of this sort of process. Consider persons who have, as the result of early irrational socialization experiences, constructed an illusory image of self as inferior. If these persons capitalize on later experiences to fashion an equally irrational notion of some brand of self-superiority, this could serve to balance the depreciated self-concept. Another example of this balancing of illusory notions relates to attitudes toward the opposite gender. A man's early experiences with his mother could result in generalized illusory images about the hostile motives of women, but these could be opposed by equally illusory ideas about women generated by the unrealistically idealized images evolving in the course of an intense romantic involvement. This sort of interactive equilibrium between fictive notions may play a much larger role in supporting social or personal stability than is realized.

Greenwald (1980) theorized that fabricated ideas or biases "helps to preserve the (individual's) knowledge system's organization" (p. 615). He analyzed in considerable detail the "totalitarian" tactics pressed into service by the "ego" to maintain self-integrity. He visualized the self as essentially a knowledge system or a base for cognitive control, with its primary intent to preserve the availability of its stored information. The compiled body of information representing the self is compared to a library. The adequate functioning of a library requires an "organized system for shelving books and recording the locations of shelved books." It also requires that "the organization existing at the time of shelving the book still be in existence at the time of searching for it" (p. 613). Greenwald (1980) focused on the need for the self to operate by highly conservative, tightly controlled rules in order to maintain stability over time. The need for stability presumably has the highest priority and often overrules standards of rationality. That is, illusory concepts that dramatize optimistic outcomes, the centrality of self, and the rigid regulation of change are said to preserve the integrity of the cognitive "library" basic to the self-system. Fictions are presumably fed into the self-system to bolster its contours and structure as a system, per se. Greenwald (1980) remarked that "the egocentricity and conservatism biases may provide a 'protective belt' that preserves the 'hard core' belief that all of one's memory is the interrelated experience of a single entity—the one called *myself*" (p. 614).

Despite the Enlightenment, fictional and irrational ideas are richly alive and well today. This implies that the fictive is intrinsically attractive. To think "irrationally" may be tempting, because it represents a form of freedom. To break out of the bonds of the logical may be as satisfying as breaking out of any restraint system. Earlier we discussed the possibility that religious schemas may be attractive because they offer a bundle of integrative and comforting beliefs, as well as depict a universe that defies the rules of rationality and fills the life space with all of the potentialities represented by magic and mysterious figures immune to the limits of conventional reason.

Considering the contrasting ways in which the two genders are socialized, one might expect males and females to have different styles of constructing defenses against the major absurdities. However, it is difficult to detect consistent gender differences with reference to death anxiety variables directly or indirectly linked with the whole issue. True, women do express more conscious death anxiety then men, but it is not clear whether this reflects a greater willingness on the part of women to admit to anxiety. Note that no consistent gender differences have been observed in the amount of unconscious death anxiety. There are hints that women may romanticize death more than do men. At another level, one finds data indicating that boys portray more lethal action in their spontaneous stories than do girls. But these few scattered findings do not add up to a meaningful picture of gender differences in attitudes toward death. Relatedly, one finds little evidence of consistent gender differences in belief in a "just world" or other broad illusory strategies.

Some gender differences have shown up in the use of specific defense mechanisms. Males are more inclined to utilize turning against others and projection, whereas females more often use turning against self. Males apparently rely more on outwardly directed aggressive tactics. One can also ponder other observations that might be pertinent. For example, women are more susceptible to depression (presumably an indication of lesser ability to utilize protective illusion) than are men; but, on the other hand, men abuse alcohol more often (presumably a chemical approach to camouflaging reality). Further, women are slightly more inclined than men to rely on the buffering effects of religious belief.

These bits and pieces are not really informative. Perhaps males use more aggressive illusory strategies than women. On the whole, though, one is, at our present stage of knowledge, hard pressed to document any gross contrasts in the ways men and women fabricate protective images.

SELF-DECEPTION

A favorite topic in the literature dealing with illusion concerns the nature of the self-deception involved in the construction of an illusory belief. A perusal of this literature indicates that the meaning of "self-deception" is obscure. Contributors to a volume edited by J. Martin (1988) have excellently analyzed its various connotations. They point out that one major axis of disagreement relates to whether self-deceivers are conceptualized as being in a paradoxical state of believing something they know is not true, or whether they are viewed in less paradoxical terms. Other dimensions of confusion and disagreement relate to whether self-deception requires a splitting of self, whether it necessarily involves unconscious distortion, whether it is "intentional" or "volitional," and so forth. One emerges from the multiple views expressed in this volume with a sense that the meaning of "self-deception" can range from motivated unconscious concealment of truth from self to a kind of cognitive obtuseness or vagueness in processing information.

Empirical studies demonstrate that persons can be "self-deceived." As defined by Gur and Sackeim (1979), self-deception exists when an individual simultaneously holds two contradictory beliefs, with one not subject to awareness and the nonawareness motivationally inspired. Note that some (e.g., Gibbins & Douglas, 1985) dispute the soundness of the Gur and Sackeim (1979) findings. We do not further review the detailed complexities of the arguments that have flourished with respect to self-deception. It is clear, however, that the major disputed issue revolves around whether one can "know" something is not true and yet, within the same time frame, "believe" it is true. Actually, we are puzzled that the possibility of such a bald state of contradiction is treated as unlikely or necessarily requiring explanation. Such states of contradiction are routinely rampant and well assimilated into schemas of what is cognitively acceptable. Some have linked the ability to function contradictorily to the fairly well-documented fact (e.g., Chanowitz & Langer, 1985) that the self is not a unitary entity. Apparently, contradictory notions and beliefs may simultaneously exist at different levels or in different sectors of the self-space. There is probably a relatively high tolerance for grossly discrepant ideas to coexist within the same self-space; and the need to significantly segregate such ideas in separate regions may arise only in selective instances.

The truth is that most societies are quite tolerant of behaviors and attitudes that functionally involve an acceptance of contradictory polarities. Certainly the history of Western culture has been marked by numerous such instances. One only has to recall the simultaneous declaration of democracy and the practice of slavery; the parallel devotion to charitable religions and ruthless business ethics; the coexistence of beliefs in the sacredness of motherhood and denunciation of sexuality, which is the *sine qua non* of human reproduction, as evil; the juxtaposition of putting women on a pedestal and not allowing them to vote; the simultaneous loyalty to science and religious (sacred) doctrine; the coexistence of good parenting values and the widespread exploitation of children; and so forth. Most codes of social behavior call for a heavy dose of immediate contradiction. That is, it is the norm to "put on" social facades that are often only slightly synchronized with internal feelings. There are many times in an average day when one musters a friendly mien on the outside, while the coexisting internal feeling is weighted with negativity and anger. Even moderately sensitive persons are quite conscious of this state of contradiction but have been socialized to accept it as a routine matter. We know, too, that ambivalence is a common attribute of human perceptions. The clinical literature teems with examples of persons who simultaneously love and hate important figures in their lives. Such ambivalence is also true of attitudes toward self.

In short, persons are all trained to be accepting of, and even tolerably comfortable with, starkly contradictory attitudes in themselves. They do not have to elaborately deceive themselves about these contradictions. Given the motivation to be contradictory, it is apparently no great effort "to go with it." Most cultures are so suffused with blatant contradictions that persons could not survive their socialization experiences unless they learned to accept such contradictions as a natural state of affairs. They implicitly learn that the rules of logic apply to only a narrow chunk of life, and that real life adaptation is impossible without mustering a *belle indifference* toward even obvious logical violations. It would appear that tolerance of irrationalities is a property of the human psyche. What requires explanation is not the universal comfort with contradiction, but rather the spasmodic efforts to confront it. As Kuhn (1962) pointed out, even the most prestigious scientific establishments, representative of the essence of logical intellectuality, tolerate the accumulation of large amounts of contradictory evidence before they reformulate floundering explanatory paradigms. Scientists in a particular discipline may, for decades, live with (and ignore) research findings that are incongruent with their favorite theories. What better illustration is there of the normality of tolerance for contradiction?

It is obvious that there can be a literal awareness of contradiction and yet "self-deception" prevails; one simply has learned to minimize or not attribute any meaningful importance to the discrepancy. That is, a normative capacity exists to be intellectually blind if there is good reason to be so. A myriad of make-believe skills facilitate slipping in and out of obtuseness and standard logic. There are probably many sectors in which even directly confronting individuals with gross discrepancies in a belief would not elicit sincere admission (or perception) of the "realness" of these discrepancies.

THE EXPERT ILLUSION SUSTAINERS

Cultures provide individuals with multiple reassuring rituals and strategies. In the case of death anxiety, widespread support is afforded by myths of "ascension" and immortality, the availability of authoritatively recommended ways of living that guarantee health and long life, and elaborate practices for concealing the existence of nonexistence. In fact, each culture cultivates specialists who devote major energies to fabricating fictive buffers for the populace. Elaborate mechanisms exist for "training" expert defenders of illusory strategies. Specialized vocations have evolved for supplying make-believe reassurance and support. By way of illustration, one immediately thinks of the shaman, the priest, the magician, the generic psychological therapist, the television writer who delivers a weekly quota of optimistic imagery, the authoritative placebo bestower, and so forth. There is quite a phalanx of such sustainers in most societies. We thought it would be interesting to look at some of them and gain perspective on certain aspects of their specialized roles.

Comedians

Because of our previous research (Fisher & Fisher, 1981), we are particularly knowledgeable about two classes of illusion protectors (viz., comedians and actors). We also decided to consider a third important class (viz., priests and ministers). Our studies of comedians and actors involved persons professionally committed to these vocations. The objective was to explore developmental and personality variables relevant to such individuals, on the basis of interviews, projective tests (Rorschach, Thematic Apperception Test), and early memories. The spectrum of data demonstrated that certain themes or concerns typify comedians and actors. Persons in both of these occupations proved to be centrally concerned with soothing and protecting others. Comedians typically took on the responsibility of making people feel less threatened by life's dangers and contradictions. They have the interminable duty to make people laugh—to convince them that even the worst catastrophe is funny.

Our study (Fisher & Fisher, 1981) disclosed that comedians grow up in families where they are expected to shield their parents (especially mother); they become experts at using humor for this purpose. We noted:

> The comedian learns as a child that by being funny and playing the part of a comic he gives his parents psychological support. His sense of obligation to them seems to get expressed, at least partially, in the feeling that he must create an atmosphere that will blunt the impact of negative forces in the world. He probably learns to stroke his parents with his funny role. (p. 71)

Comedians come to this "It is my obligation to soothe you" role by growing up with parents who expect an early renunciation of dependence and a premature shouldering of adultlike responsibilities. We stated: "What the parents expect may be paraphrased as follows: 'I want you to grow up very fast. Forget that you are a child who has the privilege of being supported and nurtured. I will be displeased if you do not live up to the self-sacrificing role I have in mind for you' " (pp. 54–55). In this context, comedians, as children, feel they are relentlessly judged as bad or good by their parents in terms of how well they accept a superresponsible assignment. Comedians are, in fact, sensitively preoccupied with good–bad imagery and view their comedy as a means of doing good. They are, by their own testimony, "healers" who help people by exposing them to threatening material (death, anality, sex) and then detoxifying it all with humor. Actually, by employing humor to prove that good and bad are relative concepts existing largely in the eye of the beholder, comedians try to neutralize the myriad ways in which persons feel targeted as bad or evil.

Actors

Data from our study (Fisher & Fisher, 1981) of actors revealed an analogous devotion to shielding others. We found that actors are, like comedians, quite preoccupied with issues of good versus bad. They, too, feel obligated to prove their virtue by protecting others against the onslaught of certain threats. They take on a mission to help the populace deny the threat of death and the possibility that all is transitory. We demonstrated, by means of objective scoring systems (applied to projective fantasy material), that actors are particularly fascinated with death imagery and modes of maintaining a sense of time permanence. Their Rorschach inkblot responses are

> infused with concern about the continuity of life, the bridging of the generations, rebirth, preservation, the integration of past, present, and future. . . . We interpreted these themes pertaining to life, death, preservation, age, birth, and time as a cluster reflecting a focus on the importance of maintaining and fostering the continuity of life from the past into the future, from one generation to the next. (p. 160)

Actors are inclined to feel a religiouslike responsibility for stabilizing within self and others a sense that the past moves smoothly into the future and that the possibility of death should not overwhelm us. They perceive their acting as a means to actualize this responsibility. They wish to reassure the audience that we are all part of a plan larger than ourselves, which guarantees the future. With respect to this matter, we commented:

> The actor becomes a creature of a larger plan, which is called the play. He becomes the creature of the playwright who has written a role for him which meshes in a prearranged way with other roles. His destiny, while he is on the stage, is in the hands of a larger power that foresees the outcome of all that will happen. . . . Finally, he gains the identification with multiple other roles and, in so doing, transcends being just the one. He can feel he is part of a collective range of quasi-selves instead of being confined to his single self. (p. 160)

Interestingly, there are suggestions that actors also learn their obligation to maintain continuity from their families. They grew up in family settings where father was often literally or psychologically absent and mother expected them to play various "fill in" roles, to compensate for father's absence, and smooth the flow of family functioning.

Priest Figures

As we have already documented, chief sustainers of illusion in most cultures are the priest figures. They are assigned a central responsibility for preserving the sacred schema guaranteeing that we are part of a larger meaningful whole, watched over by ineffable powers, and armored to some extent against somatic vulnerability. We have collected the available scientific information in the literature concerning the personalities and origins of religious figures (viz., ministers, priests, shamans, rabbis) to clarify the dynamics of certain aspects of their role behavior.

Unfortunately, the dependable conclusions from this literature are somewhat limited. However, one consistent finding is that the ministers and priests are intently dedicated to social service, helping others, and self-sacrifice (e.g., Barry & Bordin, 1967; Celmer, 1986; Maddi & Rulla, 1972; Menges & Dittes, 1965; Siegelman & Peck, 1960). Like comedians and clowns, they are preoccupied with issues of good and evil and feel it is their responsibility to be virtuous, nurturant protectors. They must bring a meaningful picture of God's guiding presence to all. There are hints that their "I must serve others" attitude represents, in part, a compensatory mode for controlling underlying, more aggressive, rebellious feelings (Maddi & Rulla, 1972; Menges & Dittes, 1965). One also finds hints that priests' mothers played a prominent part in urging commitment to a religious world view (Barry & Bordin, 1967; Menges & Dittes, 1965).

Therefore, among priests, comedians, and actors, one sees the common theme of reassuring and providing comforting, largely optimistic images about the tenor of existence. In all three instances, a motivating factor for carrying such a responsibility seems to be an internal debate about whether one is good or bad. To prove one is truly good, there must be a sincere dedication to making others feel less threatened, more protected, and solidly persuaded that there is hope up ahead. The evidence suggests that certain patterns of early interaction with parents incite the good–bad conflict and the consequent need to serve as an illusion sustainer.

SHOULD WE TEACH ILLUSION?

As we become more aware of the reliance on fictions for self-protection, we question whether this information can be advantageously used in the socialization of children. We already have witnessed that children show an interest very early in fictions and playful pretending. They seem to be aware of the importance of acquiring illusion skills and are typically encouraged to do so by their parents. However, if we know that certain classes of illusions (e.g., overoptimistic judgments of the probabilities of success) enhance adaptation, should we not be taking direct action to encourage such protective make-believe?

It is probable that most parents encourage make-believe in indirect and perhaps largely unconscious ways. But are more direct channels for inculcating illusion justified? There are some obvious instances in which parents exhort their children to accept untrue notions as true. Parents often enthusiastically convince their children of the existence of Santa Claus, the Easter Bunny, and the Tooth Fairy, although they know that they are implanting falsehoods. Prentice, Manosevitz, and Hubbs (1978) performed a systematic study of children's beliefs about Santa Claus and other imaginary figures and the relationship of these beliefs to parental attitudes. The sample of children was composed of upper-middle-class boys and girls at three age levels: 4, 6, and 8. A large majority of the 4- and 6-year-olds believed strongly in the reality of Santa Claus and the Easter Bunny. Further, only 15% of the parents tried to discourage belief in Santa Claus. Seventy-five percent of the parents were really enthusiastic in their support of the Santa Claus fiction; and "many . . . continue to engage in practices supportive of the Santa Claus myth even after it has become clear that the child no longer believes" (p. 624). There was a significant positive relationship between the children's probability of believing in Santa Claus and the parents encouraging belief. Frequently, parents justified their encouragement on the basis that it helped them to "manage or control their child's behavior" (p. 624). Actually, it would appear that some parents want their children to believe the Santa Claus myth because they feel it is good for them. They feel it provides a sense of security by giving the children a deserved childhood privilege—being innocently invested in a widely accepted form of make-believe. As cited by Prentice et al. (1978), Bettelheim (1976) strongly supports this view:

> The small child should be able to believe in Santa, or the Easter Bunny, or the Tooth Fairy. . . . Parental insistence on denying the impossible dream makes the world a terribly unfriendly place . . . to hate reality is a likely consequence of being forced to give up fantasies too early. (p. 627)

Let us return to the general question of whether parents should consciously encourage their children to accept illusory images that appear to have protective value. Should parents deliberately teach their children an unrealistic brand of optimism about the future? Should they analogously encourage fictional notions about a "just world," the assurance of reward for virtue, the potential yielding of all problems to reasoned effort, and so forth? One might argue that parents who do not truly believe in specific illusory images would not be able to communicate them convincingly. There may be some truth in this viewpoint, although parents who do not believe in Santa can still convince their offspring of his existence. One is hard pressed to find a scientific rationale for deciding whether the deliberate teaching of illusory ideas is profitable. Actually, we regard such a decision to be largely a political one. History teems with examples of political leaders who consciously chose to instill in the populace fictitious images "for their own good." Just so do some parents proceed. In any case, many parents do, in a mixed state of automaticity, camouflaged intent, and peripheral awareness, engage in a program of "teaching" their offspring illusory schemas that border on the deliberate.

FREUD'S VIEW OF ILLUSION

Freud often seemed uneasy about how to conceptualize the place of illusion in life. His basic position was that illusion detracts from optimum adjustment and, when too abundantly present, is a sign of neurosis or even more serious psychopathology. Obviously, though, he was endlessly drawn to ways in which persons utilize defense modes that call for fabricating fiction. In theorizing that dreams, selective forgetting, and "slips" are primarily wish fulfilling, he implicitly suggested that individuals are set to convince themselves that all will turn out as they wish. His wish-fulfillment formulations can be viewed as a theory about the need to pretend optimistically that events will conform to one's hopes.

In his *Future of an Illusion* (see Freud, 1961), he focused on the salience of religion as a strategy for creating a world with acceptable levels of meaning and security. But he warned that religious belief is ultimately neurotic and an unstable base. He urged that maturity requires one to confront the starkness of "reality" and to be willing to go wherever rationality leads. He saw only immaturity and deficiency in the process of illusion construction. It is, of course, the stated purpose of psychoanalytic therapy to flense illusion from the personality space. Yet, as noted earlier, psychoanalytic therapy is built around encouraging analysands to develop a transference (a dramatized bundle of supposedly unreal images anchored in early experience) to the analyst. This transference presumably becomes the vehicle for demonstrating to analysands the fanciful character of their illusions about primary figures. That is, if analysands are to succeed in therapy, they must richly cultivate their transference illusions. Somewhat paradoxically, psychoanalytic therapy requires an efflorescence of illusion. Illusion is depicted as the fulcrum for the therapy process.

Although it is true that Freud (1961) consistently insisted on dissecting illusions out of existence, one detects how attracted he was to fictions in the sense of wanting to use them to cure and provide ultimate insights. However, he was not comfortable with any concept suggesting that persons could learn to wrap themselves in fictions that would afford solid, lasting psychological advantages. But, as the following quote indicates, Freud (1961) did at times glimpse the fundamental protective value of contrived fictions:

(Nature) destroys us—coldly, cruelly, relentlessly as it seems to us. . . . It was precisely because of these dangers with which nature threatens that we came together and created civilization, its actual *raison d'etre* is to defend us against nature . . . *thus a store of ideas is created, borne for man's need to make his helplessness tolerable. . . . It can clearly be seen that the possession of these ideas protects him . . . against the dangers of nature and fate.* (p. 20, italics added)

Although Freud (1961) regarded illusion constructions as inferior forms of coping, he implicitly assumed that "neurotics" derive appreciable defensive support, albeit temporarily, from such constructions. He cited clinical contexts in which illusory notions provided sufficient reassurance to fend off more serious forms of upset. For example, he referred to individuals who defend against Oedipal temptations and terrors by building up an illusorily exaggerated picture of the distance and coldness of the parent of the opposite gender. He described fathers who defend against potentially intense incestuous anxieties by fashioning an illusory image of daughter's degree of unfriendliness and therefore unavailability. Many other analogous defensive paradigms are found in his clinical accounts. The truth is that, although Freud regarded illusion as an inferior form of defensive adaptation, he was intently aware of how universally it is employed. He knew that most people depend heavily on it throughout their lives.

MAGIC

Elaborate accounts of the history of magic have been compiled (e.g., Kieckhefer, 1990; Tambiah, 1990). Belief in the efficacy of magical practices goes far into the past and extends to the present. In essence, magic consists of illusory ideas about how extraordinary forces can be controlled and compelled to do one's bidding. The magicians of the world have applied their skills to every conceivable aspect of life: illness, fertility, madness, farming, birth defects, love, building a house, victory in battle, and so forth. Basically, magic is the prototype of illusion construction. It simply calls for conjuring up an image, ritual, or formula that is ascribed the power to accomplish some end by enlisting extraordinary imaginary assistance. Interestingly, Western religions have been sensitive about falling into the same category as magic and have struggled to construct definitions that would establish a clear distinction (Tambiah, 1990). Protestant theologians were particularly sensitive about this issue and attacked the rites of the Catholic Church (e.g., transubstantiation), because they were thought to smack of magical mumbo jumbo. They proposed that the magician compels the forces of nature, whereas true religion involves a conscious agent that controls the world and can be influenced only by prayer and supplication. However, Tambiah (1990) pointed out that the Bible "did not disbelieve in magic and did not deny that the idols might have had occult powers" (p. 19). It is apparent that, throughout the centuries, magic has permeated every aspect of fantasy and behavior and is an inescapable constituent of human modes of adaptation. Malinowski is said by Tamiah (1990) to have asserted that "magic ritualizes man's optimism when there is a hiatus in man's knowledge (and) is invoked and practiced to fill in the gap of anxiety and uncertainty when the limits of technological control are reached" (p. 22).

At times the border between magic and science has been surprisingly porous. Tamiah (1990) documented that during the scientific and philosophical revolutions of the 17th century, magical schemas existed side by side with more empirical concepts and in numerous instances were forerunners of such concepts. Mystical-magical theories frequently provided frameworks for later scientific triumphs. Tamiah (1990) pointed out that scientific models of heliocentrism, the infinity of the worlds, the circulation of blood, and specific mathematical ideas were, in their early phases, linked to magical formulations. Also, astrology significantly influenced astronomical practices. Kieckhefer (1990) described medieval Europe as a scene in which persons who identified themselves with medicine and science practiced a mongrel mixture of the magical and the empirical. For example, practitioners used certain herbs, because of their presumed natural therapeutical efficacy, to treat various diseases. However, these practitioners might have simultaneously felt it necessary to assure the therapeutic potency of the herbs by picking them at a certain phase of the moon with the left rather than the right hand, by putting them in a solution of holy water, or by reciting a special incantation while preparing them for use. Kieckhefer (1990) outlined a prescription for curing skin disease that called for mixing together four herbs and applying them to the skin. But then the physician was told to scratch the patient's neck "after sunset," pour the blood from the scratch into "running water," and then "spit three times after it and say, 'Take this disease and depart with it' " (p. 65).

With respect to the conflation of magic and science, intellectuals in medieval Europe conceptualized magic as existing in two forms: natural and demonic. Natural magic could not be differentiated clearly from science and indeed was considered to be a branch that dealt with hidden powers within nature. But demonic magic was said to enlist demons to interfere in human affairs. Kieckhefer (1990) considered that intellectuals in the 17th century who felt they were identified with a rational-empirical perspective were still heavily steeped in magical elements. A plant might be assumed to be therapeutic for an illness because of some symbolic analogy. Thus, plants with liver-shaped leaves were regarded as good for liver ailments. Plants were perhaps pictured as therapeutic by virtue of being able to capture stellar or planetary influences. Kieckhefer (1990) concluded that, in medieval Europe, it was difficult to identify the practice of magic with one specified class of magicians. Instead, important components of magic could be observed across a spectrum, which included physicians, monks, parish priests, surgeon barbers, folk healers, and ordinary folks. One of the most "noted medical authorities" of the 14th century revealed his continuing investment in magic by recommending that epileptics prevent seizures by carrying a slip of parchment with the names of the biblical magi written on it.

It is too easy to relegate belief in magic to earlier epochs. However, the available information suggests that the 20th-century world is densely infused with magical practices. Surveys indicate widespread beliefs in superstitions, the power of "good" and "bad" luck, and the protective value of various versions of amulets (e.g., t-shirts with inscriptions, lucky coins). Belief in astrological notions is still common in many cultures. Transitional objects of multiple sorts are still widely clutched by children and adults to ward off danger. A major manifestation of devotion to magic occurs in health practices and self-healing (as was also true in medieval times). Untold billions of dollars are spent on patent medicines that have no demonstrable physiological potency. Millions of persons religiously ingest patent elixirs with the purely imaginary expectation that they will be rendered healthier. Many foods, vitamins, and minerals are fancifully ascribed therapeutic efficacies that are not empirically founded. Enormous amounts of magical fantasy are invested in placebos. Such fantasy is so universal that it has proved to be a serious obstacle to the possibility of accurately measuring the physiological ("biological") potency of various drugs. No matter how carefully researchers (especially those dealing with psychotropic drugs) set up their experiments, the "placebo effects" encrust the outcomes and obscure their interpretations (Fisher & Greenberg, 1989).

In the 17th century, magic and science had overlapping boundaries. Can one see any overlap in the 20th century? The fact is that the sciences are now heavily armored against the possible intrusion of magical ideas. Magic is treated as the antithesis of science. But as one examines the workings of modern science, magical influences can be detected here and there. Probably the most visible signs of magical thinking occur where scientists are attempting to apply their lore to practical problems. In this century, many presumably scientific medical procedures have been devised on the basis of flimsy data and then wishfully imbued with the magical hopes of the innovators. Quite invalidly, procedures such as lobotomy, clitorectomy, tonsillectomy, and colonectomy have been applied fancifully (and with imaginative hopefulness) to address many forms of distress. In truth, these applications usually have been more rooted in thinly rationalized magical expectations than in credible science.

The special attitude of science in carving out a superrational domain for itself deserves comment. Science does not formally concern itself with the apparently absurd existential dilemmas. It does not get involved with matters of broad existential meaning. Esslin (1961) offered a particularly well-phrased description of this orientation:

> The modern scientific attitude . . . rejects the postulate of a wholly coherent
> and simplified explanation that must account for all the phenomena, purposes
> and moral rules of the world. In concentrating on the slow, painstaking explo-
> ration of limited areas of reality by trial and error—by the construction, test-
> ing, and discarding of hypotheses—the scientific attitude cheerfully accepts the

view that we must be able to live with the realization that large segments of knowledge and experience will remain for a long time, perhaps forever, outside our ken; that ultimate purposes cannot, and never will be, known; and that we must therefore be able to accept the fact that much that earlier metaphysical systems, mythical, religious, or philosophical, sought to explain must forever remain unexplained. From this point of view, any clinging to systems of thought that provide, or purport to provide, complete explanations of the world and man's place in it must appear childish and immature, a flight from reality into illusion and self-deception. (pp. 313–314)

In short, science strains to banish the use of illusion in explanations. It has no tolerance for even the temporary comforting value of illusion in situations where puzzlement and paradox are intimidating. Science calls for a dehumanized stance. The scientist is supposed to look at things "as they are," no matter how much discomfort they evoke. A similar kind of detachment is written into the job descriptions of the surgeon and other occupations that require objective detachment in the face of tasks that raise vital life and death issues (e.g., law enforcement, military strategy). Obviously, the antiillusory pretensions of the scientist are idealizations. In truth, the history of science is replete with examples of illusory schemas that were plugged in to soothe the scientific establishment until more valid ones could come along.

There is widespread complaint that the antiillusory strictures of science are making it harder and harder for persons to generate the illusory schemas so helpful in giving meaning to the average life. This conflict is often verbalized in the imagery of a battle between science and religion. If scientific values were ever to become so widely and completely accepted as to render illusion construction highly disreputable, would this have a net negative impact on mental health? We do not know enough to give an answer that is more than a guess. However, even if the impact were anticipated to be seriously negative, the mission of science would not permit any weakening in the resolve to banish illusion. This zeal for objectivity has payed off well in many ways, but it represents a brand of depersonalization that has, at times, stirred up a good deal of cultural pain. One need only recall the objective success of scientists in designing substances and instruments of immense destructive power, but maintaining that they, as devotees of objectivity, have no responsibility for where their "objective" ingenuity has led them.

Consider, in relation to how radically science might crowd out self-defenses based on illusion, that many individuals already have shown amazing cleverness in converting science into illusory strategies. For example, many have convinced themselves that science is an overwhelming "good" that will eventually banish life's major problems. Many have convinced themselves that they can already convert science's bank of information into assurance of somatic invulnerability (bordering on a sense of immortality). Many have intense transferences to major science figures (like Einstein) that inspire a fictive conviction that nature has been safely tamed. It would appear that the qualities of science, as antiillusory as they are, may be ingeniously manipulated to create new mythologies.

Paradoxically, as science has become increasingly abstruse and complex, it has, at least implicitly, asserted that the ordinary person does not have the capacity to understand the world as it is really constituted. Scientists speak a language far "above" the comprehension of nonscientists and leave the impression: "You have only a vague notion of what is happening in the universe. Your ideas are simplistic and childlike. You have an inaccurate and partial view of what is going on." That is, science tells average persons that their basic ideas about the nature of things are illusory. It does offer the hope that if one were to study what science has uncovered, one could attain a realistic level of knowledge. But it is understood that few persons have the ability to master sophisticated science.

If this is so, one may speculate that large segments of the population suspect they are only in partial contact with the "real picture." They are being inculcated with the notion that the greater the advances of science, the greater the disparity between what is true and what they know about this truth. Persons may increasingly surrender to the feeling that their world schemas lack credibility. There has been popular resistance to accepting this down position. This is evidenced in defensive belittlement of scientists and especially in stereotyping of the "weird professor" who lacks common sense. One can only wonder about the effects of large numbers of individuals chronically feeling that they lack a true understanding of "reality." Does it result in a generally increased tolerance for the illusory? Does it encourage greater use of illusory defensive images? These are questions well worth clarifying.

SELF-AWARENESS

Self-deception is, to some extent, facilitated by obtuseness about certain aspects of experiences. It seems to call for focused ignoring of feelings and internalized information. As we have seen, the process of constructing illusory ideas is analogously supported by deflecting attention from nonconfirmatory or contradictory information. At one level, this process can be viewed as selectively avoiding awareness of particular regions of self. It is therefore of interest that research on the effects of increasing self-awareness has come up with findings suggesting that such intensified awareness is unfriendly to illusion formation. There are studies indicating that when persons are made more self-aware (e.g., by being confronted with their mirror image), they more accurately identify their own emotional states and correctly detect the physiological effects of ingested substances. One experiment (Gibbons, Carver,

Scheier, & Harmuth, 1979) showed that subjects could more accurately judge whether they were ingesting an active substance or a placebo when their self-awareness was heightened. Persons also make more accurate predictions of their future behavior when they do so while being confronted with their mirror image (Fisher, 1989).

What we are especially curious about is the fact that intensifying self-awareness is likely to increase feelings of depression (e.g., Gibbons et al., 1985). It will be recalled that depression is associated with a dimunition in generating illusory auras. Perhaps the increase in depression resulting from augmented self-awareness is, in part, the result of concomitant diminished ability to nurture wishful, illusory images. As noted earlier, it may also be true that increased self-awareness has a depressing impact, because it necessarily results in increased awareness of one's own body. To be more body aware is to open the possibility of a heightened consciousness of somatic vulnerability (Fisher, 1989).

It is paradoxical that illusory ideas should be dampened when attention is focused more toward the self and the body. The experiences persons have with their bodies are, after all, private and not easily monitored or censored by external agents. Therefore, persons might anticipate that this would make it easier for them to fictively manipulate their private sensations and feelings. One explanation for this discrepancy might be that the intensified self-awareness activates self-criticalness and concern about living up to superego standards. Perhaps modal superego rules call for being as "real" as possible and giving in to a minimum of self-indulgent fantasies.

BELIEF IN A JUST WORLD

As outlined earlier, Lerner (1980) elaborated the most basic of all sustaining illusions: the belief that what happens in the world is just and fair. By and large, persons seem to be persuaded that one gets what one deserves. Even very young children believe in "immanent justice," that a fault will induce its own punishment. Surprisingly, the battle-scarred mature adult also seems to cling to a fundamentally "just world" schema. Despite the innumerable examples of life's injustices freely available for inspection, the "justice" stereotype persists. It would appear that if life is to be perceived as manageable (controllable, livable), it has to be experienced as meaningfully fair. The more emotionally involving a situation is, the more likely it is to invoke the "just world" assumption. Even in situations where individuals have been severely and permanently injured, they will somehow frame the event so that it can be explained as justified. The dedication to "just world" images can lead to great personal sacrifice to rectify perceived injustice and even to denial of rewards to self if the rewards seem like "too much."

Lerner (1980) described one of the most paradoxical phenomena—the need to denigrate those who are the targets of negative events (e.g., illness, loss). If persons on the receiving end of the negatives can be proved to be bad, inadequate, wrong, or to have "brought it on themselves," the situation is no longer unjust. If a person deserves the bad thing that happened, there is no injustice. The research literature indicated that most persons invest an impressive amount of ingenuity in proving, to themselves, that events do, by and large, move along fairly. Toward this end, a dazzling repertoire of defense mechanisms has evolved. Relatedly, religious concepts frequently provide useful defensive maneuvers in terms of a "just God."

Almost all societies promise justice. Both explicitly and implicitly, the culture strikes a bargain with each of its participants: "If you do what is expected and obey the rules, you will be rewarded. If you fail to do the right thing, there will be unpleasant consequences." This schema is basic to feeling that it is worthwhile to conform, to achieve, and to practice self-denial. Most social structures require such a foundation. One of the greatest potential threats to the "just world" paradigm is the inevitability of death. If life is fair, why do you ultimately die? Many of the major religious systems (especially Christianity) have focused on neutralizing this disparity. Another major threat is the gross economic inequalities in most societies. The blatant differences between the poor and the rich are there to see and to vitiate notions of life's fairness.

Lerner (1980) pointed out, however, that most cultures have camouflaged these contrasts and rendered them apparently reasonable. He reported that the illusion of the "just world" may be as strong (or even stronger) in the lower socioeconomic levels as in the upper levels. To illustrate the contortions practiced by those in the lower economic strata to insulate themselves from the "unfairness" of their environment, he noted: "The respondents from . . . lower strata were more likely to complain about people on welfare than about rich people, landlords, gangsters, Hollywood celebrities, or the lot of the poverty-stricken, elderly, or mentally ill" (p. 166). It is noteworthy that persons in the upper strata "were considerably more likely than laboring respondents to report any groups as overrewarded" (p. 166). The literature abounds with heroic distortions that persons sincerely manufacture to defend what we suggest is one of the most necessary of the modal illusions.

ABSURDITY

We have referred, again and again, to the fundamental absurdities and analyzed the various strategies employed to dodge too much awareness of them. However, we also have referred to what seems to be an irresistible impulse to peek at life absurdities, to play with notions of absurdity, and to invent scenarios in which absurdity seductively calls and even invites. We know there are infinite ways in which cultures flirt with the possibilities of absurdity. Artists have often taken the lead in giving us a taste of this potentially shocking stuff. Certainly the surrealists were determined to confront us with visions of the grotesque and an array of images that highlight lack of meaning or coherence. The theater of the absurd fervently tried to do similar things. Obviously, too, the comedians of the world have boldly bombarded us with absurd visions, but have almost always been careful to do so in a soothing, amusing way. Their message is "Yes, life is ridiculous but don't get alarmed. Your discomfort is tolerable if you will just treat the whole business as funny and laughable." At other levels, we see individuals hunting for glimpses of the absurd by taking drugs (e.g., LSD), speaking in "tongues," performing acts that suddenly place oneself in a publicly ridiculous position (e.g., wearing outlandish clothing or dramatically committing a bizarre act), immersing self in grotesque or surrealistic art messages, and so forth.

As noted earlier, one possibly seeks contact with the absurd to get the "feel of it" and thereby to attenuate its potential threat. Imbibing absurdity in small doses may hopefully build up a degree of immunity against it. Obviously, too, some persons embrace absurdity as an act of revolt, as a means of mirroring back to others that they feel they are being treated absurdly. Therapists who work with psychologically disturbed children frequently see them as engaging in just such a protest. One wonders whether psychotherapists who use "paradoxical therapy" techniques are not at least implicitly acknowledging that many so-called "neurotic symptoms" are condensed depictions (and protests) of what are felt to be ridiculous ways of living. It bears repeating that "getting into" absurdity may be a tempting means for jettisoning the usual rigidities. If things are really absurd, why worry about rules or whether events will turn out according to plan? In short, why take the defined "reality" seriously? There are many examples of individuals who have taken the plunge into this apparently liberating state of mind (e.g., in the so-called "hippy" subculture), but who have often found it to be unhappily disorganizing.

We suggest that the ability to stare briefly at the existential absurdities may be helpful in some ways. There are no scientific data about how much awareness of such absurdities is "good" for the average individual. Becker (1973) took the position that more than a limited awareness will generate terror and psychological breakdown. However, he was only speculating and his view may be overly alarmist. The sheer amount of playing with absurdity that goes on in Western cultures implies that the modal threshold for toxicity is not as low as Becker (1973) and others (e.g., Rank, 1945) assumed. As with most psychological phenomena, there are probably large individual differences in such thresholds. One may speculate that persons who are securely embedded in a social structure and a dependable work career can tolerate a moderate level of awareness of the basic existential dilemmas. All persons seem to experiment with opening themselves to intimations of such awareness and gradually learn to titrate how much they can manage.

SOME BASIC THEMES

What are the few essential themes that one can distill from the total substance of the material that has been explored? First of all, there has been a fundamental neglect of the psychological importance of the niche that humans occupy in nature. All persons live on a miniature planet in a measureless universe, they are less than dwarfs in relation to the forces "out there," the duration of their existence is momentary, and their bodies are of the same biological stuff as all animals. Some awareness of these facts probably frames each individual's self-concept and world view, and presumably endows existence with at least quasiabsurd overtones. None of the widely accepted major theories of personality or psychological functioning seriously incorporates this class of information. It is simply assumed that (aside from genetic factors) the chief shapers of personality derive from one's relationships with primary socialization figures.

Psychopathology is particularly likely to be attributed to glitches in such relationships. However, there is room for doubt. It remains quite possible that the continuous impact of being insignificant and vulnerable in the larger universe is responsible for complex defensive personality mechanisms and for a sizeable part of the anxiety, uncertainty, and "deviant" behavior endemic in human populations. Death anxiety or other variables reflective of existential absurdity may have as much (or more) influence on personality organization as some socially derived variables, such as Oedipal conflict, gender role confusion, socioeconomic status, and degree of parental authoritarianism. Further empirical studies may reveal that the scientific establishment has been as hesitant as most individuals to acknowledge the intrusive presence of the absurdities. By way of contrast, world religions have been acutely concerned with the absurdities and have devoted energetic doctrinal effort to camouflaging them and deflecting their intensity.

If the "natural" vulnerability of persons is one of the significant sources of their "psychopathology," this would imply that the degree to which tension and disturbance in any population can be controlled is limited. No matter what special defensive and compensatory strategies are mobilized, one cannot escape some sense of the actual state of affairs. To a certain extent, all persons probably have an intuition of the salient human dilemmas; and this generates anxiety plus other psychological discomforts. There may be limited elasticity in how far psychological discomfort can be reduced. This is alluded to by the earlier cited finding that, at any given point in time, a good fifth of the population is experiencing psychological pain approaching clinical proportions.

A second primary matter is the evidence that myth and illusion construction are integral to just about everything that humans think. Ideas anchored in illusion seem to reinforce most adaptive strategies. Persons are endlessly making things up to shield themselves and to put a more favorable twist on what confronts them. It will be recalled that from an early age children are fascinated with illusion and practice it over and over. Even that core structure, the self, is built up, to some extent, around illusory images and preserved by putting a wishful spin on information. Whether it be to firm up positive or negative images of self, selective slanting of incoming data is the rule. All cultures create world schemas that are largely imaginary and expressed in the rhetoric of religious and political slogans. The concept of "reality" is obscure and slippery; and most individuals have learned to play with it according to their tastes.

Another major theme that has emerged strongly is the difficulty of neatly classifying modes of adaptation as mature versus immature or psychologically "healthy" versus "unhealthy." This is especially true with respect to situations in which individuals confront one or the other of the absurdities. Defensive tactics based on illusory constructions are probably necessary. In encounters with the more extreme forms of threat (e.g., loss of primary figures, severe disablement), it is often quite sound to wrap oneself in illusory compensatory ideas. What is apparently immature in one context may be an effective "defense mechanism" in another. Multiple variables, such as age, gender, and socioeconomic status, have been shown to mediate the effectiveness of various defense mechanisms. Relativity prevails as to whether it is advantageous to be oriented toward "internal" versus "external" locus of control; whether it is advantageous to take a repressive versus sensitized attitude toward various kinds of conflictual fantasies; and whether more versus less illusory elaboration in defining events is to the advantage of persons as stress intensifies. Such relativity calls into question the assurance with which therapists and other "mental health" experts recommend particular ways of coping with tension as necessarily superior. It is far from obvious that directly confronting a troubling conflict is better than more indirectly handling it. We do not see that "repression" is generally inferior to "insight." Sometimes it is and sometimes it is not, depending on many factors.

Humans have displayed genius in concocting exotic techniques for coping with the psychological wear and tear of the complexly threatening terrain they inhabit. Not only are they exposed to dense predatory forces, but, perhaps even worse, have acquired the finely attuned capacity to scrutinize their own feelings about their exposed position. They are capable of understanding their own "no-win" position and have defensively developed an amazing repertoire of tactics for buffering this understanding. The repertoire could fill a large catalogue. It includes such cleverness as shutting out aware-ness of the unpleasant, attributing it to others rather than to self, transform-ing it into its opposite, "pretending" it is controlled by friendly powers greater than self, and ascribing magical warding off potency to self. This cleverness is all the more spectacular because it often simultaneously requires the ca-pacity to be opportunistically obtuse and simple minded.

REFERENCES

Abramowitz, C. V., Abramowitz, S. I., Robert, H. B., & Jackson, C. (1974). Differential effectiveness of directive and non-directive group therapies as a function of client internal–external control. *Journal of Consulting & Clinical Psychology, 42*, 849–853.

Ackerman, R., & DeRubeis, R. J. (1991). Is depressive realism real? *Clinical Psychology Review, 11*, 565–584.

Alexander, C. N., Chandler, H. M., Langer, E. J., Newman, R. I., & Davies, J. L. (1989). Transcendental meditation, mindfulness, and longevity: An experimental study with the elderly. *Journal of Personality and Social Psychology, 57*, 950–964.

Alexander, I. E., & Alderstein, A. M. (1960). Studies in the psychology of death. In H. P. David & J. C. Brengelmann (Eds.), *Perspectives in personality research* (pp. 65–92). New York: Springer.

Alexander, I. E., Colley, R. S., & Alderstein, A. M. (1957). Is death a matter of indifference? *Journal of Psychology, 43*, 277–283.

Alexander, I. E., & Constanzo, P. R. (1979). Death anxiety, dissent, and competence. *Journal of Personality, 47*, 734–751.

Al-Issa, I. (1977). Social and cultural aspects of hallucinations. *Psychological Bulletin, 84*, 570–587.

Allison, J., Blatt, S. J., & Zimet, C. N. (1968). *The interpretation of psychological tests.* New York: Harper & Row.

Alloy, L. B., & Abramson, L. Y. (1979). Judgment of contingency in depressed and nondepressed students: Sadder but wiser? *Journal of Experimental Psychology, 108*, 441–485.

Alloy, L. B., & Abramson, L. Y. (1982). Learned helplessness, depression, and the illusion of control. *Journal of Personality and Social Psychology, 42*, 1114–1126.

Alloy, L. B., & Abramson, L. Y. (1988). Depressive realism: Four theoretical perspectives. In L. B. Alloy (Ed.), *Cognitive processes in depression* (pp. 223–265). New York: Guilford Press.

Alloy, L. B., Abramson, L. Y., & Viscusi, D. (1981). Induced mood and the illusion of control. *Journal of Personality and Social Psychology, 41*, 1129–1140.

Allport, G. W. (1950). *The individual and his religion: A psychological interpretation.* New York: Macmillan.

Allport, G. W. (1966). Religious context of prejudice. *Journal for the Scientific Study of Religion, 5*, 447–457.

Allred, K. D., & Smith, T. W. (1989). The hardy personality: Cognitive and physiological responses to evaluative threat. *Journal of Personality and Social Psychology, 56,* 257–266.

American Psychiatric Association. (1980). *Diagnostic and statistical manual of mental disorders* (3rd ed.). Washington, DC: Author.

Anderson, E. A. (1987). Preoperative preparation for cardiac surgery facilitates recovery, reduces psychological distress, and reduces the incidence of acute postoperative hypertension. *Journal of Consulting and Clinical Psychology, 55,* 513–520.

Andrade, C., Srinath, S., & Andrade, A. C. (1989). True hallucinations in non-psychotic states. *Canadian Journal of Psychiatry, 34,* 704–706.

Andrew, J. (1970). Recovery from surgery, with and without preparatory information, for three coping styles. *Journal of Personality and Social Psychology, 15,* 223–226.

Andrews, F. M. (Ed.). (1986). *Research on the quality of life.* Ann Arbor: Institute for Social Research, The University of Michigan.

Andrews, F. M., & Withey, S. B. (1976). *Social indicators of well-being.* New York: Plenum Press.

Andrews, J. D. W. (1989). Integrating visions of reality. *American Psychologist, 44,* 803–817.

Antonovsky, A. (1979). *Health, stress, and coping.* San Francisco: Jossey-Bass.

Argyle, M., & Beit-Hallahmi, B. (1975). *The social psychology of religion.* London: Routledge & Kegan Paul.

Arieti, S. (1950). New views on the psychology and psychopathology of wit and of the comic. *Psychiatry, 13,* 43–62.

Aron, A., Aron, E. N., Tudor, M., & Nelson, G. (1991). Close relationships as including other in the self. *Journal of Personality and Social Psychology, 60,* 241–253.

Aronson, S. R. (1970). *A comparison of cognitive versus focused-activities techniques in sensitivity group training.* Unpublished doctoral dissertation, University of California, Los Angeles.

Baird, C. F. (1972). *Death fantasy in male and female college students.* Unpublished doctoral dissertation, Boston University Graduate School, Boston, MA.

Barchilon, J. (1973). Pleasure, mockery and creative integrations: Their relationship to childhood knowledge, a learning defect and the literature of the absurd. *International Journal of Psycho-Analysis, 54,* 19–34.

Barnes, G. M., & Russell, M. (1978). Drinking patterns in western New York State. *Journal for the Study of Alcoholism, 39,* 1148–1157.

Barnouw, V. (1985). *Culture and personality.* Homewood, IL: Dorsey Press.

Barry, W. A., & Bordin, E. S. (1967). Personality development and the vocational choice of the ministry. *Journal of Counseling Psychology, 14,* 395–403.

Bateson, G. (1972). *Steps to an ecology of mind.* San Francisco: Chandler.

Batson, D. C., & Ventis, L. W. (1982). *The religious experience: A social-psychological perspective.* New York: Oxford University Press.

Battista, J. R. (1982). Empirical test of Vaillant's Hierarchy of Ego Functions. *American Journal of Psychiatry, 139,* 356–357.

Battle, E., & Rotter, J. B. (1963). Children's feelings of personal control as related to social class and ethnic groups. *Journal of Personality, 31,* 482–490.

Baum, A., Fleming, R., & Singer, J. E. (1983). Coping with victimization by technological disaster. *Journal of Social Issues, 39,* 117–138.

Baum, A., & Singer, J. E. (Eds.). (1980). *Advances in environmental psychology: Vol. 2. Applications of personal control.* Hillsdale, NJ: Lawrence Erlbaum Associates.

Baumeister, R. F. (1987). How the self became a problem: A psychological review of historical research. *Journal of Personality and Social Psychology, 52,* 163–176.

Baumeister, R. F. (1989). The optimal margin of illusion. *Journal of Social and Clinical Psychology, 8,* 176–189.

Baumeister, R. F. (1990). Anxiety and deconstruction: On escaping the self. In J. M. Olson & M. P. Zanna (Eds.), *Self-inference processes: The Ontario symposium* (Vol. 6, pp. 259–291). Hillsdale, NJ: Lawrence Erlbaum Associates.

Baumeister, R. F., Shapiro, J. P., & Tice, D. M. (1985). Two kinds of identity crisis. *Journal of Personality, 53,* 407–424.

Beahrs, J. O. (1986). *Limits of scientific psychiatry: The role of uncertainty in mental health.* New York: Brunner/Mazel.

Beck, A. T. (1976). *Cognitive therapy and emotional disorders.* New York: International Universities Press.

Becker, E. (1973). *The denial of death.* New York: The Free Press.

Bellak, L. (1963). Acting out: Conceptual and therapeutic considerations. *American Journal of Psychotherapy, 17,* 375–389.

Benjamin, J. D. (1961). Some developmental observations relating to the theory of anxiety. *Journal of the American Psychoanalytic Association, 9,* 652–668.

Benson, J. S., & Kennelly, K. J. (1976). Learned helplessness: The result of uncontrollable reinforcements or uncontrollable aversive stimuli? *Journal of Personality and Social Psychology, 34,* 138–145.

Benson, P., & Spilka, B. (1973). God image as a function of self-esteem and locus of control. *Journal for the Scientific Study of Religion, 12,* 297–310.

Bentall, R. P., Jackson, H. F., & Pilgrim, D. (1988). Abandoning the concept of "schizophrenia": Some implications of validity arguments for psychological research into psychotic phenomena. *British Journal of Clinical Psychology, 27,* 303–324.

Berger, P. L. (1967). *The sacred canopy: Elements of a sociological theory of religion.* New York: Doubleday.

Bergin, A. E. (1983). Religiosity and mental health: A critical re-evaluation and meta-analysis. *Professional Psychology: Research and Practice, 14,* 170–184.

Bergin, A. E., Masters, K., & Richards, P. S. (1987). Religiousness and mental health reconsidered: A study of an intrinsically religious sample. *Journal of Counseling Psychology, 34,* 197–204.

Bermann, S., & Richardson, V. (1986–1987). Social change in the salience of death among adults in America: A projective assessment. *Omega, 17,* 195–207.

Bernstein, A. S. (1987). Orienting response research in schizophrenia: Where we have come and where we might go. *Schizophrenia Bulletin, 13,* 623–641.

Berrenberg, J. L. (1987). The Belief in Personal Control Scale: A measure of God-mediated and exaggerated control. *Journal of Personality Assessment, 51,* 194–206.

Bettelheim, B. (1976). *The uses of enchantment.* New York: Alfred A. Knopf.

Birky, I. T., & Ball, S. (1988). Parental trait influence on God as an object representation. *The Journal of Psychology, 122,* 133–137.

Bixler, E. O., Kales, A., Soldatos, C. R., Kales, J. D., & Healey, S. (1979). Prevalence of sleep disorders in the Los Angeles metropolitan area. *American Journal of Psychiatry, 136,* 1257–1262.

Blakely, K. B. (1975). *Chronic renal failure: A study of death anxiety in dialysis and kidney transplant patients.* Unpublished doctoral dissertation. University of Manitoba, Winnipeg, Manitoba (Canada).

Blankstein, K. R. (1984). Psychophysiology and perceived locus of control: Critical review, theoretical speculation, and research directions. In H. M. Lefcourt (Ed.), *Research with the locus of control construct* (Vol. 3, pp. 73–208). New York: Academic Press.

Blatt, S. J., & Wild, C. M. (1976). *Schizophrenia: A developmental analysis.* New York: Academic Press.

Block, J. (1965). *The challenge of response sets: Unconfounding meaning, acquiescence, and social desirability in the MMPI.* New York: Appleton-Century-Crofts.

Block, J. (1971). *Lives through time.* Berkeley, CA: Bancroft Books.

Blum, G. S. (1956). Defense preference in four countries. *Journal of Projective Techniques, 20,* 33–41.

Bond, M. P., Gardner, S. T., Christian, J., & Sigal, J. J. (1983). Empirical study of self-rated defense styles. *Archives of General Psychiatry, 40,* 333–338.

Bond, M. P., & Vaillant, J. S. (1986). An empirical study of the relationship between diagnosis and defense style. *Archives of General Psychiatry, 43,* 285–288.

Borkeneau, F. (1965). The concept of death. *The 20th Century, 157,* 313–329.

Bowers, K. S. (1968). Pain, anxiety, and perceived control. *Journal of Consulting and Clinical Psychology, 32,* 596–602.

Bowers, K. S., & Meichenbaum, D. (1984). *The unconscious reconsidered.* New York: Wiley.

Boyar, J. I. (1964). *The construction and partial validation of a scale for the measurement of the fear of death.* Unpublished doctoral dissertation, University of Rochester, NY.

Bradburn, N. M. (1969). *The structure of psychological well-being.* Chicago: Aldine.

Bramel, D. (1963). Selection of a target for defensive projection. *Journal of Abnormal and Social Psychology, 66,* 318–324.

Brandstatter, H. (1983). Emotional responses to other persons in everyday life situations. *Journal of Personality and Social Psychology, 45,* 871–883.

Brehm, J. W. (1966). *A theory of psychological reactance.* New York: Academic Press.

Bretherton, I. (Ed.). (1984). *Symbolic play.* New York: Academic Press.

Bretherton, I., O'Connell, B., Shore, C., & Bates, E. (1984). The effect of contextual variation on symbolic play development from 20 to 28 months. In I. Bretherton (Ed.), *Symbolic play* (pp. 271–298). New York: Academic Press.

Brett-Jones, J., Garety, P., & Hemsley, D. (1987). Measuring delusional experiences: A method and its application. *British Journal of Clinical Psychology, 26,* 257–265.

Breznitz, S. (Ed.). (1983). *The denial of stress.* New York: International Universities Press.

Briddell, D. W., Rimm, D. C., Caddy, G. R., Krawitz, G., Sholis, D., & Wunderlin, R. J. (1978). Effects of alcohol and cognitive set on sexual arousal to deviant stimuli. *Journal of Abnormal Psychology, 87,* 418–430.

Brody, L. R., Rozek, M. K., & Muten, E. O. (1985). Age, sex, and individual differences in children's defensive styles. *Journal of Clinical Child Psychology, 14,* 132–138.

Brown, J. D., & Smart, S. A. (1991). The self and social conduct: Linking self-representations to prosocial behavior. *Journal of Personality and Social Psychology, 60,* 368–375.

Brown, O. J. (1977). *Fear of death and western Protestant ethic personality traits.* Unpublished doctoral dissertation, Ohio State University, Columbus.

Bryant, F. B., & Veroff, J. (1982). The structure of psychological well-being: A sociohistorical analysis. *Journal of Personality and Social Psychology, 43,* 653–673.

Bryant, F. B., & Veroff, J. (1986). Dimensions of subjective mental health in American men and women. In F. M. Andrews (Ed.), *Research on the quality of life* (pp. 117–146). Ann Arbor: University of Michigan Press.

Bulman, R. J., & Wortman, C. B. (1977). Attributions of blame and coping in the "real world": Severe accident victims react to their lot. *Journal of Personality and Social Psychology, 35,* 351–363.

Burger, J. M. (1989). Negative reactions to increases in perceived personal control. *Journal of Personality and Social Psychology, 56,* 246–256.

Buri, J. R., & Mueller, R. A. (1987, August). *Conceptions of parents, conceptions of self, and conceptions of God.* Paper presented at the annual convention of the American Psychological Association, New York.

Burnes, K., Brown, W. A., & Keating, G. W. (1971). Dimensions of control: Correlations between MMPI and I-E scores. *Journal of Consulting and Clinical Psychology, 36,* 301.

Byrne, D. (1964). The Repression-Sensitization Scale: Rationale, reliability, and validity. In B. A. Maher (Ed.), *Progress in experimental personality research* (pp. 169–220). New York: Academic Press.

Cacioppo, J. T., & Petty, R. E. (1983). *Social psychophysiology.* New York: Guilford Press.

Caird, D. (1987). Religiosity and personality: Are mystics introverted, neurotic, or psychotic? *British Journal of Social Psychology, 26,* 345–346.

Campbell, A., Converse, P. E., & Rodgers, W. L. (1976). *The quality of American life.* New York: Russell Sage Foundation.

Campbell, J. D., & Fehr, B. (1990). Self-esteem and perceptions of conveyed impressions: Is negative affectivity associated with greater realism? *Journal of Personality and Social Psychology, 58,* 122–133.

Cantril, H. (1965). *The pattern of human concerns.* New Brunswick, NJ: Rutgers University Press.

Celmer, V. (1986). *The personality and occupational profiles of Roman Catholic priests and women who seek to become Roman Catholic priests: A test of the Holland model of vocational choice.* Unpublished doctoral dissertation, Texas Tech University, Lubbock, TX.

Chadwick, P. D. J., & Lowe, C. F. (1990). Measurement and modification of delusional beliefs. *Journal of Consulting and Clinical Psychology, 58,* 225–232.

Chaikin, A. (1985). The loneliness of the long-distance astronaut. *Discover, 6,* 20–31.

Chandler, M. J. (1975). Relativism and the problem of epistemological loneliness. *Human Development, 18,* 171–180.

Chandler, M. J. (1987). The Othello effect: Essay on the emergence and eclipse of skeptical doubt. *Human Development, 30,* 137–159.

Chandler, M. J., Paget, K. F., & Koch, D. A. (1978). The child's demystification of psychological defense mechanisms: A structural and developmental analysis. *Developmental Psychology, 14,* 197–205.

Chandler, T. A., Wolf, F. M., Cook, B., & Dugovics, D. A. (1980). Parental correlates of locus of control in fifth graders: An attempt at experimentation in the home. *Merrill-Palmer Quarterly, 26,* 183–195.

Chanowitz, B., & Langer, E. (1985). Self-protection and self-inception. In M. W. Martin (Ed.), *Self-deception and self-understanding* (pp. 117–135). Lawrence, KS: University of Kansas Press.

Cherulnik, P. D., & Citrin, M. M. (1974). Individual differences in psychological reactance: The interaction between locus of control and mode of elimination of freedom. *Journal of Personality and Social Psychology, 29,* 398–404.

Choron, J. (1963). *Death and western thought.* New York: Collier Books.

Clinchy, B., & Mansfield, A. (1985). *Justifications offered by children to support positions on issues of "fact" and "opinion."* Paper presented at the 56th annual meeting of the Eastern Psychological Association, Boston.

Colby, K. M., & Spar, J. E. (1983). *The fundamental crisis in psychiatry.* Springfield, IL: Charles Thomas.

Cole, D. A. (1989). Psychopathology of adolescent suicide: Hopelessness, coping beliefs, and depression. *Journal of Abnormal Psychology, 98,* 248–255.

Cole, D. A., & LaVoie, J. C. (1985). Fantasy play and related cognitive development in 2- to 6-year-olds. *Developmental Psychology, 21,* 233–240.

Colliver, J., Doernberg, D., Grant, S. B., Dufour, M., & Bertolucci, D. (1986). Trends in mortality from cirrhosis and alcoholism—United States, 1942–1983. *Morbidity and Mortality Weekly Report, 35*(No 45), 703–704.

Corey, L. G. (1961). An analogue of resistance to death awareness. *Journal of Gerontology, 6,* 59–60.

Costa, P. T., Jr., & McCrae, R. R. (1980). Influence of extraversion and neuroticism on subjective well-being: Happy and unhappy people. *Journal of Personality and Social Psychology, 38,* 668–678.

Costello, C. G. (1982). Fears and phobias in women: A community study. *Journal of Abnormal Psychology, 91,* 280–286.

Cramer, P. (1979). Defense mechanisms in adolescence. *Developmental Psychology, 15,* 476–477.

Cramer, P. (1983). Children's use of defense mechanisms in reaction to displeasure caused by others. *Journal of Personality, 51,* 78–94.

Cramer, P. (1987). The development of defense mechanisms. *Journal of Personality, 55,* 597–614.

Cramer, P. (1988). The Defense Mechanism Inventory: A review of research and discussion of the scales. *Journal of Personality Assessment, 52,* 142–164.

Crandall, V. C., & Crandall, B. W. (1983). Maternal and childhood behaviors as antecedents of internal–external control perceptions in young adulthood. In H. M. Lefcourt (Ed.), *Research with the locus of control construct* (Vol. 2, pp. 53–103). New York: Academic Press.

Crocker, J., Alloy, L. B., & Kayne, N. T. (1988). Attributional style, depression, and perceptions of consensus for events. *Journal of Personality and Social Psychology, 54,* 840–846.

Csikszentmihalyi, M., & Larson, R. (1984). *Being adolescent: Conflict and growth in the teenage years.* New York: Basic Books.

Cushman, P. (1991). Ideology obscured: Political uses of the self in Daniel Stern's infant. *American Psychologist, 46,* 206–219.

Cushman, P. (1990). Why the self is empty. *American Psychologist, 45,* 599–611.

Cutler, S. J. (1976). Membership in different types of voluntary associations and psychological well-being. *The Gerontologist, 16,* 335–339.

Daniels, E. B., Jr. (1973). Some notes on clowns, madness, and psychotherapy. *Psychotherapy and Psychosomatics, 24,* 465–470.

Davis, W. L., & Davis, D. E. (1972). Internal–external control and attribution of responsibility for success and failure. *Journal of Personality, 40,* 123–135.

Davis, W. L., & Phares, E. J. (1969). Parental antecedents of internal–external control of reinforcement. *Psychological Reports, 24,* 427–436.

Davison, G. C., Tsujimoto, R. N., & Glaros, A. G. (1973). Attribution and the maintenance of behavior change in falling asleep. *Journal of Abnormal Psychology, 82,* 124–133.

de Charms, R. (1979). Personal causation and perceived control. In L. C. Perlmuter & R. A. Monty (Eds.), *Choice and perceived control* (pp. 29–40). Hillsdale, NJ: Lawrence Erlbaum Associates.

Deconchy, J. (1968). God and parental images. In A. Godin (Ed.), *From cry to word* (pp. 85–94). Brussels: Lumen Vital Press.

DeVos, G. (1952). A quantitative approach to affective symbolism in Rorschach responses. *Journal of Projective Techniques, 16,* 133–150.

Diamond, M. J., & Shapiro, J. L. (1973). Changes in locus of control as a function of encounter group experiences: A study and replication. *Journal of Abnormal Psychology, 82,* 514–518.

Dickstein, L. S. (1972). Death concern: Measurements and correlates. *Psychological Reports, 30,* 563–571.

Dickstein, L. S. (1975). Self-report and fantasy correlates of death concern. *Psychological Reports, 37,* 147–158.

Dickstein, L. S., & Blatt, S. J. (1966). Death concern, futurity, and anticipation. *Journal of Consulting Psychology, 30,* 11–17.

Diener, E. (1984). Subjective well-being. *Psychological Bulletin, 95,* 524–575.

Dies, R. R. (1968). Development of a projective measure of perceived locus of control. *Journal of Projective Techniques and Personality Assessment, 32,* 487–490.

DiLalla, L. F., & Watson, M. W. (1988). Differentiation of fantasy and reality: Preschoolers' reactions to interruptions in their play. *Developmental Psychology, 24,* 286–291.

Doherty, W. J., & Baldwin, C. (1985). Shifts and stability in locus of control during the 1970s: Divergence of the sexes. *Journal of Personality and Social Psychology, 48,* 1048–1053.

Dohrenwend, B. S., & Dohrenwend, B. P. (Eds.). (1974). *Stressful life events: Their nature and effects.* New York: Wiley.

Dollinger, S. J., & Cramer, P. (1990). Children's defensive responses and emotional upset following a disaster: A projective assessment. *Journal of Personality Assessment, 54,* 116–127.

Donahue, M. J. (1985). Intrinsic and extrinsic religiousness: Review and meta-analysis. *Journal of Personality and Social Psychology, 48,* 400–419.

Donahue, M. J., & Bergin, A. E. (1983, August). *Religion, personality, and lifestyle: A meta-analysis.* Paper presented at the meeting of the American Psychological Association, Anaheim, CA.

Douglas, M. (1970). *Natural symbols: Explorations in cosmology.* New York: Pantheon.

DuCette, J., & Wolk, S. (1972). Locus of control and extreme behavior. *Journal of Consulting and Clinical Psychology, 39,* 253–258.

Duke, M. P., & Lancaster, W., Jr. (1976). A note on locus of control as a function of father absence. *Journal of Genetic Psychology, 129,* 335–336.

Dunning, D., & Story, A. L. (1991). Depression, realism, and the overconfidence effect: Are the sadder wiser when predicting future actions and events? *Journal of Personality and Social Psychology, 61,* 521–532.

Dupuy, H. (1974). *Utility of the National Center for Health Statistics General Well-Being Schedule in the assessment of self-representations of subjective well-being and distress* (National Conference on Education in Alcohol, Drug Abuse and Mental Health Programs). Washington, DC: DHEW.

Durkheim, E., & Mauss, M. (1963). *Primitive classification.* Chicago: University of Chicago Press.

Duval, S., & Wicklund, R. A. (1972). *A theory of objective self-awareness.* New York: Academic Press.

Dyal, J. A. (1984). Cross-cultural research with the locus of control construct. In H. M. Lefcourt (Ed.), *Research with the locus of control construct* (Vol. 3, pp. 209–306). New York: Academic Press.

Einhorn, H. J., & Hogarth, R. M. (1978). Confidence in judgment: Persistence of the illusion of validity. *Psychological Review, 85,* 395–416.

Eliade, M. (1967). Cultural fashions and the history of religions. In J. M. Kitagawa (Ed.), *The history of religions: Essays on the problem of understanding* (pp. 21–38). Chicago: University of Chicago Press.

Eliade, M. (1969). *The quest: History and meaning in religion.* Chicago: University of Chicago Press.

Elkind, D. (1963). The child's concept of his religious denomination: III. The Protestant child. *Journal of Genetic Psychology, 103,* 291–304.

Ellis, A. (1987). The impossibility of achieving consistently good mental health. *American Psychologist, 42,* 364–375.

Ellison, C. G., Gay, D. A., & Glass, T. A. (1989). Does religious commitment contribute to individual life satisfaction? *Social Forces, 68,* 100–123.

Elster, J. (1983). *Sour grapes: Studies in the subversion of rationality.* New York: Cambridge University Press.

Enright, R., Lapsley, D., Franklin, C., & Steuck, K. (1984). Longitudinal and cross-cultural validation of the belief–discrepancy reasoning construct. *Developmental Psychology, 20,* 143–149.

Epstein, R., & Komorita, S. S. (1971). Self-esteem, success–failure, and locus of control in Negro children. *Developmental Psychology, 4,* 2–8.

Epstein, S. (1983). The unconscious, the preconscious, and the self-concept. In J. Suls & A. G. Greenwald (Eds.), *Psychological perspectives on the self* (Vol. 2, pp. 219–247). Hillsdale, NJ: Lawrence Erlbaum Associates.

Erikson, E. H. (1977). *Toys and reason: Stages in the ritualization of experience.* New York: Norton.

Eron, L. D. (1948). Frequencies of themes and identifications in the stories of schizophrenic patients and non-hospitalized college students. *Journal of Consulting Psychology, 12,* 387–395.

Esslin, M. (1961). *The theater of the absurd.* Garden City, NY: Anchor Books.

Evans, F. J. (1985). Expectancy, therapeutic instructions, and the placebo response. In L. White, B. Tursky, & G. E. Schwartz (Eds.), *Placebo: Theory, research, and mechanisms* (pp. 215–228). New York: Guilford.

Eysenck, H. J., Wakefield, J. A., Jr., & Friedman, A. F. (1983). Diagnosis and clinical assessment. In M. R. Rosenzweig & L. W. Porter (Eds.), *Annual review of psychology* (Vol. 34, pp. 167–193). Palo Alto, CA: Annual Reviews, Inc.

Farberow, N. L. (Ed.). (1980). *The many faces of suicide.* New York: McGraw-Hill.

Farley, G. A. (1970). *An investigation of death anxiety and the sense of competence.* Unpublished doctoral dissertation, Duke University, Durham, NC.

Feifel, H., & Branscomb, A. B. (1973). Who's afraid of death? *Journal of Abnormal Psychology, 81,* 282–288.

Feifel, H., & Hermann, L. J. (1973). Fear of death in the mentally ill. *Psychological Reports, 33,* 931–938.

Fein, G. G. (1975). A transformational analysis of pretending. *Developmental Psychology, 11,* 291–296.

Fein, G. G. (1981). Pretend play in childhood: An integrative review. *Child Development, 52,* 1095–1118.

Feldman, J. B. (1978). *The utilization of the subliminal psychodynamic activation method in the further examination of conscious and unconscious measures of death anxiety.* Unpublished doctoral dissertation, Case Western Reserve University, Cleveland, OH.

Felson, R. B. (1989). Parents and the reflected appraisal process: A longitudinal analysis. *Journal of Personality and Social Psychology, 56,* 965–971.

Felton, B. J., & Revenson, T. A. (1984). Coping with chronic illness: A study of illness controllability and the influence of coping strategies on psychological adjustment. *Journal of Consulting and Clinical Psychology, 52,* 343–353.

Fenichel, O. (1945). *The psychoanalytic theory of neurosis.* New York: Norton.

Fenigstein, A. (1984). Self-consciousness and the overperception of self as a target. *Journal of Personality and Social Psychology, 47,* 860–870.

Fischer, K. W., & Pipp, S. L. (1984). Development of the structures of unconscious thought. In K. S. Bowers & D. Meichenbaum (Eds.), *The unconscious reconsidered* (pp. 88–148). New York: Wiley.

Fisher, S. (1967). Projective methodologies. *Annual Review of Psychology, 18,* 165–190.

Fisher, S. (1970). *Body experience in fantasy and behavior.* New York: Appleton-Century-Crofts.

Fisher, S. (1973). *The female orgasm: Psychology, physiology, fantasy.* New York: Basic Books.

Fisher, S. (1986). *Development and structure of the body image* (Vols. 1 and 2). Hillsdale, NJ: Lawrence Erlbaum Associates.

Fisher, S. (1989). *Sexual images of the self: The psychology of erotic sensations and illusions.* Hillsdale, NJ: Lawrence Erlbaum Associates.

Fisher, S., & Fisher, R. L. (1981). *Pretend the world is funny and forever: A psychological analysis of comedians, clowns, and actors.* Hillsdale, NJ: Lawrence Erlbaum Associates.

Fisher, S., & Greenberg, R. P. (1979). Body opening symptoms and right–left sets. *Journal of Nervous and Mental Disease, 167,* 422–427.

Fisher, S., & Greenberg, R. P. (1985). *The scientific credibility of Freud's theories and therapy.* New York: Columbia University Press.

Fisher, S., & Greenberg, R. P. (1989). *The limits of biological treatments for psychological distress.* Hillsdale, NJ: Lawrence Erlbaum Associates.

Fisher, S., Wright, D. M., & Moelis, I. (1979). Effects of maternal themes upon death imagery. *Journal of Personality Assessment, 43,* 595–599.

Fiske, S. T., Pratto, F., & Pavelchak, M. A. (1983). Citizens' images of nuclear war: Content and consequences. *Journal of Social Issues, 39,* 41–65.

Fogelson, R. D. (1982). Person, self, and identity: Some anthropological retrospects, circumspects, and prospects. In B. Lee (Ed.), *Psychosocial theories of the self* (pp. 67–109). New York: Plenum.

Folkman, S. (1984). Personal control and stress and coping processes: A theoretical analysis. *Journal of Personality and Social Psychology, 46,* 839–852.

Ford, C. E., & Neale, J. M. (1985). Learned helplessness and judgments of control. *Journal of Personality and Social Psychology, 49,* 1330–1336.

Foulkes, D. (1982). *Children's dreams: Longitudinal studies.* New York: Wiley.

Foy, D. W., Sipprelle, R. C., Rueger, D. B., & Carroll, E. M. (1984). Etiology of posttraumatic stress disorder in Vietnam veterans: Analysis of premilitary, military, and combat exposure influences. *Journal of Consulting and Clinical Psychology, 52,* 79–87.

Francis, L. J. (1985). Personality and religion: Theory and measurement. In L. B. Brown (Ed.), *Advances in the psychology of religion* (pp. 171–181). New York: Pergamon Press.

Frank, J. D. (1961). *Persuasion and healing.* Baltimore: Johns Hopkins University Press.

Frank, R. G., Umlauf, R. L., Wonderlich, S. A., Askanazi, G. S., Buckelew, S. P., & Elliott, T. R. (1987). Differences in coping styles among persons with spinal cord injury: A cluster-analytic approach. *Journal of Consulting and Clinical Psychology, 55,* 727–731.

Frankl, V. E. (1955). *The doctor and the soul.* New York: Knopf.

Freedman, B., & Chapman, L. J. (1973). Early subjective experience in schizophrenic episodes. *Journal of Abnormal Psychology, 82,* 46–54.

Freedman, R., Adler, L. E., Gerhardt, G. A., Waldo, M., Baker, N., Rose, G. M., Drebing, C., Nagamoto, H., Bickford-Wimer, P., & Franks, R. (1987). Neurobiological studies of sensory gating in schizophrenia. *Schizophrenia Bulletin, 13,* 669–678.

Freud, S. (1953). Three essays on sexuality. In J. Strachey (Ed. and Trans.), *The standard edition of the complete psychological works of Sigmund Freud* (Vol. 7, pp. 135–243). London: Hogarth Press. (Original work published 1905)

Freud, S. (1959a). Character and anal erotism. In J. Strachey (Ed. and Trans.), *The standard edition of the complete psychological works of Sigmund Freud* (Vol. 9, pp. 167–176). London: Hogarth Press. (Original work published 1908)

Freud, S. (1959b). Obsessive actions and religious practices. In J. Strachey (Ed. and Trans.), *The standard edition of the complete psychological works of Sigmund Freud* (Vol. 9, pp. 115–128). London: Hogarth Press. (Original work published 1907)

Freud, S. (1961). The future of an illusion. In J. Strachey (Ed. and Trans.), *The standard edition of the complete psychological works of Sigmund Freud* (Vol. 21, pp. 3–56). London: Hogarth Press. (Original work published 1927)

Fromm, E. (1941). *Escape from freedom.* New York: Holt, Rinehart & Winston.

Fromm, E. (1950). *Psychoanalysis and religion.* New Haven, CT: Yale University Press.

Fulton, R. (1965). *Death and identity.* New York: Wiley.

Galanter, M. (1982). Charismatic religious sects and psychiatry: An overview. *American Journal of Psychiatry, 139,* 1539–1548.

Galanter, M., & Buckley, P. (1978). Evangelical religion and meditation: Psychotherapeutic effects. *The Journal of Nervous and Mental Disease, 166,* 685–691.

Galanter, M., Rabkin, R., Rabkin, J., & Deutsch, A. (1979). The "Moonies": A psychological study of conversion and membership in a contemporary religious sect. *American Journal of Psychiatry, 136,* 165–170.

Garber, J., & Seligman, M. E. P. (Eds.). (1980). *Human helplessness: Theory and applications.* New York: Academic Press.

Gardner, R. W., & Moriarty, A. (1968). *Personality development at preadolescence.* Seattle: University of Washington Press.

Garrett, A. M., & Willoughby, R. H. (1972). Personal orientation and reactions to success and failure in urban Black children. *Developmental Psychology, 7,* 92.

Gartner, J., Larson, D. B., & Allen, G. D. (1991). Religious commitment and mental health: A review of the empirical literature. *Journal of Psychology and Theology, 19,* 6–25.

Gediman, H. K. (1971). The concept of stimulus barrier: Its review and reformulation as an adaptive ego function. *International Journal of Psycho-Analysis, 52,* 243–257.

Geer, J. H., Davison, G. C., & Gatchel, R. I. (1970). Reduction of stress in humans through nonveridical perceived control of aversive stimulation. *Journal of Personality and Social Psychology, 16,* 731–738.

Gergen, K. J. (1982). From self to science: What is there to know? In J. Suls (Ed.), *Psychological perspectives on the self* (Vol. 1, pp. 129–149). Hillsdale, NJ: Lawrence Erlbaum Associates.

Geyer, M. A., & Braff, D. L. (1987). Startle habituation and sensorimotor gating in schizophrenia and related animal models. *Schizophrenia Bulletin, 13,* 643–668.

Gibbins, K., & Douglas, W. (1985). Voice recognition and self-deception: A reply to Sackeim and Gur. *Journal of Personality and Social Psychology, 48,* 1369–1372.

Gibbons, F. X., Carver, C. S., Scheier, M. R., & Harmuth, S. E. (1979). Self-focused attention and the placebo effect: Fooling some of the people some of the time. *Journal of Experimental Social Psychology, 15,* 263–274.

Gibbons, F. X., Smith, T. W., Ingram, R. E., Pearce, K., Brehm, S. S., & Schroeder, C. G. (1985). Self-awareness and self-confrontation: Effects of self-focused attention on members of a clinical population. *Journal of Personality and Social Psychology, 48,* 662–675.

Gibbs, H. W., & Achterberg-Lawlis, J. (1978). Spiritual value and death anxiety: Implications for counseling with terminal cancer patients. *Journal of Counseling Psychology, 25,* 563–569.

Giffin, H. (1984). The coordination of meaning in the creation of a shared make-believe reality. In I. Bretherton (Ed.), *Symbolic play* (pp. 73–100). New York: Academic Press.

Gill, M. M. (1979). The analysis of the transference. *Journal of the American Psychoanalytic Association, 27* (Supplement), 263–288.

Glass, D. C., & Carver, C. S. (1980). Helplessness and the Coronary-Prone Personality. In J. Garber & M. Seligman (Eds.), *Human helplessness* (pp. 223–243). New York: Academic Press.

Glass, D. C., Singer, J. E., & Friedman, L. N. (1969). Psychic cost of adaptation to an environmental stressor. *Journal of Personality and Social Psychology, 12,* 200–210.

Godin, A., & Hallez, M. (1965). Parental images and divine paternity. In A. Godin (Ed.), *From religious experience to a religious attitude* (pp. 65–96). Chicago: Loyola University Press.

Golding, S. L., Atwood, G. E., & Goodman, R. A. (1966). Anxiety and two cognitive forms of resistance to the idea of death. *Psychological Reports, 18,* 359–364.

Goleman, D. (1985). The psychology of self-deception. *Vital lies, simple truths.* New York: Simon & Schuster.

Golin, S., Terrell, F., & Johnson, B. (1977). Depression and the illusion of control. *Journal of Abnormal Psychology, 86,* 440–442.

Golin, S., Terrell, F., Weitz, J., & Drost, P. L. (1979). The illusion of control among depressed patients. *Journal of Abnormal Psychology, 88,* 454–457.

Golomb, C. (1979). Pretend play: A cognitive perspective. In N. R. Smith & M. B. Franklin (Eds.), *Symbolic functioning in childhood* (pp. 101–116). New York: Wiley.

Gorsuch, R. L. (1988). Psychology of religion. In M. R. Rosenzweig & L. W. Porter (Eds.), *Annual review of psychology* (Vol. 39, pp. 201–221). Palo Alto, CA: Annual Reviews, Inc.

Gottschalk, L. A. (1979). Drug effects in the assessment of affective states in man. In L. A. Gottschalk (Ed.), *The content analysis of verbal behavior: Further studies* (pp. 499–537). New York: Spectrum Publications.

Gottschalk, L. A., Haer, J. L., & Bates, D. E. (1972). Effect of sensory overload on psychological state. *Archives of General Psychiatry, 27,* 451–457.

Gottschalk, L. A., & Gleser, G. C. (1969). *The measurement of psychological states through the content analysis of verbal behavior.* Berkeley: University of California Press.

Gough, H. G., & Heilbrun, A. B. (1965). *The adjective check list manual.* Palo Alto, CA: Consulting Psychologists Press.

Gozali, J., & Sloan, J. (1971). Control orientation as a personality dimension among alcoholics. *Quarterly Journal of Studies on Alcohol, 32,* 159–161.

Greeley, A. M. (1975). *The sociology of the paranormal: A reconnaissance.* Beverly Hills, CA: Sage.

Greenberg, J., Pyszczynski, T., Solomon, S., Rosenblatt, A., Veeder, M., Kirkland, S., & Lyon, D. (1990). Evidence for terror management theory: II. The effects of mortality salience on reactions to those who threaten or bolster the cultural worldview. *Journal of Personality and Social Psychology, 58,* 308–318.

Greenberg, R. P., & Fisher, S. (1973). A muscle awareness model for changes in Rorschach human movement responses. *Journal of Personality Assessment, 37,* 512–518.

Greenberger, E. (1965). Fantasies of women confronting death. *Journal of Consulting Psychology, 29,* 252–260.

Greenwald, A. G. (1980). The totalitarian ego: Fabrication and revision of personal history. *American Psychologist, 35,* 604–618.

Greenwald, A. G. (1982). Is anyone in charge? Personanalysis versus the principle of personal unity. In J. Suls (Ed.), *Psychological perspectives on the self* (Vol. 1, pp. 151–184). Hillsdale, NJ: Lawrence Erlbaum Associates.

Gregory, W. L., Chartier, G. M., & Wright, M. H. (1979). Learned helplessness and learned effectiveness: Effects of explicit response cues on individuals differing in personal control expectancies. *Journal of Personality and Social Psychology, 37,* 1982–1992.

Griffith, E. E. H., English, T., & Mayfield, V. (1980). Possession, prayer, and testimony: Therapeutic aspects of the Wednesday night meeting in a Black church. *Psychiatry, 43,* 120–128.

Griffith, E. E. H., Mahy, G. E., & Young, J. L. (1986). Psychological benefits of Spiritual Baptist "mourning": II. An empirical assessment. *American Journal of Psychiatry, 143,* 226–229.

Griffith, R. M., Miyagi, O., & Tago, A. (1958). The universality of typical dreams: Japanese vs. Americans. *American Anthropologist, 60,* 1173–1179.

Gross, M. L. (1978). *The psychological society.* New York: Random House.

Gur, R. C., & Sackeim, H. A. (1979). Self-deception: A concept in search of a phenomenon. *Journal of Personality and Social Psychology, 37,* 147–169.

Gurin, G., Verott, J., & Feld, S. (1960). *Americans view their mental health.* New York: Basic Books.

Haan, N. (with contributions by P. Joffe, R. F. Morrissey, & M. P. Naditch). (1977). *Coping and defending: Processes of self-environment organization.* New York: Academic Press.

Haer, J. L. (1970). Alterations in consciousness induced by sensory overload. *Journal for the Study of Consciousness, 3,* 161–169.

Hahn, R. A. (1985). A sociocultural model of illness and healing. In L. White, B. Tursky, & G. E. Schwartz (Eds.), *Placebo: Theory, research, and mechanisms* (pp. 167–195). New York: Guilford Press.

Haitsma, K. V. (1986). Intrinsic religious orientation: Implications in the study of religiosity and personal adjustment in the aged. *The Journal of Social Psychology, 126,* 685–687.

Hale, W. D., & Cochran, C. D. (1986). Locus of control across the adult lifespan. *Psychological Reports, 59,* 311–313.

Hale, W. D., Hedgepeth, B. E., & Taylor, E. B. (1985–1986). Locus of control and psychological distress among the aged. *International Journal of Aging and Human Development, 21,* 1–8.

Hall, C. S. (1951). What people dream about. *Scientific American, 184,* 60–63.

Hall, C. S. (1966). A comparison of the dreams of four groups of hospitalized mental patients with each other and with a normal population. *Journal of Nervous and Mental Disease, 143,* 135–139.

Hall, C. S., & Van de Castle, R. L. (1966). *The content analysis of dreams.* New York: Appleton-Century-Crofts.

Hamilton, S. B., Chavez, E. L., & Keilin, W. G. (1986). Thought of Armageddon: The relationship between attitudes toward the nuclear threat and cognitive/emotional responses. *International Journal of Mental Health, 15,* 189–207.

Hanada, K., & Takahashi, S. (1983). Multi-institutional collaborative studies of diagnostic reliability of DSM-III. In R. Spitzer, J. Williams, & A. Sodal (Eds.), *International perspectives on DSM-III* (pp. 273–290). Washington, DC: American Psychiatric Press.

Handal, P. J., Peal, R. L., Napoli, J. G., & Austrin, H. R. (1984–1985). The relationship between direct and indirect measures of death anxiety. *Omega, 15,* 245–262.

Handal, P. J., & Rychlak, J. F. (1971). Curvilinearity between dream content and death anxiety and the relationship of death anxiety to repression-sensitization. *Journal of Abnormal Psychology, 77,* 11–16.

Harris, P. L., Donnelly, K., Guz, G. R., & Pitt-Watson, R. (1986). Children's understanding of the distinction between real and apparent emotion. *Child Development, 57,* 895–909.

Harwicke, N. J. (1980). *Body barrier: Relation to beliefs about sickness and death.* Unpublished doctoral dissertation, Illinois Institute of Technology, Chicago.

Hay, D., & Morisy, A. (1978). Reports of ecstatic, paranormal, or religious experience in Great Britain and the United States: A comparison of trends. *Journal for the Scientific Study of Religion, 17,* 255–268.

Hayslip, B., Jr., & Stewart-Bussey, D. (1986–1987). Locus of control-levels of death anxiety relationships. *Omega, 17,* 41–50.

Heilbrun, A. B., & Brown, N. (1978). Fabrication of delusional thinking in normals. *Journal of Abnormal Psychology, 24,* 422–425.

Heilbrun, A. B., Jr., & Pepe, V. (1985). Awareness of cognitive defenses and stress management. *British Journal of Medical Psychology, 58,* 9–17.

Helgeland, J. (1984–1985). The symbolism of death in the later middle ages. *Omega, 25*, 145–160.

Heller, D. (1986). *The children's God*. Chicago: University of Chicago Press.

Hersch, P. D., & Scheibe, K. E. (1967). Reliability and validity of internal–external control as a personality dimension. *Journal of Consulting Psychology, 31*, 609–613.

Hetherington, E. M., Cox, M., & Cox, R. (1979). Play and social interaction in children following divorce. *Journal of Social Issues, 35*, 26–49.

Hilgard, E. R. (1977). *Divided consciousness: Multiple controls in human thought and action*. New York: Wiley.

Hole, R. W., Rush, A. J., & Beck, A. T. (1979). A cognitive investigation of schizophrenic delusions. *Psychiatry, 42*, 312–319.

Holroyd, K. A., & Andrasek, F. (1978). Coping and the self-control of chronic tension headache. *Journal of Consulting and Clinical Psychology, 46*, 1036–1045.

Holt, R. R. (Ed.). (1968). *Diagnostic psychological testing* (rev. ed.). New York: International Universities Press.

Holzman, P. S. (1987). Recent studies of psychophysiology in schizophrenia. *Schizophrenia Bulletin, 13*, 49–75.

Hooper, T., & Spilka, B. (1970). Some meanings and correlates of future time and death among college students. *Omega, 1*, 149–156.

Houston, B. K. (1972). Control over stress, locus of control and response to stress. *Journal of Personality and Social Psychology, 21*, 249–255.

Houston, B. K., & Holmes, S. (1974). Effect of avoidant thinking and reappraisal for coping with threat involving temporal uncertainty. *Journal of Personality and Social Psychology, 30*, 382–388.

Howell, W. (1976). *Attitudes toward death and toward the future in aged and young adults*. Unpublished doctoral dissertation, Michigan State University, Lansing.

Hui, C. H. (1982). Locus of control: A review of cross-cultural research. *International Journal of Intercultural Relations, 6*, 301–323.

Hull, J. G. (1981). A self-awareness model of the causes and effects of alcohol consumption. *Journal of Abnormal Psychology, 90*, 586–600.

Hull, J. G., & Bond, C. F. (1986). Social and behavioral consequences of alcohol consumption and expectancy: A meta-analysis. *Psychological Bulletin, 99*, 347–360.

Hunsberger, B. (1985). Religion, age, life satisfaction, and perceived sources of religiousness: A study of older persons. *Journal of Gerontology, 40*, 615–620.

Hurlburt, R. T. (1979). Random sampling of cognitions and behavior. *Journal of Research in Personality, 13*, 103–111.

Huzinga, J. (1949). *Humo ludens: A study of play-element in culture*. London: Routledge & Kegan Paul.

Ihilevich, D., & Gleser, G. C. (1986). *Defense mechanisms: Their classification, correlates, and measurement with the Defense Mechanism Inventory*. Owasco, MI: DMI Associates.

Ilfeld, F. W. (1977). Current social stressors and symptoms of depression. *American Journal of Psychiatry, 134*, 161–166.

Immergluck, L. (1964). Determinism–freedom in contemporary psychology: An ancient problem revisited. *American Psychologist, 19*, 270–281.

Inglehart, R., & Rabier, J. (1986). Aspirations adapt to situations—but why are the Belgians so much happier than the French? A cross-cultural analysis of the subjective quality of life. In F. M. Andrews (Ed.), *Research on the quality of life* (pp. 1–84). Ann Arbor, MI: Institute for Social Research, University of Michigan.

James, W. (1910). *Psychology: The briefer course*. New York: Holt.

Janoff-Bulman, R. (1985). The aftermath of victimization: Rebuilding shattered assumptions. In C. R. Figley (Ed.), *Trauma and its wake* (pp. 15–35). New York: Brunner/Mazel.

Janoff-Bulman, R., & Marshall, G. (1982). Mortality, well-being, and control: A study of an aged population of institutionalized elderly. *Personality and Social Psychology Bulletin, 8*, 691–698.

Jarvis, G. K., & Northcott, H. C. (1987). Religion and differences in morbidity and mortality. *Social Science and Medicine, 25*, 813–824.

Jensen, G. F., & Erickson, M. L. (1979). The religious factor and delinquency: Another look at the hellfire hypothesis. In R. Wuthnow (Ed.), *The religious dimension* (pp. 157–177). New York: Academic Press.

Jimakas, M. J. (1980). *Fear of death in schizophrenics and normals.* Unpublished doctoral dissertation, United States International University, San Diego, CA.

Johnson, W. G., Ross, J. M., & Mastria, M. A. (1977). Delusional behavior: An attributional analysis of development and modification. *Journal of Abnormal Psychology, 86*, 421–426.

Jolley, J. C., & Taulbee, S. J. (1986). Assessing perceptions of self and God: Comparison of prisoners and normals. *Psychological Reports, 59*, 1139–1146.

Jospe, M. (1978). *The placebo effect in healing.* Lexington, MA: Lexington Books.

Juni, S. (1982). The composite measure of the Defense Mechanism Inventory. *Journal of Personality Assessment, 44*, 484–486.

Juni, S., & Masling, J. (1980). Reaction to aggression and the Defense Mechanism Inventory. *Journal of Personality Assessment, 44*, 484–486.

Kagan, J., & Moss, H. A. (1962). *Birth to maturity.* New York: Wiley.

Kanfer, F. H., & Seidner, M. L. (1973). Self-control: Factors enhancing tolerance of noxious stimulation. *Journal of Personality and Social Psychology, 25*, 381–389.

Kaplan, M. F. (1968). Elicitation of information and response biases of repressors, sensitizers, and neutrals in behavior prediction. *Journal of Personality, 36*, 84–91.

Kapleau, P. (1967). *The three pillars of Zen.* Boston: Beacon.

Karasau, T. B., & Steinmuller, R. I. (1978). *Psychotherapeutics in medicine.* New York: Grune & Stratton.

Kastenbaum, R. (1979). *Between life and death.* New York: Springer.

Kastenbaum, R., & Costa, P. T., Jr. (1977). Psychological perspectives on death. *Annual Review of Psychology, 28*, 225–249.

Katkovsky, W., Crandall, V. C., & Good, S. (1967). Parental antecedents of children's beliefs in internal–external control of reinforcements in intellectual achievement situations. *Child Development, 28*, 765–776.

Kellner, R. (1986). *Somatization and hypochondriasis.* Westport, CT: Praeger Publishers.

Kendler, K. S., Glazer, W. M., & Morgenstern, H. (1983). Dimensions of delusional experience. *American Journal of Psychiatry, 140*, 466–469.

Khavari, K. A., & Harmon, T. M. (1982). The relationship between the degree of professed religious belief and use of drugs. *The International Journal of the Addictions, 17*, 847–857.

Kieckhefer, R. (1990). *Magic in the middle ages.* New York: Cambridge University Press.

Kihlstrom, J. F. (1984). Conscious, subconscious, unconscious: A cognitive perspective. In K. S. Bowers & D. Meichenbaum (Eds.), *The unconscious reconsidered* (pp. 149–211). New York: Wiley.

Kihlstrom, J. F. (1985). Hypnosis. In M. R. Rosenzweig & L. W. Porter (Eds.), *Annual review of psychology* (Vol. 36, pp. 385–418). Palo Alto, CA: Annual Reviews, Inc.

Kilbourne, B., & Richardson, J. T. (1984). Psychotherapy and new religions in a pluralistic society. *American Psychologist, 39*, 237–251.

King, G. W. (1986). *Statistical abstract of the United States* (107th ed.) (p. 106). Washington, DC: United States Bureau of the Census.

Kline, P. (1987). The scientific status of the DMT. *British Journal of Medical Psychology, 60*, 53–59.

Koenig, H. G., Kvale, J. N., & Ferrel, C. (1988). Religion and well-being in later life. *The Gerontologist, 28*, 18–28.

Kogan, N., & Wallach, M. A. (1961). Age changes in values and attitudes. *Journal of Gerontology, 16*, 272–280.

Kramer, B. M., Kalick, S. M., & Milburn, M. A. (1983). Attitudes toward nuclear weapons and nuclear war: 1945–1982. *Journal of Social Issues, 39*, 7–24.

Kramer, M. (1970). Manifest dream content in normal and psychopathologic states. *Archives of General Psychiatry, 22,* 149–159.

Krause, N. (1986). Stress and coping: Reconceptualizing the role of locus of control beliefs. *Journal of Gerontology, 41,* 617–622.

Krebs, D., Denton, K., & Higgins, N. C. (1988). On the evaluation of self-knowledge and self-deception. In K. B. MacDonald (Ed.), *Sociobiological perspectives on human development* (pp. 103–139). New York: Springer-Verlag.

Kreiger, S. R., Epting, F. R., & Leitner, L. M. (1974). Personal constructs, threat and attitudes toward death. *Omega, 5,* 299–310.

Kubler-Ross, E. (1969). *On death and dying.* New York: Macmillan.

Kuhn, D., Pennington, N., & Leadbeater, B. (1983). Adult thinking in developmental perspective. In P. B. Baltes & O. G. Brim, Jr. (Eds.), *Life-span development and behavior* (Vol. 6, pp. 33–76). New York: Academic Press.

Kuhn, T. S. (1962). *The structure of scientific revolutions.* Chicago: University of Chicago Press.

Kuhn, T. S. (1976). *The Copernican revolution.* Cambridge, MA: Harvard University Press.

Kuiper, N. A. (1978). Depression and causal attributions for success and failure. *Journal of Personality and Social Psychology, 36,* 236–246.

Kutchins, H., & Kirk, S. A. (1986). The reliability of DSM-III: A critical review. *Social Work Research & Abstracts, 21,* 3–12.

Langer, E. J. (1975). The illusion of control. *Journal of Personality and Social Psychology, 32,* 311–328.

Langer, E. J. (Ed.). (1983). *The psychology of control.* Beverly Hills: Sage.

Langer, E. J., Janis, I. L., & Wolfer, J. A. (1975). Reduction of psychological stress in surgical patients. *Journal of Experimental Social Psychology, 11,* 155–165.

Langer, E. J., & Rodin, J. (1976). The effects of choice and enhanced personal responsibility for the aged: A field experiment in an institutional setting. *Journal of Personality and Social Psychology, 34,* 191–198.

Langner, T. S. (1962). A twenty-two item screening score of psychiatric symptoms indicating impairment. *Journal of Health and Human Behavior, 3,* 269–276.

Lasch, C. (1984). *The minimal self: Psychic survival in troubled times.* New York: Norton.

Layne, C. (1983). Painful truths about depressives' cognitions. *Journal of Clinical Psychology, 39,* 848–853.

Lazarus, R. S. (1983). The costs and benefits of denial. In S. Breznitz (Ed.), *The denial of stress* (pp. 1–30). New York: International Universities Press.

Lefcourt, H. M. (1967). Effects of cue explication upon persons maintaining external control expectancies. *Journal of Personality and Social Psychology, 5,* 372–378.

Lefcourt, H. M. (1982). *Locus of control: Current trends in theory and research.* Hillsdale, NJ: Lawrence Erlbaum Associates.

Lefcourt, H. M., Hogg, E., & Sordoni, C. (1975). Locus of control, field dependence and the conditions arousing objective versus subjective self-awareness. *Journal of Research in Personality, 9,* 21–36.

Leighton, D. C., Harding, J. S., Macklin, D. B., Macmillan, A. M., & Leighton, A. H. (1963). *The character of danger.* New York: Basic Books.

Lerner, M. J. (1971). Observers' evaluation of a victim: Justice, guilt and veridical perception. *Journal of Personality and Social Psychology, 20,* 127–135.

Lerner, M. J. (1980). *The belief in a just world: A fundamental delusion.* New York: Plenum Press.

Leslie, A. M. (1987). Pretense and representation: The origins of "theory of mind." *Psychological Review, 94,* 412–426.

Lester, D. (1967). Fear of death of suicidal persons. *Psychological Reports, 20,* 1077–1078.

Lester, D., & Lester, G. (1970). Fear of death, fear of dying, and threshold differences for death words and neutral words. *Omega, 1,* 175–179.

Lester, D., & Schumacher, J. (1969). Schizophrenia and death concern. *Journal of Projective Techniques and Personality Assessment, 33,* 403–405.

Levenson, H. (1973). Multidimensional locus of control in psychiatric patients. *Journal of Consulting and Clinical Psychology, 41,* 397–404.

Levin, J. S., & Schiller, P. L. (1987). Is there a religious factor in health? *Journal of Religion and Health, 26,* 9–36.

Levin, J. S., & Vanderpool, H. Y. (1987). Is frequent religious attendance *really* conducive to better health? Toward an epidemiology of religion. *Social Science and Medicine, 24,* 589–600.

Levinson, D. J., with Darrow, C. N., Klein, E. B., Levinson, M. H., & McKee, B. (1978). *The seasons of a man's life.* New York: Alfred A. Knopf.

Levinson, D. J., & Malone, M. J. (1980). *Toward explaining human culture: A critical review of the findings of worldwide cross-cultural research.* New Haven: Human Relations Area Files, Inc.

Lewinsohn, P. M., Chaplin, W., & Barton, R. (1980). Social competence and depression: The role of illusory self-perceptions. *Journal of Abnormal Psychology, 89,* 203–212.

Lieberman, P., & Baker, F. (1985). The reliability of psychiatric diagnosis in the emergency room. *Hospital and Community Psychiatry, 36,* 3–12.

Lifton, R. J. (1964). On death and death symbolism: The Hiroshima disaster. *Psychiatry, 27,* 191–210.

Lifton, R. J. (1967). *Life in death: Survivors of Hiroshima.* New York: Random House.

Lindeman, C. A., & Van Aernam, B. (1971). Nursing intervention with the presurgical patient: The effects of structured and unstructured preoperative teaching. *Nursing Research, 20,* 319–332.

Linehan, M. M., Goodstein, J. L., Nielsen, S. L., & Chiles, J. A. (1983). Reasons for staying alive when you are thinking of killing yourself: The Reasons for Living Inventory. *Journal of Consulting and Clinical Psychology, 51,* 276–286.

Link, B., & Dohrenwend, B. P. (1980). Formulation of hypotheses about the true prevalence of demoralization in the United States. In B. P. Dohrenwend, B. S. Dohrenwend, M. S. Gould, B. Link, R. Neugebauer, & R. Wunsch-Hitzig (Eds.), *Mental illness in the United States: Epidemiological estimates* (pp. 114–132). New York: Praeger Special Studies, Praeger Scientific.

Lipowski, Z. J. (1975, May/June). Sensory and information inputs overload: Behavioral effects. *Comprehensive Psychiatry, 16,* 199–221.

Lipp, L., Kolstoe, R., James, W., & Randall, H. (1968). Denial of disability and internal control of reinforcement: A study using a perceptual defense paradigm. *Journal of Consulting and Clinical Psychology, 32,* 72–75.

Lloyd, C. (1980). Life events and depressive order reviewed: I. Events as predisposing factors. *Archives of General Psychiatry, 37,* 529–535.

Lockard, J. S. (1988). Origins of self-deception. In J. S. Lockard & D. L. Paulhus (Eds.), *Self-deception: An adaptive mechanism?* (pp. 14–22). New York: Prentice-Hall.

Loeb, R. C. (1975). Concomitants of boys' locus of control examined in parent–child interactions. *Developmental Psychology, 11,* 353–358.

Lonetto, R. (1980). *Children's conceptions of death.* New York: Springer.

Lonetto, R., & Templer, D. I. (1986). *Death anxiety.* Washington, DC: Hemisphere.

Lorr, M., Klett, J. C., & McNair, D. M. (1963). *Syndromes of psychosis.* New York: Macmillan.

Lowenthal, M. F., Thurnher, M., Chiriboga, D., & Associates (1975). *Four stages of life.* San Francisco: Jossey-Bass.

Lowry, R. J. (1965). *Male–female differences in attitudes towards death.* Unpublished doctoral dissertation, Brandeis University, Waltham, MA.

Lucas, R. A. (1974). A comparative study of measures of general anxiety and death anxiety among three medical groups including patient and wife. *Omega, 5,* 233–243.

Lumpkin, J. R. (1986). The relationship between locus of control and age: New evidence. *Journal of Social Behavior and Personality, 1,* 245–252.

Lyerly, S. B., Ross, S., Krugman, A. D., & Clyde, D. J. (1964). Drugs and placebos: The effects of instructions upon performance and mood under amphetamine sulphate and chloral hydrate. *Journal of Abnormal and Social Psychology, 68,* 321–327.

Lynn, S. J., Rhue, J. W., & Weekes, J. R. (1990). Hypnotic involuntariness: A social cognitive analysis. *Psychological Review, 97,* 169–184.

Maccoby, E. E., & Jacklin, C. N. (1974). *The psychology of sex differences.* Stanford, CA: Stanford University Press.

MacDonald, A. P., Jr. (1971). Internal–external locus of control: Parental antecedents. *Journal of Consulting and Clinical Psychology, 37,* 141–147.

MacDonald, K. B. (Ed.). (1988). *Sociobiological perspectives on human development.* New York: Springer-Verlag.

MacLeod, C., Mathews, A., & Tata, P. (1986). Attentional bias in emotional disorders. *Journal of Abnormal Psychology, 95,* 15–20.

Maddi, S. R., & Rulla, L. M. (1972). Personality and the Catholic religious vocation: I. Self and conflict in female entrants. *Journal of Personality, 40,* 104–122.

Marcia, J. E. (1976). Identity six years after: A follow-up study. *Journal of Youth and Adolescence, 5,* 145–160.

Marcia, J. E. (1980). Identity in adolescence. In J. Adelson (Ed.), *Handbook of adolescent psychology* (pp. 159–187). New York: Wiley.

Marks, G. (1984). Thinking one's abilities are unique and one's opinions are common. *Personality and Social Psychology Bulletin, 10,* 203–208.

Marks, G., & Miller, N. (1987). Ten years of research on the false-consensus effect: An empirical and theoretical review. *Psychological Bulletin, 102,* 72–90.

Markus, H. (1980). The self in thought and memory. In D. M. Wegner & R. R. Vallacher (Eds.), *The self in social psychology* (pp. 102–130). New York: Oxford University Press.

Markus, H., & Nurius, P. (1986). Possible selves. *American Psychologist, 41,* 954–969.

Markus, H., & Sentis, L. J. (1982). The self in social information processing. In J. Suls (Ed.), *Psychological perspectives on the self* (Vol. 1, pp. 41–70). Hillsdale, NJ: Lawrence Erlbaum Associates.

Markus, H., & Wurf, E. (1987). The dynamic self-concept: A social psychological perspective. *Annual Review of Psychology, 38,* 299–337.

Martin, J. (1988). *Who am I this time? Uncovering the fictive personality.* New York: Norton.

Martin, M. W. (1985). *Self-deception and self-understanding.* Lawrence, KS: University of Kansas Press.

Martin, T. O. (1982–1983). Death anxiety and social desirability among nurses. *Omega, 13,* 51–58.

Maslach, C. (1974). Social and personal bases of individuation. *Journal of Personality and Social Psychology, 29,* 411–425.

Maslow, A. H. (1962). Lessons from the peak-experiences. *Journal of Humanistic Psychology, 2,* 9–18.

Matas, L., Arend, R. A., & Sroufe, A. (1978). Continuity of adaptation in the second years: The relationship between quality of attachment and later competence. *Child Development, 49,* 547–556.

Mathews, A., May, J., Mogg, K., & Eysenck, M. (1990). Attention bias in anxiety: Selective search or defective filtering? *Journal of Abnormal Psychology, 99,* 166–173.

McClain, E. W. (1978). Personality differences between intrinsically religious and nonreligious students: A factor analytic study. *Journal of Personality Assessment, 42,* 159–166.

McClelland, D. C. (1963). The harlequin complex. In R. White (Ed.), *The study of lives* (pp. 94–119). New York: Atherton Press.

McClelland, D. C. (1989). Motivational factors in health and disease. *American Psychologist, 44,* 675–683.

McClelland, D. C., Atkinson, J. W., Clark, R. A., & Lowell, E. L. (1953). *The achievement motive.* New York: Appleton-Century-Crofts.

McClure, J. (1991). *Explanations, accounts, and illusions.* New York: Cambridge University Press.

McGhee, P. E. (1971). Development of the humor-response: A review of the literature. *Psychological Bulletin, 76,* 328–348.

McGlashan, T. H., Evans, F. J., & Orne, M. T. (1969). The nature of hypnotic analgesia and place-bo response to experimental pain. *Psychosomatic Medicine, 31*, 227–246.

McGuire, W. J., & McGuire, C. V. (1982). Significant others in self-space: Sex differences and developmental trends in the social self. In J. Suls (Ed.), *Psychological perspectives on the self* (Vol. 1, pp. 71–96). Hillsdale, NJ: Lawrence Erlbaum Associates.

Meissner, W. W. (1958). Affective response to psychoanalytic death symbols. *Journal of Abnormal and Social Psychology, 56*, 295–299.

McMordie, W. R. (1981). Religiosity and fear of death: Strength of belief system. *Psychological Reports, 49*, 921–922.

Meltzoff, J., & Kornreich, M. (1970). *Research in psychotherapy.* New York: Atherton Press.

Meltzoff, J., Singer, J. L., & Korchin, S. J. (1952). Motor inhibition and Rorschach movement responses: A test of the sensori-tonic theory. *Journal of Personality, 21*, 400–410.

Menaghan, E. (1982). Measuring coping effectiveness. A panel analysis of marital problems and coping efforts. *Journal of Health and Social Behavior, 23*, 220–234.

Menges, R., & Dittes, J. D. (1965). *Psychological studies of clergymen: Abstracts of research.* New York: Thomas Nelson & Sons.

Messer, S. B., & Winskur, M. (1980). Some limits to the integration of psychoanalytic and behavior therapy. *American Psychologist, 35*, 818–827.

Mikulincer, M., Florian, V., & Tolmacz, R. (1990). Attachment styles and fear of personal death: A case study of affect regulation. *Journal of Personality and Social Psychology, 58*, 273–280.

Miller, D. R., & Swanson, G. E. (1966). *Inner conflict and defense.* New York: Schocken.

Mirsky, A. F., & Duncan, C. C. (1986). Etiology and expression of schizophrenia: Neurobiological and psychosocial factors. In M. R. Rosenzweig & L. W. Porter (Eds.), *Annual review of psychology* (Vol. 37, pp. 291–319). Palo Alto, CA: Annual Reviews, Inc.

Mischel, W. (1981). Metacognition and the rules of delay. In J. H. Flavell & L. Ross (Eds.), *Social cognitive development: Frontiers and possible futures* (pp. 240–271). Cambridge, MA: Cambridge University Press.

Mishara, B. L., Baker, A. H., & Mishara, T. T. (1976). The frequency of suicide attempts: A retrospective approach applied to college students. *American Journal of Psychiatry, 133*, 841–844.

Monts, J., Zurcher, L. A., Jr., & Nydegger, R. V. (1977). Interpersonal self-deception and personality correlates. *Journal of Social Psychology, 103*, 91–99.

Moran, G. S. (1987). Some functions of play and playfulness: A developmental perspective. *Psychoanalytic Study of the Child, 42*, 11–29.

Moriarity, J. J. P. (1974). *Death anxiety in hysteric and obsessive personalities.* Unpublished doctoral dissertation, University of Detroit, MI.

Mull, C. S., Cox, C. L., & Sullivan, J. A. (1987). Religion's role in the health and well-being of well elders. *Public Health Nursing, 4*, 151–159.

Mumford, E., Schlesinger, E. J., & Glass, G. V. (1982). The effects of psychological intervention on recovery from surgery and heart attacks: An analysis of the literature. *American Journal of Public Health, 72*, 141–151.

Nagamoto, H. T., Adler, L. E., Waldo, M. C., & Freedman, R. (1989). Sensory gating in schizophrenics and normal controls: Effects of changing stimulation interval. *Biological Psychiatry, 25*, 549–561.

Ndetei, D. M., & Vadher, A. (1984). Frequency and clinical significance of delusions across cultures. *Acta Psychiatria Scandinavica, 70*, 73–76.

Nelson, E. R., & Craighead, E. W. (1977). Selective recall of positive and negative feedback, self-control behaviors, and depression. *Journal of Abnormal Psychology, 86*, 379–388.

Nelson, M. (1971). The concept of God and feelings toward parents. *Journal of Individual Psychology, 27*, 46–49.

Nelson, M., & Jones, E. (1957). An application of the Q-Technique to the study of religious concepts. *Psychological Reports, 3*, 293–297.

Nemiah, J. C. (1957). The psychiatrist and rehabilitation. *Archives of Physical Medicine and Rehabilitation, 38*, 143–147.

Ness, R. C., & Wintrob, R. M. (1980). The emotional impact of fundamentalist religious participation: An empirical study of intragroup variation. *American Journal of Orthopsychiatry, 50,* 302–315.

Neustadt, W. E. (1982). *Death anxiety in elderly nursing home residents and amount of contact received from staff: A correlation study.* Unpublished master's thesis, University of Oregon, Eugene.

Newcomb, M. D. (1986). Nuclear attitudes and reactions: Associations with depression, drug use, and quality of life. *Journal of Personality and Social Psychology, 50,* 906–920.

Nicholson, H. C., & Edwards, K. (1979). *A comparison of four statistical methods for assessing similarity of God concepts to parental images.* Paper presented at the annual meeting of the Society for the Scientific Study of Religion.

Nicolich, L. M. (1977). Beyond sensorimotor intelligence: Assessment of symbolic maturity through analysis of pretend play. *Merrill-Palmer Quarterly, 23,* 89–99.

Nisbett, R. E., & Ross, L. (1980). *Human inference: Strategies and shortcomings of social judgment.* Englewood Cliffs, NJ: Prentice-Hall.

Noam, G. G., & Recklitis, C. J. (1990). The relationship between defenses and symptoms in adolescent psychopathology. *Journal of Personality Assessment, 54,* 311–327.

Norem, K., & Cantor, N. (1986). Anticipatory and post hoc cushioning strategies: Optimism and defensive pessimism in "risky" situations. *Cognitive Therapy and Research, 10,* 347–362.

Norman, J., & Harris, M. W. (1981). *The private life of the American teenager.* New York: Rawson, Wade Publishers.

Nowicki, S., Jr., & Roundtree, J. (1971). Correlates of locus of control in a secondary school population. *Developmental Psychology, 4,* 477–478.

Nucci, L. (1981). Conceptions of personal issues: A domain distinct from moral or societal concepts. *Child Development, 52,* 114–121.

Nuechterlein, K. H., & Dawson, M. E. (1984). Information processing and attentional functioning in the developmental course of schizophrenic disorders. *Schizophrenia Bulletin, 10,* 160–203.

O'Connor, B. P., & Vallerand, R. J. (1989). Religious motivation in the elderly: A French-Canadian replication and an extension. *Journal of Social Psychology, 130,* 53–59.

Olson, J. M., & Hafer, C. L. (1990). Self-inference processes: Looking back and ahead. In J. M. Olson & M. P. Zanna (Eds.), *Self-inference processes* (pp. 293–320). Hillsdale, NJ: Lawrence Erlbaum Associates.

Oltmanns, T. F., & Maher, B. A. (Eds.). (1988). *Delusional beliefs.* New York: Wiley.

Orbach, I., & Glaubman, H. (1979). Children's perception of death as a defensive process. *Journal of Abnormal Psychology, 88,* 671–674.

Ortega y Gasset, J. (1957). *The revolt of the masses.* New York: Norton.

Osarchuk, M., & Tatz, S. (1973). Effect of induced fear of death on belief in afterlife. *Journal of Personality and Social Psychology, 27,* 256–260.

Overton, W. F. (1984). World views and their influence on psychological theory and research: Psychological theory and research. Kuhn-Lakatos-Laudan. *Advances in Child Development and Behavior, 18,* 191–226.

Palmore, E., & Luikart, C. (1972). Health and social factors related to life satisfaction. *Journal of Health and Social Behavior, 13,* 68–80.

Pandina, R. J., White, H. R., & Yorke, J. (1981). Estimation of substance use involvement: Theoretical considerations and empirical findings. *International Journal of the Addictions, 16,* 1–24.

Papousek, M., Papousek, H., & Harris, B. J. (1987). The way to the origins of play. In D. Gorlitz & J. F. Wohlwill (Eds.), *Curiosity, imagination, and play* (pp. 215–245). Hillsdale, NJ: Lawrence Erlbaum Associates.

Parish, T. S., & Nunn, G. D. (1983). Locus of control as a function of family type and age at onset of father absence. *Journal of Psychology, 113,* 187–190.

Park, C., Cohen, L. H., & Herb, L. (1990). Intrinsic religiousness and religious coping as life stress moderators for Catholics versus Protestants. *Journal of Personality and Social Psychology, 59,* 562–574.

Pattison, E. M., Lapins, N. A., & Doerr, H. A. (1973). Faith healing. *Journal of Nervous and Mental Disease, 157,* 397–409.

Paulhus, D. L., & Levitt, K. (1987). Socially desirable responding triggered by affect: Automatic egotism? *Journal of Personality and Social Psychology, 52,* 245–259.

Pearlin, L. I., & Schooler, C. (1978). The structure of coping. *Journal of Health and Social Behavior, 19,* 2–21.

Pennebaker, J. W. (1990). *Opening up: The healing power of confiding in others.* New York: Morrow.

Pepler, D. J. (1982). Play and divergent thinking. In D. J. Pepler & K. H. Rubin (Eds.), *The play of children: Current theory and research* (pp. 64–78). Basel: S. Karger.

Pepler, D. J., & Rubin, K. H. (Eds.). (1982). *The play of children: Current theory and research.* Basel: S. Karger.

Peterson, C., & Bossio, L. M. (1991). *Health and optimism.* New York: The Free Press.

Phares, E. J. (1971). Internal–external control and the reduction of reinforcement value after failure. *Journal of Consulting and Clinical Psychology, 37,* 386–390.

Phares, E. J. (1976). *Locus of control in personality.* Morristown, NJ: General Learning Press.

Phares, E. J., Ritchie, D. E., & Davis, W. L. (1968). Internal–external control and reaction to threat. *Journal of Personality and Social Psychology, 10,* 402–405.

Phares, E. J., Wilson, K. G., & Klyver, N. W. (1971). Internal–external control and the attribution of blame under neutral and distractive conditions. *Journal of Personality and Social Psychology, 18,* 285–288.

Piaget, J. (1962). *Play, dreams and imitation in childhood.* New York: Norton.

Piaget, J., & Inhelder, B. (1956). *The child's concept of space.* London: Routledge & Kegan.

Piazza, T., & Glock, C. Y. (1979). Images of God and their social meanings. In R. Wuthnow (Ed.), *The religious dimension* (pp. 69–91). New York: Academic Press.

Pinder, M. M., & Hayslip, B., Jr. (1981). Cognitive, attitudinal, and affective aspects of death and dying in adulthood: Implications for care providers. *Educational Gerontology, 6,* 107–124.

Pitcher, E. G., & Prelinger, E. (1963). *Children tell stories: An analysis of fantasy.* New York: International Universities Press.

Plutchik, R., Kellerman, H., & Conte, H. R. (1979). A structural theory of ego defenses and emotions. In C. E. Izard (Ed.), *Emotions in personality and psychopathology* (pp. 229–257). New York: Plenum.

Pollak, J. M. (1979–1980). Correlates of death anxiety: A review of empirical studies. *Omega, 10,* 97–121.

Posey, T. B., & Losch, M. E. (1983–1984). Auditory hallucinations of hearing voices in 375 normal subjects. *Imaginations, Cognition, and Personality, 3,* 99–113.

Premack, D., & Woodruff, G. (1978). Does the chimpanzee have a theory of mind? *Behavioral and Brain Sciences, 4,* 515–526.

Prentice, N. M., Manosevitz, M., & Hubbs, L. (1978). Imaginary figures of early childhood: Santa Claus, Easter Bunny, and the Tooth Fairy. *American Journal of Orthopsychiatry, 48,* 618–628.

Proudfoot, W., & Shaver, P. (1975). Attribution theory and the psychology of religion. *Journal for the Scientific Study of Religion, 14,* 317–330.

Pruyser, P. W. (1983). *The play of the imagination.* New York: International Universities Press.

Pyszczynski, T. (1982). Cognitive strategies for coping with uncertain outcomes. *Journal of Research in Personality, 16,* 386–399.

Randour, M. L., & Bondanza, J. (1987). The concept of God in the psychological formation of females. *Psychoanalytic Psychology, 4,* 301–313.

Rank, O. (1945). *Will therapy and truth and reality.* New York: Knopf.

Reid, D. W. (1984). Participatory control and the chronic-illness adjustment process. In H. M. Lefcourt (Ed.), *Research with the locus of control construct* (Vol. 3, pp. 361–389). New York: Academic Press.

Rhudick, P. J., & Dibner, A. S. (1961). Age, personality, and health correlates of death concerns in normal aged individuals. *Journal of Gerontology, 16*, 44–49.

Rhue, J. W., & Lynn, S. J. (1987). Fantasy proneness: Developmental antecedents. *Journal of Personality, 55*, 121–137.

Richardson, J. T. (1985). Psychological and psychiatric studies of new religions. In L. B. Brown (Ed.), *Advances in the psychology of religion* (pp. 209–223). New York: Pergamon.

Richardson, V., Bermann, S., & Piwowarski, M. (1983). Projective assessment of the relationships between the salience of death, religion, and age among adults in America. *Journal of General Psychology, 109*, 149–156.

Richardson, V., & Sands, R. (1986–1987). Death attitudes among mid-life women. *Omega, 17*, 327–341.

Rieff, P. (1966). *The triumph of the therapeutic.* New York: Harper & Row.

Riegel, K. F. (1973). Dialectic operations. The final period of cognitive development. *Human Development, 16*, 346–370.

Rizley, R. (1978). Depression and distortion in the attribution of causality. *Journal of Abnormal Psychology, 87*, 32–48.

Rizzuto, A. M. (1979). *The birth of the living God: A psychoanalytic study.* Chicago: University of Chicago Press.

Robbins, M. C., & Kilbride, P. L. (1971). Sex differences in dreams in Uganda. *Journal of Cross-Cultural Psychology, 2*, 406–408.

Robins, L. N., Helzer, J. E., Weissman, M. M., Orvaschel, H., Gruenberg, E., Burke, J. D., Jr., & Regier, D. A. (1984). Lifetime prevalence of specific psychiatric disorders in three sites. *Archives of General Psychiatry, 41*, 949–958.

Rodin, J. (1986). Health, control, and aging. In M. M. Baltes & P. B. Baltes (Eds.), *The psychology of control and aging* (pp. 139–165). Hillsdale, NJ: Lawrence Erlbaum Associates.

Rodin, J., & Langer, E. J. (1977). Long-term effects of a control-relevant intervention with the institutionalized aged. *Journal of Personality and Social Psychology, 35*, 897–902.

Rodin, J., Rennert, K., & Solomon, S. K. (1980). Intrinsic motivation for control: Fact or fiction? In A. Baum & J. E. Singer (Eds.), *Advances in environmental psychology* (pp. 131–148). Hillsdale, NJ: Lawrence Erlbaum Associates.

Rodin, J., & Salovey, P. (1989). Health psychology. In M. R. Rosenzweig & L. W. Porter (Eds.), *Annual review of psychology* (Vol. 40, pp. 533–579). Palo Alto, CA: Annual Reviews, Inc.

Rohsenow, D. J., & O'Leary, M. R. (1978). Locus of control research on alcoholic populations: A review. I. Development, scales, and treatment. *International Journal of the Addictions, 13*, 55–78.

Roof, W. C. (1979). Concepts and indicators of religious commitment: A critical review. In R. Wuthnow (Ed.), *The religious dimension* (pp. 17–45). New York: Academic Press.

Rosenberg, M. (1965). *Society and the adolescent self-image.* Princeton, NJ: Princeton University Press.

Rosenblatt, A., Greenberg, J., Solomon, S., Pyszczynski, T., & Lyon, D. (1989). Evidence for terror management theory: I. The effects of mortality salience on reactions to those who violate or uphold cultural values. *Journal of Personality and Social Psychology, 57*, 681–690.

Rosenhan, D. (1973). On being sane in insane places. *Sciences, 179*, 250–258.

Rosenthal, R. (1966). *Experimental effects in behavioral research.* New York: Appleton-Century-Crofts.

Rosenzweig, S. (1945). The picture association method and its application in study of reactions to frustration. *Journal of Personality, 14*, 3–23.

Ross, L., Rodin, J., & Zimbardo, P. G. (1969). Toward an attribution therapy: The reduction of fear through induced cognitive-emotional misattribution. *Journal of Personality and Social Psychology, 12*, 279–288.

Ross, M. W. (1983). Clinical profiles of Hare Krishna devotees. *American Journal of Psychiatry, 140*, 416–420.

Ross, S., & Buckalew, L. W. (1985). Placebo agentry: Assessment of drug and placebo effects. In L. White, B. Tursky, & G. E. Schwartz (Eds.), *Placebo: Theory, research, and mechanisms* (pp. 67–82). New York: Guilford Press.

Roth, D. L., & Ingram, R. E. (1985). Factors in the Self-Deception Questionnaire: Associations with depression. *Journal of Personality and Social Psychology, 48,* 243–251.

Rothbaum, F., Weisz, J. R., & Snyder, S. S. (1982). Changing the world and changing the self: A two-process model of perceived control. *Journal of Personality and Social Psychology, 42,* 5–37.

Rotter, J. B. (1966). Generalized expectancies for internal versus external control of reinforcement. *Psychological Monographs, 80*(Whole No. 609).

Rotter, J. B., Seeman, M., & Liverant, S. (1962). Internal versus external control of reinforcement. A major variable in behavior therapy. In N. F. Washburne (Ed.), *Decisions, values, and groups* (Vol. 2, pp. 473–516). London: Pergamon.

Rozensky, R. H., Rehm, L. P., Pry, G., & Roth, D. (1977). Depression and self-reinforcement behavior in hospitalized patients. *Journal of Behavioral, Therapy, and Experimental Psychiatry, 8,* 31–34.

Rubens, R., & Lapidus, L. (1978). Schizophrenic patterns of arousal and stimulus barrier functioning. *Journal of Abnormal Psychology, 87,* 199–211.

Rubin, K. H. (1982). Early play theories revisited: Contributions to contemporary research and theory. In D. J. Pepler & K. H. Rubin (Eds.), *The play of children: Current theory and research* (pp. 4–14). New York: S. Karger.

Rychlak, J. F. (1973). Time orientation in the positive and negative free fantasies of mildly abnormal versus normal high school males. *Journal of Consulting and Clinical Psychology, 41,* 175–180.

Sackeim, H. A. (1983). Self-deception, self-esteem, and depression: The adaptive value of lying to oneself. In J. Masling (Ed.), *Empirical studies of psychoanalytic theories* (Vol. 1, pp. 101–158). Hillsdale, NJ: Lawrence Erlbaum Associates.

Sackeim, H. A., & Gur, R. C. (1978). Self-deception, self-confrontation, and consciousness. In G. E. Schwartz & D. Shapiro (Eds.), *Consciousness and self-regulation: Advances in research* (Vol. 2, pp. 139–197). New York: Plenum Press.

Sackeim, H. A., & Gur, R. C. (1979). Self-deception, other-deception, and self-reported psychopathology. *Journal of Consulting and Clinical Psychology, 47,* 213–215.

Saltz, E., & Brodie, J. (1982). Pretend-play training in childhood: A review and critique. In D. J. Pepler & K. H. Rubin (Eds.), *The play of children: Current theory and research* (pp. 97–112). New York: S. Karger.

Santy, P. (1983). The journey out and in: Psychiatry and space exploration. *American Journal of Psychiatry, 140,* 519–527.

Sanua, V. D. (1969). Religion, mental health, and personality: A review of empirical studies. *American Journal of Psychiatry, 125,* 1203–1213.

Sarbin, T. R., & Mancuso, J. C. (1980). *Schizophrenia: Medical diagnosis or moral verdict?* New York: Pergamon Press.

Sarnoff, I., & Corwin, S. M. (1959). Castration anxiety and the fear of death. *Journal of Personality, 27,* 374–385.

Scarlett, W. G., & Wolf, D. (1979). When it's only make-believe: The construction of a boundary between fantasy and reality in storytelling. In E. Winner & H. Gardner (Eds.), *Fact, fiction, and fantasy in childhood* (pp. 29–40). San Francisco: Jossey-Bass.

Schafer, R. B. (1976). *A new language for psychoanalysis.* New Haven, CT: Yale University Press.

Schafer, R. B., & Keith, P. M. (1985). A causal model approach to the symbolic interactionist view of the self-concept. *Journal of Personality and Social Psychology, 48,* 963–969.

Scheier, M. F., & Carver, C. S. (1987). Dispositional optimism and physical well-being: The influence of generalized outcome expectancies on health. *Journal of Personality, 55,* 169–210.

Scheier, M. F., Magovern, G. J., Abbott, R. A., Matthews, K. A., Owens, J. F., Lefebvre, R. C., & Carver, C. S. (1989). Dispositional optimism and recovery from coronary artery bypass surgery: The beneficial effects on physical and psychological well-being. *Journal of Personality and Social Psychology, 57,* 1024–1040.

Scherer, K. R., & Tannenbaum, P. H. (1986). Emotional experiences in everyday life: A survey approach. *Motivation and Emotion, 10,* 295–314.

Schibuk, M., Bond, M., & Bouffard, R. (1989). The development of defenses in childhood. *Canadian Journal of Psychiatry, 34,* 581–587.

Schlegal, R. P., & Sanborn, M. D. (1979). Religious affiliation and adolescent drinking. *Journal of Studies on Alcohol, 40,* 693–703.

Schneiderman, L. (1956). The estimation of one's own bodily traits. *Journal of Social Psychology, 44,* 89–99.

Schulz, R. (1978). *The psychology of death, dying, and bereavement.* Reading, MA: Addison-Wesley.

Schwab, J. J., & Schwab, M. E. (1978). *Sociocultural roots of mental illness: An epidemiologic survey.* New York: Plenum Press.

Schwartz, P. K. (1980). *A study of the relationship between attachment–separation and the fear of death.* Unpublished doctoral dissertation, California School of Professional Psychology, Los Angeles.

Searles, H. F. (1961). Schizophrenia and the inevitability of death. *Psychiatric Quarterly, 35,* 631–665.

Seeman, J. (1989). Toward a model of positive health. *American Psychologist, 44,* 1099–1109.

Seligman, M. E. P. (1975). *Helplessness: On depression, development, and death.* San Francisco: W. H. Freeman.

Shapiro, D. (1965). *Neurotic styles.* New York: Basic Books.

Shaver, P., Lenauer, M., & Sadd, S. (1980). Religiousness, conversion, and subjective well-being: The "healthy-minded" religion of modern American women. *American Journal of Psychiatry, 137,* 1563–1568.

Sheikh, A. A., Kunzendorf, R. G., & Sheikh, K. S. (1989). Healing images: From ancient wisdom to modern science. In A. A. Sheikh & K. S. Sheikh (Eds.), *Eastern and western approaches to healing* (pp. 395–565). New York: Wiley.

Sheikh, A. A., & Sheikh, K. S. (Eds.). (1989). *Eastern and western approaches to healing: Ancient wisdom and modern knowledge.* New York: Wiley.

Sherrod, L., & Singer, J. L. (1979). The development of make-believe play. In J. H. Goldstein (Ed.), *Sports, games, and play* (pp. 1–28). Hillsdale, NJ: Lawrence Erlbaum Associates.

Shrauger, J. S., & Schoenman, T. J. (1979). Symbolic interactionist view of self-concept: Through the looking glass darkly. *Psychological Bulletin, 86,* 549–576.

Siegelman, M., & Peck, R. F. (1960). Personality patterns related to occupational roles. *Genetic Psychology Monographs, 61,* 291–349.

Siller, J. (1969). Psychological situation of the disabled with spinal cord injuries. *Rehabilitation Literature, 30,* 290–296.

Silver, R. L., & Wortman, C. B. (1980). Coping with undesirable life events. In J. Garber & M. E. P. Seligman (Eds.), *Human helplessness* (pp. 279–375). New York: Academic Press.

Silverman, J. (1972). Stimulus intensity modulation and psychological dis-ease. *Psychopharmacologia, 24,* 42–80.

Silverman, L. H., Lachmann, F. M., & Milich, R. H. (1982). *The search for oneness.* New York: International Universities Press.

Singer, J. L. (with E. Biblow, J. T. Freyberg, S. Gottlieb, & M. A. Pulaski). (1973). *The child's world of make-believe.* New York: Academic Press.

Singer, J. L., & McCraven, V. G. (1961). Some characteristics of adult daydreaming. *Journal of Psychology, 51,* 151–164.

Sjoback, H. (1973). *The psychoanalytic theory of defensive processes.* New York: Wiley.

Skinner, E. A., & Connell, J. P. (1986). Control understanding: suggestions for a developmental framework. In M. M. Baltes & P. B. Baltes (Eds.), *The psychology of control and aging* (pp. 35–69). Hillsdale, NJ: Lawrence Erlbaum Associates.

Slade, P. D., & Bentall, R. P. (1988). *Sensory deception: A scientific analysis of hallucination.* Baltimore, MD: The John Hopkins University Press.

Slezak, M. E. (1980). *Attitudes toward euthanasia as a function of death fears and demographic variables.* Unpublished doctoral dissertation, California School of Professional Psychology, Fresno.

Smith, J. (1981). Self and experience in Maori culture. In P. Heelas & A. Look (Eds.), *Indigenous psychologies* (pp. 145–158). New York: Academic Press.

Smith, N. R., & Franklin, M. B. (Eds.). (1979). *Symbolic functioning in childhood.* Hillsdale, NJ: Lawrence Erlbaum Associates.

Smith, R. E. (1970). Changes in locus of control as a function of life crisis resolution. *Journal of Abnormal Psychology, 75,* 328–332.

Smith, R. E. (1989). Effects of coping skills training on generalized self-efficacy and locus of control. *Journal of Personality and Social Psychology, 56,* 228–233.

Smith, T. W. (1979). Happiness: Time trends, seasonal variations, intersurvey differences, and other mysteries. *Social Psychology Quarterly, 42,* 18–30.

Solantaus, T., Rimpela, M., & Taipale, V. (1984). The threat of war in the minds of 12–18-year-olds in Finland. *The Lancet, April 7,* 784–785.

Solomon, S., Greenberg, J., & Pyszczynski, T. (1991). In M. P. Zanna (Ed.), *Advances in experimental social psychology* (Vol. 24, pp. 93–150). New York: Academic Press.

Speece, M. W., & Brent, S. B. (1984). Children's understanding of death: A review of three components of a death concept. *Child Development, 55,* 1671–1686.

Spence, D. (1982). *Narrative truth and historical truth.* New York: W. W. Norton.

Spencer, J. (1975). The mental health of Jehovah's Witnesses. *British Journal of Psychiatry, 126,* 556–559.

Spilka, B., Hood, R., & Gorsuch, R. (1985). *The psychology of religion: An empirical approach.* Englewood Cliffs, NJ: Prentice-Hall.

Spinetta, J. J., & Rigler, D. (1972). The child-abusing parent: A psychological review. *Psychological Bulletin, 77,* 296–304.

Spitzer, R. L., Endicott, J., & Robins, E. (1978). Research diagnostic criteria: Rationale and reliability. *Archives of General Psychiatry, 35,* 773–782.

Srole, L., Langner, T. S., Michael, S. T., Kirkpatrick, P., Opler, M. K., & Rennie, T. A. C. (1975). *Mental health in the metropolis: The Midtown Manhattan Study. Book 1.* New York: Harper Torchbooks.

Srole, L., Langner, T. S., Michael, S. T., Kirkpatrick, P., Opler, M. K., & Rennie, T. A. C. (1977). *Mental health in the metropolis: The Midtown Manhattan Study. Book 2.* New York: Harper Torchbooks.

Stambrook, M., & Parker, K. C. H. (1987). The development of the concept of death in childhood: A review of the literature. *Merrill-Palmer Quarterly, 33,* 133–157.

Steele, C. M. (1988). The psychology of self-affirmation: Sustaining the integrity of the self. *Advances in Experimental Social Psychology, 21,* 261–302.

Steinitz, L. Y. (1980). Religiosity, well-being, and *Weltanschauung* among the elderly. *Journal for the Scientific Study of Religion, 19,* 60–67.

Straus, A. S. (1982). The structure of the self in Northern Cheyenne culture. In B. Lee (Ed.), *Psychological theories of the self* (pp. 111–128). New York: Plenum Press.

Strauss, J. S. (1969). Hallucinations and delusions as points on continua function: Rating scale evidence. *Archives of General Psychiatry, 21,* 581–586.

Strunk, O. (1959). Perceived relationships between parental and deity concepts. *Psychological Newsletter, 10,* 222–226.

Sullivan, H. S. (1953). *The interpersonal theory of psychiatry.* New York: Harper & Row.

Suls, J., & Fletcher, B. (1985). The relative efficacy of avoidant and nonavoidant coping strategies: A meta-analysis. *Health Psychology, 4,* 249–288.

Sunderberg, N. D., Latkin, C. A., Littman, R. A., & Hagan, R. A. (1990). Personality in a religious commune: CPIs in Rajneeshpuram. *Journal of Personality Assessment, 55,* 7–17.

Swann, W. B., Jr. (1983). Self-verification: Bringing social reality into harmony with the self. In J. Suls & A. G. Greenwald (Eds.), *Psychological perspectives on the self* (Vol. 2, pp. 33–66). Hillsdale, NJ: Lawrence Erlbaum Associates.

Swann, W. B., Jr. (1987). Identity negotiation: Where two roads meet. *Journal of Personality and Social Psychology, 53,* 1038–1051.

Swann, W. B., Jr., Griffin, J. J., Jr., Predmore, S. C., & Gaines, B. (1987). The cognitive–affective crossfire: When self-consistency confronts self-enhancement. *Journal of Personality and Social Psychology, 52,* 881–889.

Swann, W. B., Jr., & Hill, C. A. (1982). When our identities are mistaken: Reaffirming self-conceptions through social interaction. *Journal of Personality and Social Psychology, 43,* 59–66.

Swann, W. B., Jr., Pelham, B. W., & Krull, D. S. (1989). Agreeable fancy or disagreeable truth? Reconciling self-enhancement and self-verification. *Journal of Personality and Social Psychology, 57,* 782–791.

Swann, W. B., Jr., & Predmore, S. C. (1985). Intimates as agents of social support: Sources of consolation or despair? *Journal of Personality and Social Psychology, 49,* 1609–1617.

Swann, W. B., Jr., & Read, S. J. (1981). Acquiring self-knowledge: The search for feedback that fits. *Journal of Personality and Social Psychology, 41,* 1119–1128.

Swartz, L. (1985). Anorexia nervosa as a culture-bound syndrome. *Social Science and Medicine, 20,* 725–730.

Szasz, T. S. (1961). *The myth of mental illness: Foundations for a theory of personal conduct.* New York: Hoeber & Harper.

Tamayo, A., & Dugas, A. (1977). Conceptual representations of mother, father, and God according to sex and field of study. *The Journal of Psychology, 97,* 79–84.

Tambiah, S. J. (1990). *Magic, science, religion, and the scope of rationality.* New York: Cambridge University Press.

Taylor, S. E. (1979). Hospital patient behavior: Reactance, helplessness, or control? *Journal of Social Issues, 35,* 156–184.

Taylor, S. E. (1983). Adjustment to threatening events: A theory of cognitive adaptation. *American Psychologist, 38,* 1161–1173.

Taylor, S. E. (1989). *Positive illusions: Creative self-deception and the healthy mind.* New York: Basic Books.

Taylor, S. E., & Brown, J. (1988). Illusion and well-being: A social psychological perspective on mental health. *Psychological Bulletin, 103,* 193–210.

Telch, M. J., Lucas, J. A., & Nelson, P. (1989). Nonclinical panic in college students: An investigation of prevalence and symptomatology. *Journal of Abnormal Psychology, 98,* 300–306.

Templer, D. I. (1971). Death anxiety as related to depression and health of retired persons. *Journal of Gerontology, 26,* 521–523.

Tennen, H., & Herzberger, S. (1987). Depression, self-esteem, and the absence of self-protective attributional biases. *Journal of Personality and Social Psychology, 52,* 72–80.

Thomas, C. B., & Duszynski, K. R. (1985). Are words of the Rorschach predictors of disease and death? The case of "whirling." *Psychosomatic Medicine, 47,* 201–211.

Thomas, D. L. (1988). *The religion and family connection: Social science perspective.* Provo, UT: Religious Study Center, Brigham Young University.

Thomas, K. (1971). *Religion and the decline of magic.* New York: Charles Scribner's.

Thomas, L. E., & Cooper, P. E. (1980). Incidence and psychological correlates of intense spiritual experiences. *Journal of Transpersonal Psychology, 12,* 75–85.

Thompson, C. (1981). Will it hurt if I can control it? A complex answer to a simple question. *Psychological Bulletin, 80,* 89–101.

Thorson, J. A., & Powell, F. C. (1989). Death anxiety and religion in an older male sample. *Psychological Reports, 64,* 985–986.

Tiger, L. (1979). *Optimism: The biology of hope.* New York: Simon & Schuster.

Tobacyk, J., & Milford, G. (1983). Belief in paranormal phenomena: Assessment instrument development and implications for personality functioning. *Journal of Personality and Social Psychology, 44,* 1029–1037.

Tolor, A., & Jalowiec, J. E. (1968). Body boundary, parental attitudes, and internal–external expectancy. *Journal of Consulting and Clinical Psychology, 32,* 206–209.

Torrey, E. F. (1986). *Witchdoctors and psychiatrists.* New York: Harper & Row.

Triandis, H. C., McCusker, C., & Hui, C. H. (1990). Multimethod probes of individualism and collectivism. *Journal of Personality and Social Psychology, 59,* 1006–1020.

Tudor, T. (1970). *The concept of repression: The results of two experimental paradigms.* Unpublished doctoral dissertation, University of Texas, Austin.

Ullman, C. (1982). Cognitive and emotional antecedents of religious conversion. *Journal of Personality and Social Psychology, 43,* 183–192.

Ullman, C. (1988). Psychological well-being among converts in traditional and nontraditional religious groups. *Psychiatry, 51,* 312–322.

Underwood, G. (1982). Attention and awareness: Cognitive and motor skills. In G. Underwood (Ed.), *Aspects of consciousness* (Vol. 3, pp. 111–145). New York: Academic Press.

Ungerer, J. A., Zelazo, P. R., Kearsley, R. B., & O'Leary, K. (1981). Developmental changes in the representation of objects in symbolic play from 18 to 34 months of age. *Child Development, 52,* 186–195.

Vaillant, G. E. (1977). *Adaptation to life.* New York: Little, Brown, & Co.

Vaillant, G. E. (Ed.). (1986). *Empirical studies of ego mechanisms of defense.* Washington, DC: American Psychiatric Press.

Vaillant, G. E., & Drake, R. E. (1985). Maturity of ego defenses in relation to DSM-III Axis II personality disorder. *Archives of General Psychiatry, 42,* 587–601.

Valins, S., & Nisbett, R. E. (1971). Attribution processes in the development and treatment of emotional disorders. (Published by General Learning Corporation.)

Vergote, A., & Aubert, C. (1972). Parental images and representations of God. *Social Campus, 19,* 431–444.

Vergote, A., & Tamayo, A. (Eds.). (1980). *The parental figures and the representation of God.* The Hague: Mouton.

Vergote, A., Tamayo, A., Pasquali, L., Bonaimi, M., Pattyn, A., & Custers, A. (1969). Concept of God and parental images. *Journal for the Scientific Study of Religion, 8,* 79–87.

Veroff, J., Douvan, E., & Kulka, R. A. (1981). *The inner American: A self-portrait from 1957 to 1976.* New York: Basic Books.

Walser, C. B. (1984). *Death anxiety and separation anxiety in borderline and schizophrenic patients.* Unpublished doctoral dissertation, California School of Professional Psychology, Berkeley.

Watson, C. G., & Buranen, C. (1979). The frequencies of conversion reaction symptoms. *Journal of Abnormal Psychology, 88,* 209–211.

Watson, D., & Clark, L. A. (1984). Negative affectivity: The disposition to experience aversive emotional states. *Psychological Bulletin, 96,* 465–490.

Watts, W., & Free, L. A. (1973). *State of the nation.* New York: Universe Books.

Weinstein, N. D. (1980). Unrealistic optimism about future life events. *Journal of Personality and Social Psychology, 39,* 806–820.

Weissman, M. M., & Myers, J. K. (1978). Affective disorders in a U.S. urban community. *Archives of General Psychiatry, 35,* 1304–1311.

Wells, V. E., Klerman, G. L., & Deykin, E. Y. (1987). The prevalence of depressive symptoms in college students. *Social Psychiatry, 22,* 20–28.

West, D. A., Kellner, R., & Moore-West, M. (1986). The effects of loneliness: A review of the literature. *Comprehensive Psychiatry, 27,* 351–363.

Westermeyer, J. (1985). Psychiatric diagnosis across cultural boundaries. *American Journal of Psychiatry, 142,* 798–805.

Westermeyer, J. (1987). Cultural factors in clinical assessment. *Journal of Consulting and Clinical Psychology, 55*, 471–478.

Westman, A. S., & Brackney, B. (1990). Relationships between indices of neuroticism, attitudes toward and concepts of death, and religiosity. *Psychological Reports, 66*, 1039–1043.

White, L., Tursky, B., & Schwartz, G. E. (1985). *Placebo: Theory, research, and mechanisms.* New York: Guilford Press.

Whitehead, H. (1987). Renunciation and reformulation. Ithaca, NY: Cornell University Press.

Wicklund, R. A. (1975). Objective self-awareness: *Advances in Experimental Social Psychology, 8*, 233–275.

Wickramasekera, I. (1985). A conditional response model of the placebo effect: Predictions from the model. In L. White, B. Tursky, & G. E. Schwartz (Eds.), *Placebo: Theory, research, and mechanisms* (pp. 255–287). New York: Guilford Press.

Wiehe, V. R. (1986). *Loco parentis* and locus of control. *Psychological Reports, 59*, 169–170.

Wills, T. A. (1981). Downward comparison principles in social psychology. *Psychological Bulletin, 90*, 245–271.

Winget, C., & Kramer, M. (1979). *Dimensions of dreams.* Gainesville: University Presses of Florida.

Winner, E., & Gardner, H. (Eds.). (1979). *Fact, fiction, and fantasy in childhood.* San Francisco: Jossey-Bass.

Winnicott, D. W. (1958). *Collected papers.* New York: Basic Books.

Winnicott, D. W. (1971). *Playing and reality.* London: Tavistock.

Witkin, H. A., Dyk, R. B., Faterson, H. F., Goodenough, D. R., & Karp, S. A. (1962). *Psychological differentiation: Studies of development.* New York: Wiley.

Witter, R. A., Stock, W. A., Okun, M. A., & Haring, M. J. (1985). Religion and subjective well-being in adulthood: A quantitative synthesis. *Review of Religious Research, 26*, 332–342.

Wolf, D., & Grollman, S. H. (1982). Ways of playing: Individual differences in imaginative style. In D. J. Pepler & K. H. Rubin (Eds.), *The play of children: Current theory and research* (pp. 46–63). Basel: S. Karger.

Wulff, D. M. (1991). *Psychology of religion: Classic and contemporary views.* New York: Wiley.

Wuthnow, R. (1979). *The religious dimension: New directions in quantitative research.* New York: Academic Press.

Yates, R., III, Kennelly, K., & Cox, S. H. (1975). Perceived contingency of parental reinforcements, parent–child relations, and locus of control. *Psychological Reports, 36*, 139–146.

Zentall, S. S., & Zentall, T. R. (1983). Optimal stimulation: A model of disordered activity and performance in normal and deviant children. *Psychological Bulletin, 94*, 446–471.

Zern, D. (1984). The powerful connections of religiousness with both cultural complexity and pressures to obey cultural norms. *Genetic Psychology Monographs, 110*, 207–227.

Zern, D. (1987). The relationship of religious involvement to a variety of indicators of cognitive ability and achievement in college students. *Adolescence, 22*, 883–895.

Zilboorg, G. (1943). Fear of death. *Psychoanalytic Quarterly, 12*, 465–475.

Zuckerman, D. M., Kasl, S. V., & Ostfeld, A. M. (1984). Psychosocial predictors of mortality among the elderly poor. *American Journal of Epidemiology, 119*, 410–423.

Author Index

Page numbers in *italics* denotes complete bibliographical information.

SUBJECT INDEX

A

Absurdity, 1–10, 20–21, 49, 147–149,
   192–194
  death, 20–21
  inevitable life frustrations, 1–4, 49
  need to deny, 1–10
  psychopathology, 147–149
Actors, 181–182
Alexithymia, 136
Ambivalence, 178–179
Attribution theory, 143–144

B

Body opening symptoms, 168–169
Boundaries, 136–141, 169

C

Comedians, 180–181
Comedic strategies, 1–3, 147–148
Contradiction, tolerance for, 178–180

D

Death anxiety, 3–4, 20–48, 171, 177–178
  body awareness, 21–22

  defense against, 31–36, 44–48
  conscious level, 28–30
  gender differences, 177–178
  hypochondriasis, 21–22
  measurement, 22–26
  multiple manifestations, 36–40
  nuclear threat, 42–43
  religious defenses, 31–34, 41–42
  sex differences, 26
  terror management, 34–35
  unconscious level, 26–28
Defense mechanisms, 106–127, 178
  categories, 107–110
  developmental patterns, 120–123
  complexity, 117–119
  illusory implications, 106–110, 125–127
  masculinity–femininity correlates, 124
  maturity level, 110–120
  perceptual style correlates, 123–124
  locus of control correlates, 124
  personality correlates, 123–125
  self-esteem correlates, 124
  sex differences, 178
Delusion sustainers, 180–183
Depression, 5–10
Depressive realism, 5–10, 134
Discomfort with realism, 4–10
Discomfort in being human, 11–19
  demoralization, 14–16
  dreams, 17–18

235